GA Publishers' Awards 2014

In 2014 the first edition of *Teaching Geography Creatively* won the Geographical Association gold award for the best geography teaching resources of the year. The prestigious gold award is only awarded to materials of sufficient merit and is not awarded every year. The judges commented:

'The judges found this publication to be dynamic and engaging, with lots of practical approaches for geography teaching in the classroom. Teachers will be able to dip into the book then introduce and apply the ideas to their own setting.

This publication will be valuable for experienced and specialist teachers of geography with responsibility for leadership and implementation of geography in the primary setting. This book will also be useful for teachers of varying levels of expertise, including student teachers and those who lack the confidence to teach exciting geography lessons.'

TEACHING GEOGRAPHY CREATIVELY

Teaching Geography Creatively **was Winner of the Geographical Association Gold Award 2014.**

This fully updated second edition of *Teaching Geography Creatively* is a stimulating source of guidance for busy trainee and experienced teachers. Packed full of practical approaches for bringing the teaching of geography to life, it offers a range of innovative ideas for exploring physical geography, human geography and environmental issues.

Underpinned by the latest research and theory, expert authors from schools and universities explore the inter-relationship between creativity and learning, and consider how creativity can enhance pupils' motivation, self-image and well-being. Two brand new chapters focus on creative approaches to learning about the physical world, as well as the value of alternative learning settings.

Further imaginative ideas include:

- games and starter activities as entry points for creative learning
- how to keep geography messy
- the outdoors and learning beyond the classroom
- how to teach geography using your local area
- the links between geography and other areas of the curriculum
- looking at geography, creativity and the future
- fun and games in geography
- engaging with the world through picture-books
- teaching about sustainability.

With contemporary, cutting-edge practice at the forefront, *Teaching Geography Creatively* is an essential read for all trainee and practising teachers, offering a variety of practical strategies to create a fun and stimulating learning environment. In the process it offers a pedagogy that respects the integrity of children as joyful and imaginative learners and which offers a vision of how geography can contribute to constructing a better and more equitable world.

Stephen Scoffham is a visiting reader in sustainability and education at Canterbury Christ Church University, UK. A leading member of the Geographical Association, he is the author of many books for teachers and children on primary geography, and a school atlas consultant.

THE LEARNING TO TEACH IN THE PRIMARY SCHOOL SERIES

Series Editor: Teresa Cremin, The Open University, UK

Teaching is an art form. It demands not only knowledge and understanding of the core areas of learning, but also the ability to teach these creatively and foster learner creativity in the process. The Learning to Teach in the Primary School Series draws upon recent research which indicates the rich potential of creative teaching and learning, and explores what it means to teach creatively in the primary phase. It also responds to the evolving nature of subject teaching in a wider, more imaginatively framed twenty-first-century primary curriculum.

Designed to complement the textbook *Learning to Teach in the Primary School*, the well-informed, lively texts in this series offer support for student and practising teachers who want to develop more creative approaches to teaching and learning. Uniquely, the books highlight the importance of the teachers' own creative engagement and share a wealth of research informed ideas to enrich pedagogy and practice.

Titles in the series:

Teaching Geography Creatively, 2nd edition
Edited by Stephen Scoffham

Teaching Science Creatively, 2nd edition
Dan Davies and Deb McGregor

Teaching English Creatively, 2nd edition
Teresa Cremin

Teaching Mathematics Creatively, 2nd edition
Linda Pound and Trisha Lee

Teaching Religious Education Creatively
Edited by Sally Elton-Chalcraft

Teaching Physical Education Creatively
Angela Pickard and Patricia Maude

Teaching Music Creatively
Pam Burnard and Regina Murphy

Teaching History Creatively
Edited by Hilary Cooper

TEACHING GEOGRAPHY CREATIVELY

Second edition

Edited by
Stephen Scoffham

Routledge
Taylor & Francis Group

LONDON AND NEW YORK

First published 2017
by Routledge
2 Park Square, Milton Park, Abingdon, Oxon OX14 4RN

and by Routledge
711 Third Avenue, New York, NY 10017

Routledge is an imprint of the Taylor & Francis Group, an informa business

First edition published by Routledge 2013

British Library Cataloguing in Publication Data
A catalogue record for this book is available from the British Library

Library of Congress Cataloging in Publication Data
Names: Scoffham, Stephen, editor.
Title: Teaching geography creatively / edited by Stephen Scoffham.
Description: Second edition. | London ; New York, NY : Routledge, 2017.
Identifiers: LCCN 2016010187| ISBN 9781138952119 (hardback) | ISBN 9781138952126 (pbk.) | ISBN 9781315667775 (ebook)
Subjects: LCSH: Geography—Study and teaching (Primary)
Classification: LCC G73 .T4216 2017 | DDC 372.89/1—dc23LC record available at http://lccn.loc.gov/2016010187

ISBN: 978-1-138-95211-9 (hbk)
ISBN: 978-1-138-95212-6 (pbk)
ISBN: 978-1-315-66777-5 (ebk)

Typeset in Times New Roman
by FiSH Books Ltd, Enfield

MIX
Paper from
responsible sources
FSC
www.fsc.org   FSC® C013056

Printed and bound in Great Britain by
TJ International Ltd, Padstow, Cornwall

CONTENTS

List of figures ix
About the contributors xiii
Series editor's foreword xv
Acknowledgements xx

1 Geography and creativity: making connections 1
STEPHEN SCOFFHAM

2 Fun and games in geography 12
TERRY WHYTE

3 Engaging with the world through picture-books 30
ANNE M. DOLAN

4 Playful approaches to learning out of doors 44
SHARON WITT

5 Mental maps: learning about places around the world 58
SIMON CATLING

6 Representing places in maps and art 76
MARGARET MACKINTOSH

7 Landscapes and sweet geography 88
NIKI WHITBURN

8 Creative approaches to learning about the physical world 104
SUSAN PIKE

CONTENTS ▥ ▨ ▦ ■

9   Geography and history in the local area   118
     ANTHONY BARLOW

10   Geography and mathematics: a creative approach   131
     JANE WHITTLE

11   Geography and the creative arts   147
     JULIA TANNER

12   Geography and music: a creative harmony   163
     ARTHUR J. KELLY

13   Geography and sustainability education   177
     PAULA OWENS

14   Keeping geography messy   192
     STEPHEN PICKERING

15   Inside, outside and beyond the classroom   205
     STEPHEN SCOFFHAM WITH JONATHAN BARNES, PETER VUJAKOVIC
     AND PAULA OWENS

16   Geography, creativity and the future   222
     STEPHEN SCOFFHAM AND JONATHAN BARNES

     Appendix: National Curriculum links   232
     Index   235

FIGURES

1.1   When ideas from two different modes or lines of thinking interact it
      generates humour, surprise and creative sparks   3
1.2   Creative teachers use a range of techniques and activities to engage
      children   6
1.3   Creative activities that balance skills and challenge can generate a
      sense of flow or deep engagement   8
2.1   Geographical jokes are one example of word games   15
2.2   An example of an odd-one-out quiz   17
2.3   Dingbats for Washing-ton and rain-bow   18
2.4   Acrostics for 'river' and 'St Lucia'   19
2.5   Examples of limericks that include place names   21
2.6   Reveal picture of the leaning tower of Pisa   23
3.1   Through their drawings, children interpret and make sense of
      storybooks in different ways   31
3.2   Inspired by *Shackleton's Journey*, children at Egloskerry Primary
      School, Cornwall created an artwork of the *Endurance* and its crew
      stranded in the ice   34
3.3   Five-point response strategy (five-finger strategy)   39
4.1   Playful opportunities for place-making can promote 'happy
      geographers'   46
4.2   An example of using the Planning for Real® approach to create an
      outdoor performance area   48
4.3   Looking for signs of elves in Captain Phillimore's Woods, Hampshire   53
4.4   The Sea Call: one child's poetic response to playful place encounters   54
5.1   Barnaby Bear's address tells us where to find him   59
5.2   Creative activities to explore the meaning of an address   60
5.3   Locational knowledge for the primary years   62
5.4   Roads, homes and hills are key features in this local area map,
      drawn by a ten-year-old from memory   63
5.5   Africa and North and South America are key features in this map
      of the world, drawn by a seven-year-old from memory   63

FIGURES ▦ ▦ ▦ ■

5.6	Local fieldwork helps to develop children's mental maps	65
5.7	Four ways to investigate 'my world' knowledge	66
5.8	Activities to help children learn about the world	67
5.9	Children using a Maximap to explore the world map	68
5.10	Which of these world maps is the 'right way up'?	69
5.11	Re-orientating the world map can be a highly creative process	70
5.12	Ten engaging ways to develop locational awareness	70
5.13	Creating happy mappers	73
6.1	Close-up of some of the squares of the map created by pupils at Clinton C of E Primary School, Merton, Okehampton, Devon	77
6.2	Imagined landscapes by pupils from several participating schools in North Devon	78
6.3	Communal life and landscape around the village of Tigua, Ecuador, with the volcano Cotopaxi dominating the scene	80
6.4	Nita's painting of her husband's country tells how women follow the tracks of the goanna to their nest then dig for eggs	81
6.5	A ten-year-old's overpainting of an oblique aerial view of the Eden Project, Cornwall	83
6.6	It is important to encourage children to look at their surroundings from different perspectives	86
7.1	The 'treasure chest' on the left has coloured minerals and the one on the right has sparkly minerals	90
7.2	Which biscuit is easier to break up?	91
7.3	The crispie cake on the left was easier to 'erode'; it had less chocolate matrix to hold it together	94
7.4	Echinoid, trilobite, ammonite fossil biscuits	99
7.5	Soil and sand seascape painting	102
8.1	Some sample questions which children ask about physical geography	105
8.2	Common misconceptions in physical geography	106
8.3	Some of the children's questions about the River Tolka (Drumcondra National School)	109
8.4	Children's enquiry questions sorted into groups (Drumcondra National School)	110
8.5	Investigating a local river (Drumcondra National School)	110
8.6	Children's questions about rocks (Newtown National School)	111
8.7	Investigating rocks in the locality (Newtown National School)	112
8.8	Setting up school grounds for outdoor learning about the physical world (St Colmcille's National School)	114
9.1	Roberts proposes a concise framework for enquiry learning	120
9.2	Questions about Barrow Bridge that informed my lesson planning	122
9.3	Children's initial ideas about why people settled in Barrow Bridge	122
9.4	Pupils made drawings of different sections of the river, which they joined together	123
9.5	How pupil responses and creative engagement was part of the enquiry and fieldwork process	124
9.6	Extracts from the blog about the Barrow Bridge fieldwork by Year 3 pupils, with key vocabulary highlighted	126
9.7	Pupils creating a junk model map	127

9.8	The fieldwork inspired the children to create a game	128
10.1	Pupils' responses to the question 'What is maths?'	134
10.2	Pupils' reflection ideas following the trail	135
10.3	A Year 2 student from International School of Bologna, racing to complete the peg trail in under two minutes	137
10.4	An example of a maths map, completed by a Year 3 student	138
10.5	International School of Bologna Year 3 students measuring the height of a bush	138
10.6	International School of Bologna Year 1 students sorting leaves into different types	139
10.7	Geocaching motivates pupils and develops skills such as wayfinding and using compass directions	141
11.1	The Kinaesthetic Adventure Learning Park creates engrossing and memorable learning experiences	149
11.2	The mystery map and old manuscript that the contractors claimed to unearth when they built the park	150
11.3	Making a model of Tower Bridge	156
11.4	Artists whose paintings have influenced our perceptions of places	158
11.5	Some opportunities for applying creative arts approaches in authentic geographical learning experiences	159
12.1	Music is linked to place at a profound level	165
13.1	Creativity and criticality are complementary but different aspects of purposeful learning	180
13.2	Some principles of 'living geography'	181
13.3	Year 3 student, International School of Bologna, collecting information about the school grounds	182
13.4	A letter from a Year 3 pupil, Eastchurch School, Isle of Sheppey, Kent, following a visit to a local nature reserve	184
13.5	Extract from initial planning sheet, Southborough Primary School: the true story of Little Red Riding Hood	187
13.6	Thinking about wind turbines from different viewpoints – from a Year 4 pupil from Eastchurch School, Isle of Sheppey, Kent	189
14.1	Year 3 and 4 children recreated their home town with everything they could lay their hands on	194
14.2	The children raided the PE store to create their maps	194
14.3	Statements that might be used in a set of 'living map' cards	195
14.4	Person specifications for the travel agent simulation	197
14.5	How is the Earth like an apple?	198
14.6	Climate change could have disastrous implications for wildlife	199
14.7	There are strong links between notions of care and sustainability	201
14.8	The four Ds of the enquiry cycle	202
15.1	A collection of fridge magnets is one way to develop children's locational knowledge	207
15.2	Pupils at Woolmore Primary School, Tower Hamlets, listen to sounds and assess the quality of the environment while on a trail	211
15.3	Some children considered ways of redesigning the street outside their school as part of their project on the local community	213

CONTENTS ▨ ▨ ▪ ▪

15.4 Toy creatures such as dinosaurs enable children to create miniature
     words that engage their imagination   215
15.5 Student teachers from Winchester University exploring and
     responding to place in the Brecon Beacons   217
15.6 Creativity is best promoted by slower forms of learning   218
16.1 We are currently consuming around 50 per cent more resources than
     the Earth can provide and the trend is ever upwards   223
16.2 Interpreting place through different perspectives or 'lenses', deepens
     geographical thinking   225
16.3 Sustainability and futures thinking in the UK national curricula   229

CONTRIBUTORS

Anthony Barlow is senior lecturer in primary geography education and BA Primary Education Programme convener at the University of Roehampton. He is co-chair of the Early Years and Primary phase committee of the Geographical Association (GA). He has a fascination with trees.

Jonathan Barnes is a visiting senior research fellow at Canterbury Christ Church University and a National Teaching fellow. He currently works as education consultant to Migrant Help UK. He is author of *Cross Curricular Learning 3–14* (now in its third edition) and the forthcoming *Applying Cross-curricular Approaches Creatively*.

Simon Catling is emeritus professor of primary education in the School of Education, Oxford Brookes University. A past president of the Geographical Association, he is author of *Mapstart,* co-author of *Teaching Primary Geography* and edited *Research and Debates in Primary Geography*. Though retired, he continues to research and write.

Anne M. Dolan is a lecturer in primary geography at Mary Immaculate College, University of Limerick, Ireland. Her research interests include geographical education, geo-literacy and creativity in education. She is the author of *You, Me and Diversity: Picturebooks for Teaching Development and Intercultural Education* (Trentham Books and IOE Press, London).

Arthur J. Kelly is a senior lecturer in education at Chester University. He is a member of the editorial board of the journal *Primary Geography* and is a moderator for the Primary Geography Quality Mark, a national scheme benchmarking geographical teaching and learning.

Margaret Mackintosh was senior lecturer in primary geography education at Plymouth University. She is a member of the Geographical Association's Early Years and Primary phase committee and serves on the editorial board of *Primary Geography*.

Paula Owens is an education consultant. A former primary and deputy head teacher, Paula worked for the Geographical Association for many years leading the Primary

Geography Quality Mark and curriculum development. She is a member of the Geography Expert Subject Advisory Group and the *Primary Geography* editorial board.

Stephen Pickering is senior lecturer in primary education at the University of Worcester and course leader for primary and outdoor education. He is a fellow of the Royal Society of Arts and a consultant for the Geographical Association (GA) where he sits on the GA's *Primary Geography* editorial board.

Susan Pike is a lecturer in geography education at the Institute of Education, Dublin City University. She teaches geography education at undergraduate and post-graduate levels. Her research interests include all aspects of children's learning in geography as well as teacher education. She is the author of *Learning Primary Geography: Ideas and Inspirations from Classrooms*.

Stephen Scoffham is a visiting reader in sustainability and education at Canterbury Christ Church University, UK. A leading member of the Geographical Association, he is the author of many books for teachers and children on primary geography, and a school atlas consultant.

Julia Tanner spent her career in teaching and teacher education, and now works as an education trainer, consultant, and author, specialising in primary humanities, outdoor learning, and effective pedagogy. She is a member of the Geographical Association's Early Years and Primary phase committee, and Publications Board.

Peter Vujakovic is professor of geography at Canterbury Christ Church University. He has written widely on cartography and information graphics and has recently run a national workshop on primary school atlases as co-convener of the British Cartographic Society's Map Design Special Interest Group.

Niki Whitburn is a former senior lecturer at Bishop Grosseteste University, Lincoln, now retired. She has also previously worked for Earth Science Teachers' Association as chair of their council and a member of their Primary team.

Jane Whittle is a classroom teacher and technology integration coach at the International School of Bologna. She is co-author of a number of texts including *Back2Front: The Americas* and *The Everyday Guide to Teaching Geography: Story*.

Terry Whyte is senior lecturer in the Faculty of Education, Canterbury Christ Church University. He has written in books, journals and electronic publications about his research and his approach to education in which learning, creativity and fun are intrinsically linked.

Sharon Witt is senior lecturer in education at the University of Winchester. Her research interests include playful, experiential approaches to primary geography and place responsive education. She is a member of the Early Years and Primary phase committee of the Geographical Association and the Geography Expert Subject Advisory Group.

SERIES EDITOR'S FOREWORD

Teresa Cremin

Over recent decades teachers working in accountability cultures across the globe have been required to focus on raising standards, setting targets, and 'delivering' prescribed curricula and pedagogy. The language of schooling, Mottram and Hall (2009: 109) assert, has predominantly focused upon 'oversimplified, easily measurable notions of attainment' which, they argue, has had a homogenising effect, prompting children and their development to be discussed 'according to levels and descriptors', rather than as children, as unique learners. Practitioners, positioned as passive recipients of the prescribed agenda appear to have had their hands tied, their voices quietened and their professional autonomy both threatened and constrained. At times, the relentless quest for higher standards has obscured the personal and affective dimensions of teaching and learning, fostering a mindset characterised more by compliance and conformity than curiosity and creativity.

However, creativity too has been in the ascendant in recent decades; in many countries efforts have been made to re-ignite creativity in education, since it is seen to be essential to economic and cultural development. This impetus for creativity can be traced back to the National Advisory Committee on Creative and Cultural Education (NACCCE 1999), which recommended a core role for creativity in teaching and learning. Primary schools in England were encouraged to explore ways to offer more innovative and creative curricula (DfES 2003) and new national curricula in Scotland also foregrounded children's critical and creative thinking. Additionally, initiatives such as Creative Partnerships, an English government-funded initiative to nurture children's creativity, inspired some teachers to reconstruct their pedagogy (Galton 2010). Many other schools and teachers, encouraged by these initiatives, and determined to offer creative and engaging school experiences, have exercised the 'power to innovate' (Lance 2006). Many have proactively sought ways to shape the curriculum responsively, appropriating national policies in their own contexts and showing professional commitment and imagination, despite, or perhaps because of, the persistent performative agenda (e.g. Cremin *et al.* 2015; Neelands 2009; Jeffrey and Woods 2009).

Schools continue to be exhorted to be more innovative in curriculum construction and national curricula afford opportunities for all teachers to seize the space, exert their professionalism and shape their own curricula in collaboration with the young people with whom they are working. Yet for primary educators, tensions persist, not only because the dual policies of performativity and creativity appear contradictory, but also perhaps because teachers' own confidence as creative educators, indeed as creative individuals, has been radically reduced by the constant barrage of change and challenge. As Csikszentmihalyi (2011) notes, teachers lack a theoretically underpinned framework for creativity that can be developed in practice; they need support to develop as artistically engaged, research-informed curriculum co-developers. Eisner (2003) asserts that teaching is an art form, an act of improvisation (Sawyer 2011), and that teachers benefit from viewing themselves as versatile artists in the classroom, drawing on their personal passions and creativity as they teach creatively.

As Joubert too observes:

> Creative teaching is an art. One cannot teach teachers didactically how to be creative; there is no fail safe recipe or routines. Some strategies may help to promote creative thinking, but teachers need to develop a full repertoire of skills which they can adapt to different situations.
>
> (Joubert 2001: 21)

However, creative teaching is only part of the picture, since teaching for creativity also needs to be acknowledged and their mutual dependency recognised. The former focuses more on teachers using imaginative approaches in the classroom (and beyond) in order to make learning more interesting and effective, the latter, more on the development of children's creativity (NACCCE 1999). Both rely upon an understanding of the notion of creativity and demand that professionals confront the myths and mantras which surround the word. These include the commonly held misconceptions that creativity is the preserve of the arts or arts education, and that it is confined to particularly gifted individuals.

Creativity, an elusive concept, has been multiply defined by educationalists, psychologists and neurologists, as well as by policy makers in different countries and researchers in different cultural contexts (Glăveanu 2015). Debates resound about its individual and/or collaborative nature, the degree to which it is generic and/or domain specific, and the differences between the 'big C' creativity of genius and the 'little c' creativity of the everyday. Notwithstanding these issues, most scholars in the field believe it involves the capacity to generate, reason and critically evaluate novel ideas and/or imaginary scenarios. As such, it encompasses thinking through and solving problems, making connections, inventing and reinventing, and flexing one's imaginative muscles in all aspects of learning and life.

In the primary classroom, creative teaching and learning have been associated with innovation, originality, ownership and control (Woods and Jeffrey 1996; Jeffrey 2006) and creative teachers have been seen, in their planning and teaching, and in the ethos which they create, to afford high value to curiosity and risk taking, to ownership, autonomy and making connections (Craft *et al.* 2014; Cremin *et al.* 2009; Cremin 2015). Such teachers often work in partnership with others: with children, other teachers and experts from beyond the school gates (Cochrane and Cockett 2007; Davies *et al.* 2012; Thomson *et al.* 2012). These partnerships offer new possibilities, with teachers acquiring some of the repertoire of pedagogic practices – the 'signature pedagogies' that artists use (Thomson and Hall 2015). Additionally, in research exploring possibility thinking, which Craft (2000) argues drives creativity in education, an intriguing interplay between teachers and children has been observed. In this body of work, children and teachers have been involved in immersing themselves in playful contexts, posing questions, being imaginative, showing self-determination, taking risks and innovating – together (Burnard *et al.* 2006; Cremin *et al.* 2006, 2013; Chappell *et al.* 2008; Craft *et al.* 2012). As McWilliam (2008) argues, teachers can choose not to position themselves as the all-knowing 'sage on the stage', or the facilitator-like 'guide on the side'. They can choose, as creative practitioners do, to take up a role of the 'meddler in the middle', co-creating curricula in innovative and responsive ways that harness their own and foster the children's creativity. A new pedagogy of possibility beckons.

The Learning to Teach in the Primary School series, which accompanies and complements the edited textbook *Learning to Teach in the Primary School* (Cremin and Arthur 2014), seeks to support teachers in developing as creative practitioners, assisting them in exploring the synergies between and potential for teaching creatively and teaching for creativity. The series does not merely offer practical strategies for use in the classroom, though these abound, but more importantly seeks to widen teachers' and student teachers' knowledge and understanding of the principles underpinning creative approaches, principles based on research. It seeks to mediate the wealth of research evidence and make accessible and engaging the diverse theoretical perspectives and scholarly arguments available, demonstrating their practical relevance and value to the profession. Those who aspire to develop further as creative and curious educators will find much of value to support their own professional learning journeys and markedly enrich their pedagogy and practice right across the curriculum.

ABOUT THE SERIES EDITOR

Teresa Cremin (Grainger) is a Professor of Education (literacy) at the Open University and a past president of UKRA (2001–2) and UKLA (2007–9). She is currently a director of the Cambridge Primary Review Trust, co-convener of the BERA Creativity SIG and a trustee of Booktrust and UKLA. In addition, Teresa is a Fellow of the Royal Society for the Arts, the English Association and the Academy of Social Sciences.

Teresa's work involves research, publication and consultancy in literacy and creativity. Many of her current projects seek to explore the nature and characteristics of creative pedagogies, including for example, examining immersive theatre and related teaching techniques, children's make believe play in the context of story-telling and story acting, their everyday lives and literacy practices, and the nature of literary discussions in extracurricular reading groups. Additionally, Teresa is researching creative science practice with learners aged 3–8 years and possibility thinking as a driver for creative learning. Teresa is also passionate about (and still researching) teachers' own creative development and their identity positioning in the classroom as readers, writers, and creative human beings.

Teresa has written and edited over 25 books, and numerous papers and professional texts, most recently editing with colleagues *Researching Literacy Lives*: *Building home-school communities* (2015, Routledge), *Teaching English Creatively*

(2nd edn 2015, Routledge), *Building Communities of Engaged Readers: Reading for Pleasure* (2014, Routledge) and *The International Handbook of Research into Children's Literacy, Learning and Culture* (2013, Blackwell). *Storytelling in Early Childhood: Enriching Language, Literacy and Classroom Culture* is forthcoming (2016, Routledge). In addition her book publications since 2000 include *Writing Voices: Creating Communities of Writers* (2012, Routledge), *Learning to Teach in the Primary School* (2014, Routledge), *Teaching Writing Effectively: Reviewing Practice* (2011, UKLA), *Drama, Reading and Writing: Talking Our Way Forwards* (2009, UKLA), *Jumpstart Drama* (2009, David Fulton), *Creative Teaching for Tomorrow: Fostering a Creative State of Mind* (2009, Future Creative), *Documenting Creative Learning 5–11* (2007, Trentham), *Creativity and Writing: Developing Voice and Verve* (2005, Routledge), *Teaching English in Higher Education* (2007, NATE and UKLA), *Creative Activities for Character, Setting and Plot, 5–7, 7–9, 9–11* (2004, Scholastic) and *Language and Literacy: A Routledge Reader* (2001, Routledge).

REFERENCES

Burnard, P., Craft, A. and Cremin, T. (2006) Possibility thinking. *International Journal of Early Years Education* 14(3): 243–62.

Chappell, K., Craft, A., Burnard, P. and Cremin, T (2008) Question-posing and Question-responding: the heart of possibility thinking in the early years. *Early Years* 283: 267–86.

Cochrane, P. and Cockett, M. (2007) *Building a Creative School: A Dynamic Approach to School Improvement*. Stoke: Trentham Books.

Craft, A. (2000). *Creativity Across the Primary Curriculum*. London: Routledge.

Craft, A., Cremin, T., Burnard, P., Dragovic, T. and Chappell, K. (2012) Possibility thinking: culminative studies of an evidence-based concept driving creativity? *Education 3–13* 41(5): 538–56.

Craft, A., Cremin, T., Hay, P. and Clack, J. (2014) Creative Primary Schools: developing and maintaining pedagogy for creativity. *Ethnography and Education* 9(1): 16–34.

Cremin, T. (2015) Creative teachers and creative teaching. In A. Wilson (ed.), *Creativity in Primary Education*, pp. 33–44. London: Sage.

Cremin, T. and Arthur, J. (eds) (2014) *Learning to Teach in the Primary School* (3rd edition). London: Routledge.

Cremin, T., Burnard, P. and Craft, A. (2006) Pedagogy and possibility thinking in the early years. *International Journal of Thinking Skills and Creativity* 1(2): 108–19.

Cremin, T., Barnes, J. and Scoffham, S. (2009) *Creative Teaching for Tomorrow: Fostering a Creative State of Mind*. Deal: Future Creative.

Cremin, T., Chappell, K. and Craft, A. (2013) Reciprocity between narrative, questioning and imagination in the early and primary years: examining the role of narrative in possibility thinking. *Thinking Skills and Creativity* 9: 136–51.

Cremin, T., Glauert, E., Craft, A., Compton, A. and Stylianidou, F. (2015) Creative little scientists: exploring pedagogical synergies between inquiry-based and creative approaches in early years science. *Education 3–13* 43(4): 404–19.

Cremin, T., Mottram, M., Powell, S., Collins, R. and Drury, R. (2015) *Researching Literacy Lives: Building Home School Communities*. London: Routledge

Csikszentmihalyi, M. (2011) A systems perspective on creativity and its implications for measurement. In R. Schenkel and O. Quintin (eds), *Measuring Creativity*, pp. 407–14. Brussels: European Commission.

Davies, D., Jindal-Snape, D., Collier, C., Digby, R., Hay, P. and Howe, A. (2012) Creative environments for learning in schools. *Thinking Skills and Creativity* 8(1): 80–91.

DfES (2003) *Excellence and Enjoyment: A Strategy for Primary Schools*. Nottingham: Department for Education and Skills.

Eisner, E. (2003) Artistry in education. *Scandinavian Journal of Educational Research* 47(3): 373–84.

Galton, M. (2010) Going with the flow or back to normal? The impact of creative practitioners in schools and classrooms. *Research Papers in Education* 25(4): 355–75.

Glăveanu, V., Sierra, Z. and Tanggaard, L. (2015) Widening our understanding of creative pedagogy: a North–South dialogue. *Education 3-13* 43(4): 360–70.

Jeffrey, B. (ed.) (2006) *Creative Learning Practices: European Experiences*. London: Tufnell Press.

Jeffrey, B. and Woods, P. (2009) *Creative Learning in the Primary School*. London: Routledge.

Joubert, M. M. (2001) The art of creative teaching: NACCCE and beyond. In A. Craft, B. Jeffrey and M. Liebling (eds), *Creativity in Education*, pp. 17–34. London: Continuum.

Lance, A. (2006) Power to innovate? A study of how primary practitioners are negotiating the modernisation agenda. *Ethnography and Education* 1(3): 333–44.

Mottram, M. and Hall, C. (2009) Diversions and diversity: does the personalisation agenda offer real opportunities for taking children's home literacies seriously? *English in Education* 43(2): 98–112.

McWilliam, E. (2008) Unlearning how to teach *Innovations in Education and Teaching International* 45(3) 263-269.

NACCCE (1999) *All Our Futures: Creativity, Culture and Education*. London: Department for Education and Employment.

Neelands, J. (2009) Acting together: ensemble as a democratic process in art and life. *Research in Drama Education* 14(2): 173–89.

Sawyer, K. (ed.) (2011) *Structure and Improvisation in Creative Teaching*. New York: Cambridge University Press.

Thomson, P. and Hall, C. (2015) Everyone can imagine their own Gellert: the democratic artist and 'inclusion' in primary and nursery classrooms. *Education 3–13* 43(4): 420–32.

Thomson, P., Hall, C., Jones, K. and Sefton-Green, J. (2012) *The Signature Pedagogies Project: Final Report*. London: Creativity, Culture and Education. Available at www.creativetallis.com/uploads/2/2/8/7/2287089/signature_pedagogies_report_final_version_11.3.12.pdf (accessed 1 June 2012).

Woods, P. and Jeffrey, B. (1996) *Teachable Moments: The Art of Creative Teaching in Primary Schools*. Buckingham: Open University Press.

ACKNOWLEDGEMENTS

This book has been a joy to work on. The affirmative nature of the subject and the unstinting engagement of all those involved in producing it have urged me on to do my very best. Teresa Cremin made the initial contact and had the vision to see how we could build on our joint research into learning and creativity. The first edition of *Teaching Geography Creatively*, which resulted from these endeavours, won the Geographical Association Gold Award for new teaching materials in 2014. The second edition, which you now have before you, builds on this earlier version and extends the argument for an approach to primary geography which is infused with an environmental ethic and which places the learner at the heart of education. These books have been brought to life by a wonderful and supportive team at Routledge. Helen Pritt and Rhiannon Findlay worked on the first edition. Clare Ashworth and Sarah Tuckwell worked on this revised edition.

The idea for an edited (rather than a single-authored) book emerged at the Charney Manor research conference on primary geography held in February 2011. The overwhelmingly positive response from friends and colleagues who were present at that time convinced me to take on the task of editing the scripts. Some members of the original writing team were experienced and well-established authors; others were writing a book chapter for the first time. All contributed wonderfully imaginative ideas, responded positively to my suggestions and proved immensely quick to answer emails. They have continued to do so as we have updated and revised the text. Thanks to all of you for being such a pleasant, generous and agreeable author team. I truly believe this book is imbued with the spirit of the Charney Manor conferences, which have meant so much to all of us who have attended them and which have been held annually (with just a few breaks) since 1995.

Stephen Scoffham
Canterbury Christ Church University
March 2016

GEOGRAPHY AND CREATIVITY
Making connections

Stephen Scoffham

This chapter explores what we mean by creativity. It begins by considering some of the different definitions and features of creative thought and how these might relate to classroom practice. It is suggested that creative learning experiences have the potential to enrich the curriculum and enhance personal well-being. The rich possibilities that are offered by geography are outlined. The chapter concludes by arguing that creative approaches involving joyful and imaginative learning set in a values context, will build children's capacities in the face of an increasingly uncertain future.

INTRODUCTION

Creativity is an elusive concept. It is treasured by many educationalists as one of the key elements of effective teaching, yet remains ill-defined and poorly understood. Historically, creativity was associated with the act of creation, which was seen as a divine gift. The notion that the world was created by God is a central tenet in many religious texts. We learn from the Bible, for example, how, in the beginning, God created the heavens and Earth, progressively adding light, water, sky and living things. Certainly, there are good reasons why people in the past might have wanted to invoke superhuman powers to explain the magic and beauty of life in all its diversity. How else could these wonders have come about? Interestingly, the association between creation and creativity is embedded in our language. Both terms are derived from the same Latin verb *creare*, which means to produce or to make. It is no coincidence that the word 'creature' also shares the same linguistic root. Small wonder then that we sometimes feel uncomfortable when we are invited to be creative. The student who, when asked to note her responses to a heritage site, roundly declared 'I don't do creativity!' was reflecting this unease. Her fear was that she would be unable to come up with something that required exceptional talents or gifts.

In modern times the meaning of creativity has shifted considerably. While the idea that creativity implies a special gift still informs popular usage, it has also taken on a more prosaic dimension. Solving the problems that make up our everyday lives has come to be seen as a creative activity. As we think of solutions, suggest alternatives and imagine what might happen in the future, we are drawing on our creative powers. In education, especially, creativity has come to be associated with thinking and learning. Scoffham and

Barnes (2007: 13), for example, argue that creativity is a 'fundamental aspect of human thought'. This means that, rather than being restricted to the expressive arts, creativity has relevance for all curriculum areas.

The overlap between creativity and human thought places it at the centre of the educational agenda. Moreover, there is an increasing realisation that creativity is not fixed. Some years ago, a key UK government report, *All Our Futures* (NACCCE 1999: 28), made the point that 'all people are capable of creative achievement in some area of activity'. It now seems that we can develop our creative capacities whatever area we are involved in. Drawing on research, Lucas and Claxton (2011) argue that our mental attitude and temperament are not set in stone but are capable of change. Not only do they offer compelling evidence to support this claim, but they also outline practical strategies for effecting change. This is encouraging news because teachers are in a prime position to construct situations in which creativity is likely to flourish.

DEFINITIONS OF CREATIVITY

There are many definitions of creativity. In educational circles the definition that was put forward by the National Advisory Committee on Creative and Cultural Education (NACCCE 1999) has gained considerable currency and informed much subsequent thinking. The committee argued that creativity always involves the four following characteristics:

(a)   thinking and behaving imaginatively;
(b)   purposeful activity directed towards an objective;
(c)   processes that generate something which is original;
(d)   outcomes that are of value in relation to the objective.

This led the NACCCE to define creativity as 'imaginative activity fashioned so as to produce outcomes that are both original and of value' (*ibid.*: 30).

The NACCCE definition places considerable stress on products and outcomes and underplays the role of experimentation and flexibility. Sometimes we simply do not know where our thoughts are heading. Craft (2000) draws attention to this aspect of creativity in what she calls 'possibility thinking'. This involves both solving problems and raising questions. She also reminds us that creativity is not a single process but involves multiple dimensions that include looking into ourselves as well as outwards towards our surroundings. De Bono (2010), who coined the term 'lateral thinking', takes a different approach when he highlights the importance of making connections and seeking alternatives. He stresses how creativity involves going beyond the obvious to generate novel solutions. One of de Bono's particular interests is to develop strategies that allow people to pool their thoughts. His 'thinking hats' is a neat device for avoiding the limiting effect of binary approaches. Another enduring insight comes from Koestler (1964), who emphasises the link between creativity, surprise and humour. The way that two ideas, often from different subjects or discipline areas, can come together to generate a creative spark underpins his notion of bi-sociation (Figure 1.1).

There is increasing recognition that creativity needs to be viewed in a cultural context. Western interpretations tend to emphasise the role of the individual and are orientated towards products and innovation. Eastern perspectives are more likely to focus on team and group endeavour. They may also emphasise personal fulfilment, the expression

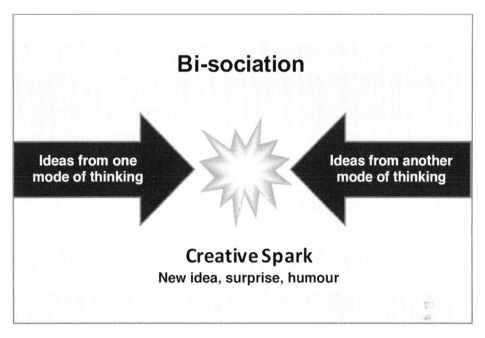

■ **Figure 1.1** When ideas from two different modes or lines of thinking interact it generates humour, surprise and creative sparks
Source: after Koestler (1964)

of inner truths and a sense of oneness with the world. Hinduism, for example, interprets creativity in spiritual or religious terms and sees time and history as cyclical. In education, where many teachers will be working with pupils from multicultural backgrounds, the dangers of adopting a one-size-fits-all approach to creativity will be immediately apparent.

To conclude, it is perhaps best to think of creativity as having a number of different dimensions ranging from the cognitive to the social and emotional. Choosing to focus on one aspect of creativity may lead us to neglect the others. However, it is generally accepted across cultures that creativity is a positive concept. There is also significant agreement that creativity is strongly associated with play, imagination and the emotions, and that it leads to new ways of seeing and thinking. These ideas are explored further in the following section.

Play

Young children are well known for their curiosity and their desire for play. They have a seemingly insatiable interest in the world around them and are constantly asking questions that adults find alternatively charming and annoying. Their questions appear charming because they often suggest unusual or unexpected connections. They are annoying partly because children ask them so persistently and partly because we often don't know the answers ourselves; or if we do, we find it hard to express them in terms children can understand.

One of the great qualities of play is that it is experimental, flexible and entertaining. Katz (2004) declares that play is about making and remaking the world. Young children are particularly good at this. Schools and teachers are sometimes accused of undermining children's natural capacity for inventiveness, but this is perhaps unfair. As children become older they come to recognise how ideas can fit together in useful patterns and networks. In other words, experience teaches them how best to approach different situations, and their capacity for unusual or divergent thought is reduced in consequence.

Generating ideas

Creativity is also strongly associated with generating new ideas. Some people, such as famous musicians, artists, scientists and mathematicians, have been so successful at devising new ideas that they have changed the way we see the world. This is sometimes termed 'big C' creativity, and it is, by definition, a comparatively rare phenomenon. By contrast, the kind of creativity we are likely to engage in on an everyday basis is known as 'small C' creativity. Both 'big C' and 'small C' creativity are about being original, even if the scale and impact are vastly different. It is also important to note that coming up with new ideas can be a highly stimulating and rewarding process. In his review of the primary school curriculum, Alexander (2010: 213) reports that children 'valued those subjects that sparked their curiosity and encouraged them to explore'. We are all attracted by novelty, and the complaint that something is boring usually arises because it is repetitive and lacks challenge. Developing new ways of thinking is stimulating even if it may also be unsettling.

Imagination

Using imagination is another aspect of creativity. This can take make different forms. It may involve asking unusual questions, envisaging alternatives or re-examining something that is taken for granted and seeing it in a different light. Coming up with new ideas can be fun, but unless these ideas are applied in some way they remain in the world of fantasy. The problem is that it is not always clear at the time whether a new idea is useful or not. Thus divergent thinking can oscillate between appearing highly creative on the one hand and whacky and weird on the other. Perhaps this is why genius and madness are often associated in the popular imagination. There are times when the boundary between the two is surprisingly thin.

Emotions

Creativity is not purely intellectual activity. Harnessing our emotional energies is an essential part of creativity and it involves accessing layers of thought that lie beneath the surface of everyday cognition. Drawing on evidence from neuroscience, Immordino-Yang and Damasio (2007) argue that while creativity may be informed by high reason, it is fundamentally based on a platform of emotional thought in both social and non-social contexts. They go on to argue that motivation – the dynamo that drives our learning – derives from emotional rather than cognitive neural networks. Craft (2000) makes a similar point when she declares that the sources of creativity are not always conscious or rational. She reminds us that 'the intuitive, spiritual and emotional also feed creativity' and that these are themselves 'fed by the bedrock of impulse' (*ibid.*: 31).

Intuition

There is a sense in which creativity involves a particular type of thought. It involves making links and connections, allowing ideas to emerge and being open to suggestion. Lucas and Claxton (2011) draw on a metaphor used by neuroscientists to suggest that we can view mental processes as a landscape that can be made either steeper or flatter according to our state of mind. Definite modes of thinking correspond to a steep, mountainous landscape while more playful and dreamy modes relate to a gentler, flatter terrain. There are times when we need focused thinking that channels our thinking down deep valleys, but the flatter terrain is better at handling ambiguities. As Lucas and Claxton explain, 'because the land is flat, neural patterns are much more able to bleed into one another, so you can find connections which are less stereotyped or conventional' (*ibid*.: 75). It is also important to be able to switch between different modes so as to get the benefit of both. People who are less creative tend to be stuck in one mode. Being flexible and receptive to new ideas is part of a creative mindset.

CREATIVITY IN PRACTICE

So what does creativity look like in a classroom context? One distinction that has proved useful is the difference between (a) teaching creatively and (b) teaching for creativity.

Teaching creatively focuses attention on the teacher; it involves teachers drawing on their own skills and abilities to make learning more stimulating. Self-image is important here. Research shows that when teachers regard themselves as creative it can enhance their practice (Cremin *et al.* 2009). Confidence is important too. Working alongside other colleagues or with non-teacher practitioners such as artists, musicians, engineers and town planners is often an affirmative experience that can release latent talents. Your own enthusiasm, curiosity and desire to learn are liable to be much more important than being theatrical or showy.

Teaching for creativity, by contrast, directs attention to the learner and the quality of their experience. A focus on creativity is likely to involve giving pupils greater control over their learning. It may also favour collaborative and co-operative approaches in which children spark ideas off each other. Providing different entry points, encouraging pupils to ask questions and getting them to make connections are key strategies. Research suggests that a combination of teaching methods is likely to be more effective than any single approach. In their study of creative teachers, Cremin *et al.* (2009) found that over 30 techniques and activities were used in just a few lessons (Figure 1.2).

Teaching creatively is not an easy option. It requires good subject knowledge so that teachers are able to answer questions imaginatively, have the confidence to engage with unfamiliar material and identify new learning opportunities as and when they occur. Of course, we cannot actually make children think or learn creatively. However, we can, as Barnes (2015) points out, provide the conditions where creativity is more likely to flourish. Careful lesson planning in which pupils are exposed to an appropriate stimulus and provided with a supportive environment where they can develop their ideas is important. There will be times when individual study is appropriate but opportunities for group and team work also need to be exploited. Collaboration helps to trigger new ideas and sharing findings can prompt further thoughts. As Perkins (2010) concludes, learning from 'the team' is often more effective than learning 'solo'.

Child-initiated activity	Explanation	Library research
Discovery	Problem-solving	Personal computer
Reverse/open questioning	Investigations	Fieldwork
Music	Conversation	Breaks for 'brain gym'
Practical activities	Time for reflection	Photographs
Construction	Shared/individual writing	Videos
Demonstration	Stories	Map work
Electronic games	Poems	Competitions
Worksheets	Role play	Presentations
Edible and visual aids	Drama	Tests
Classroom displays	Dance	Class league tables
Interactive whiteboards	Crosswords	Merit marks

▒ **Figure 1.2** Creative teachers use a range of techniques and activities to engage children
Source: after Cremin *et al.* (2009)

It is also important to recognise that there are different stages in creative thought. An initial period of drafting and incubation is followed by a period of development and testing that leads eventually to some form of iteration. The timescale is very variable. Tentative ideas and suggestions can be extremely fragile and appear silly or inappropriate until they are refined. The final resolution will be much more robust. The NACCCE (1999: 34) observe, 'At the right time and in the right way, rigorous critical appraisal is essential. At the wrong point, criticism and the cold hand of realism can kill an emerging idea.' Judging the moment is one of the arts of teaching.

Creative teaching presents teachers with other challenges. When pupils engage in deep learning it leads them to reappraise their basic concepts. This can result in a period of uncertainty and confusion. Festinger (1957) uses the term 'cognitive dissonance' to describe. the disturbance that occurs when our assumptions and expectations are challenged in some way. Pupils need a supportive environment that encourages them to speculate and experiment. This in turn will serve to build their self-confidence and mental resilience. As one teacher remarked, 'It's all about taking chances … letting them take risks with their own learning' (Cremin *et al.* 2009: 25). In the way that they relate to pupils and structure learning, teachers can generate the social and educational environment that will provide the necessary nurture and support.

CREATIVITY MATTERS

Central government has an enduring interest in creativity and creative teaching. The Roberts (2006) report and Warwick Commission (2015) summarise some of the key arguments:

1 The creative industries employ over two million people in the UK, account for around 8 per cent of the economy and are important drivers of economic growth.
2 There is a strong moral case for giving children creative experiences. These help pupils to develop their sense of personal identity and can prepare them for twenty-first-century society.

3   A focus on creativity has the potential to reengage young people who are at risk of opting out of learning altogether and thereby supports the inclusion and diversity agendas.

Another powerful force that is serving to move creativity to the forefront of the educational agenda is technology. Within a generation, electronic communications have come to dominate modern life. We are linked to people in different parts of the world through texts, emails, information searches, e-commerce, gaming and social-networking sites. We can develop ideas in conjunction with people we have never met and we can occupy multiple spaces and realities. Craft (2011) argues that the digital revolution is empowering children by extending their opportunities and developing their talents. It invites activity, participation, engagement and interpretation – all key elements of creativity. It also promotes possibility thinking by allowing us to hold ideas alongside each other, bring different pieces of information together and make leaps and connections between ideas. Technology is thus pushing the boundaries of both how we learn and how we understand the world. Digital environments favour parallel rather linear processing, emphasise graphics over text and invite collaboration rather than isolation. A major challenge for schools and educators is to decide how best to respond to these opportunities. The digital revolution is leading to patterns of thinking and ways of behaving that are difficult to control and hard to assess.

Creativity matters to us all. One leading psychologist makes the bold claim that creativity is a 'central source of meaning in our lives' (Csikszentmihalyi 1997: 2). It is through human ingenuity, he argues, that we have developed language, science, technology and all those other achievements that distinguish us from the rest of the animal kingdom. Furthermore, when we are engaged in creative activity we feel more fully alive than at other times in our lives. Csikszentmihalyi has coined the term 'flow' to characterise those moments when we are so deeply involved in something that nothing else seems to matter. On these occasions our self-awareness is diminished, time seems altered and action and awareness are merged. At the same time our motivation is so intense that we stop worrying about failure and we pursue what we are doing not because of any benefits it might bring but for its own sake. Csikszentmihalyi suggests that flow activities are most likely to occur when there is a reasonable balance between the skills we have at our disposal and the challenges that confront us. If there is too much challenge we are likely to give up. If there is too little, we tend to become bored (Figure 1.3). There are important implications for education. One of them is that creative activity is not a substitute for developing skills and knowledge. Quite the contrary: it thrives on them. Another is that creative activity is intricately linked with learning.

The link between creativity and well-being merits further attention. For example, one study has found that walking significantly enhances the generation of novel yet appropriate ideas. The benefits, which appear to be long-lasting, accrue whether the exercise is taken outside in the street or inside on a treadmill (Oppezzo and Schwartz 2014). It is also tantalising to think that if pupils are engaged in creative activities on a daily basis it could maximise their longer-term sense of fulfilment and satisfaction. This in turn has the potential to trigger an upward spiral of growth and personal development. At a time when there are considerable concerns about the quality and experience of childhood (Layard and Dunn 2009; Children's Society 2015), a focus on creativity could offer a valuable way of enhancing well-being.

It is, however, important to sound a note of caution. Creativity on its own is not necessarily a force for good. Flow experiences can be derived from both worthwhile and distasteful experiences. Education and learning can be channelled towards indoctrination as well as enlightenment. Barnes *et al.* offer this advice:

> Before embarking upon any creative journey in schools we need first to discuss, agree and document what we believe is good and right and true and beautiful. This is not as difficult as it sounds in a school setting, but ensuring that creativity is used for the good of all is a major challenge for the future of our world.
>
> (Barnes *et al.* 2008: 133)

Creativity, then, is a capacity or capability we can harness in different ways. It is what distinguishes us from machines and has given rise to some of our finest achievements. We need to ensure that it is applied constructively and placed within a moral framework. As we enter the first decades of the twenty-first century, many people would argue that thinking creatively about sustainability and the environment should be particularly high on our list of priorities.

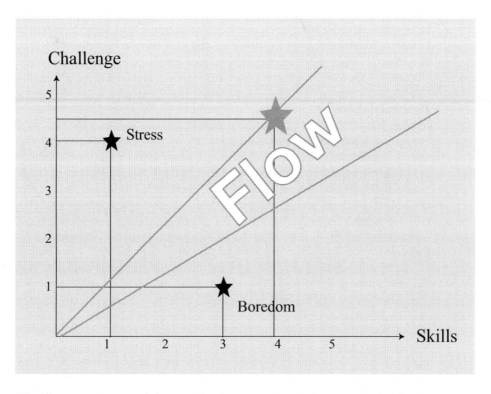

▨ **Figure 1.3** Creative activities that balance skills and challenge can generate a sense of flow or deep engagement

CREATIVITY AND GEOGRAPHY

So how can creativity and geography best be brought together? Once we acknowledge that in curriculum terms creativity isn't restricted to the performing arts, the opportunities immediately open out. To begin with, geography has a unique role as a synthesis subject. Historically, it has two major branches – physical and human. Physical geography studies the natural world and leans towards the sciences. Human geography studies how people live their lives and leans towards the humanities. The fusion of these two perspectives – how people affect the environment and how the environment affects people – stands at the heart of the subject. This means that there is an in-built creative tension. The different perspectives feed off each other.

At the same time, geography is about the contemporary world; what it is like today and how it might change in the future. Devising narratives to explain current events is a fundamentally creative endeavour. It involves drawing on different sources of information, offering alternative explanations, speculating about trends and acknowledging diversity and different cultural viewpoints. Digital technologies have a key role in helping geographers analyse and present data they collect. Modern geographers don't aspire to offer a single, immutable truth; instead they seek to provide a range of interpretations and perspectives that are systematic and rigorous, and which have validity within their own terms.

On a more practical level, geography is celebrated for its use of visual and graphical techniques such as charts and diagrams. Maps are its particular hallmark. Yet even the most accurate of these has a significant subjective element. Scoffham (2016) points out that when making a map, the cartographer has to decide what to include, what to leave out and how best to portray information about places using signs and symbols. This means that as well as being an analytical tool, maps can be seen as an art form in their own right. A comparison between the different official map surveys of western European countries makes this point extremely clearly.

If the content of geography offers rich creative possibilities, the way that it is delivered and promoted in school can be equally fruitful. There are many different situations and environments that will provide pupils with creative learning opportunities. Asking and answering questions are key techniques, along with active learning and practical investigations. Fieldwork and geographical enquires both involve raising problems and can be powerful catalysts for learning. The skilful teacher will take pupils on a journey that involves not only finding out about the world around them in imaginative ways, but also learning about themselves as they probe deep into emotional and existential domains. Geography is as much about asking questions as discovering answers. It involves learning *from* the world as well as learning *about* it.

The connection between geography and creativity is affirmed by many leading specialists. For example, in a speech launching a new geography initiative, the broadcaster and presenter Michael Palin once reflected on what geography meant for him. Geography, he declared, is 'a fusion of the power of the imagination and the hard truths of science'. It is about 'sunsets and eclipses, mountains, dreamlines, dancing dervishes, painted churches'. What could be more important, Palin asks, than exploring 'the living, breathing essence of the world we live in' and learning more about the past, present and future (Palin 2008: 5)? Using imagination and science to find out deeper truths about the planet is a highly creative endeavour. It certainly requires us to use our capacities to the full as we use different modes of thinking to make innovative links and connections.

CONCLUSION

Teachers who specialise in primary geography often do not think of themselves as being particularly creative. This is partly because creativity is still widely associated with the expressive arts and partly because it is easy to overlook the creativity that is latent in many teaching situations. It is time for this to change. By devising a challenging but supportive teaching environment, teachers can help pupils to develop their creative potential and to actually become more creative in their thinking. Not only does this have the potential to yield rich educational benefits, it is also more fun and engaging for the pupils involved.

Recognising that geography, along with other subjects, is a highly creative endeavour is essentially liberating and will enrich your teaching. As we proceed through the twenty-first century towards a future that is increasingly punctuated by uncertainty, there are good reasons why we need to help pupils to develop flexible and responsive modes of thinking. Our ability to use information, rather than information itself, will be of crucial importance in solving problems and devising imaginative solutions to them. Digital technology has an important part to play in helping us to develop creative responses.

Creative approaches to teaching geography could be seen as simply interpreting the prescribed curriculum in an imaginative way. However, a pedagogy which places creativity at the heart of joyful and ethical learning has much more to offer than this. In particular it:

▨ respects the integrity of children and gives them a meaningful voice in structuring their learning according to their needs;
▨ engages children with issues and questions which they themselves think are important and worthwhile;
▨ acknowledges that learning involves spiritual and emotional as well as cognitive dimensions;
▨ recognises that knowledge is constantly changing and needs to be continually reconstructed;
▨ addresses controversial issues and problems as part of a flexible contemporary curriculum;
▨ approaches learning in a spirit of grounded optimism, hope and enjoyment;
▨ provides children with time and space to develop their ideas free from the pressures of assessment and targets;
▨ helps children to build their identity and see meaning in their lives as they find out about themselves and their surroundings;
▨ builds children's capacity to anticipate and respond to future challenges both locally and globally; and
▨ places learning in the context of universal values in which children come to care about the world and its future.

Creativity is one of the attributes that human beings possess in abundance. Thinking back to the start of this chapter, there can be no question that 'we don't do creativity'. The link between creativity and learning is so close that the two cannot be meaningfully separated. Creativity is central to geography just as it is to every other subject in the curriculum. Furthermore, harnessing our creative abilities is a highly fulfilling process. There is nothing conceited in recognising creativity in your teaching. Nor does it have to be daunting. As the following chapters indicate, there are lots of different ways of going about it.

REFERENCES

Alexander, R. (2010) *Children, Their World, Their Education*. London: Routledge.

Barnes, J. (2015) *Cross-Curricular Learning 3–14* (3rd edn). London: Routledge.

Barnes, J., Hope, G. and Scoffham, S. (2008) A conversation about creative teaching and learning. In A. Craft, T. Cremin and P. Burnard (eds), *Creative Learning 3–11 and How We Document It*, pp. 1–64. Stoke-on-Trent: Trentham.

Children's Society (2015) *The Good Childhood Report*. London: Children's Society.

Craft, A. (2000) *Creativity Across the Primary Curriculum*. London: Routledge-Falmer.

Craft, A. (2011) *Creativity and Education Futures: Learning in a Digital Age*. Stoke-on-Trent: Trentham.

Cremin, T., Barnes, J. and Scoffham, S. (2009) *Creative Teaching for Tomorrow*. Deal: Future Creative.

Csikszentmihalyi, M. (1997) *Creativity: Flow and the Psychology of Discovery and Invention*. London: HarperPerennial.

De Bono, E. (2010) *Six Thinking Hats*. London: Penguin.

Festinger, L. (1957) *A Theory of Cognitive Dissonance*. London: Stanford University Press.

Immordino-Yang, M. H. and Damasio, A. (2007) We feel, therefore we learn: the relevance of affective and social neuroscience to education. *Mind, Brain and Education* 1(1): 3–10.

Katz, C. (2004) *Growing Up Global*. Minneapolis, MN: University of Minnesota Press.

Koestler, A. (1964) *The Act of Creation*. London: Hutchinson.

Layard, R and Dunn, J. (2009) *A Good Childhood*. London: Penguin.

Lucas, B. and Claxton, G. (2011) *New Kinds of Smart*. Maidenhead: Open University Press.

NACCCE (1999) *All Our Futures: Creativity, Culture and Education*. London: DfEE.

Oppezzo, M. and Schwartz, D. L. (2014) Give your ideas some legs: the positive effect of walking on creative thinking. *Journal of Experimental Psychology, Learning, Memory and Cognition* 40(4): 1142–52.

Palin, M. (2008) Geography action plan at Speaker's House. *Mapping News* 33: 4–5.

Perkins, D. (2010) *Making Learning Whole*. San Francisco, CA: Jossey-Bass.

Roberts, P. (2006) *Nurturing Creativity in Young People: A Report to Government to Inform Policy*. London: DfES.

Scoffham, S. (2016) Devising maps and atlases for schools. In Kent, A. and Vujakovic, P. (eds) *Routledge Handbook of Mapping and Cartography*, London: Routledge.

Scoffham, S. and Barnes, J. (2007) Written evidence to House of Commons Education and Skills Committee. In *Creative Partnerships and the Curriculum*, Eleventh Report of Session 2006–07. London: Stationery Office.

Warwick Commission (2015) *Enriching Britain: Culture, Creativity and Growth*. Coventry: Warwick Commission. Available at www2.warwick.ac.uk/research/warwickcommission/futureculture/finalreport (accessed 14 January 2016).

CHAPTER 2

FUN AND GAMES IN GEOGRAPHY

Terry Whyte

Activities and games are an excellent way of tapping into children's sense of fun and linking together both everyday and academic geography. They can be presented as warm-up exercises, provide the main focus for lessons linked to specific learning objectives or as a series of entry points either within or outside the framework of a normal lesson. This chapter focuses on the advantages of using games and play within geography teaching and the importance of developing starter activities and entry points for lessons.

INTRODUCTION

Children coming into the classroom on any day of the week will have been directly or indirectly affected by the geography around them. They will have experienced the start of a new day, eaten breakfast sourced from various local and global locations, made decisions about routes and journeys, interacted with issues such as road safety, communicated with others with similar or different cultures and identities, encountered a variety of landscapes and experienced the physical manifestations of the weather. Whether or not they identify it, geography is all around them.

Geography is often defined as the interaction between people and places. It follows that children (and adults) are geographers in an everyday sense of the word. These familiar experiences allow children to build up a useful knowledge base about their surroundings from which greater understandings can be developed. Such everyday geography can be seen as routine and taken very much for granted (Moran 2008), but it also can be 'novel, fascinating, wondrous and important' (Catling and Willy 2009: 9). Very often, children have a natural interest and curiosity for their world around them. Harnessing their enthusiasm can be a powerful and creative way to teach geography.

Using children's experiences and knowledge in isolation will not necessarily allow them to gain the skills required to understand geography as a discipline, nor the ability to apply their understanding in practice. Catling and Martin (2011) argue that what is required is an equality between academic and everyday knowledge. Government requirements provide scope for this to happen. The Early Years Foundation Stage includes elements of geography in many of the learning goals (especially Knowledge and Understanding of the World) and supports the integration of subjects. Meanwhile the geography curriculum for Key Stages 1 and 2 aims to 'inspire in pupils a curiosity and fascination about the world that will remain with them for the rest of their lives' (DfE 2013). If we view creativity as dynamic and generative, and also perhaps intuitive, then being involved in games and fun activities has the potential to support imaginative teaching, curiosity, fascination and learning.

WHY ENJOYMENT MATTERS

Children seem to have a natural sense of fun, often relate comfortably to their environment and enjoy games and play. Read and MacFarlane (2000) identify three dimensions of fun: expectation, engagement and endurability.

- *Expectation.* When they encounter a new activity, children have expectations of the degree of fun it will give them. These expectations can affect their level of engagement from the outset, and they often judge what happens against their expectations.
- *Engagement.* Engagement denotes the children's actual involvement where smiles, laughter and co-operation are evident (or not, as the case may be).
- *Endurability.* Endurability relates to children's memory of what they did and the enjoyment it brought them, which might hopefully be repeated. Ask children (or adults) to think about activities that they enjoy; their responses are likely to include the elements outlined above. Simply using humour as part of your everyday teaching is a good way to start.

Fun can be achieved through play. We all play, but children seem to be particularly good at it. What is play? Perhaps it can be seen as those activities that absorb children and in which they participate with enthusiasm. Csikszentmihalyi (1981: 14) alludes to the freedom one can experience when playing when he describes it as a 'subset of life and arrangement in which one can practice behavior without dreading its consequences'. Brown (2009) highlights the importance of the emotional side of play when he links it to stress reduction.

Play is international. All children in all cultures engage in activities that could be construed as play and they all use pretence as a way of interacting with their world (Hyder 2005). For Whitehead (2012: 3), 'play is one of the highest achievements of the human species, alongside language, culture and technology'. Without it, he argues, none of these achievements would be possible!

There are close links between play and creativity. Through play, pupils and their teachers engage in a co-creative process that involves spontaneous originality, emotional reactions and the production of a range of outcomes. Russ (2004) talks about how play can promote divergent thinking, while Wood (2009) argues that play and creativity, while not synonymous, share important characteristics. Dobson (2004) believes that play is important to a child's development and learning, encompassing creative, emotional and social aspects. The link between play and learning has fascinated psychologists. Piaget regarded play as a pleasurable process that allowed children to practice what had previously been learnt but which did not necessarily result in new learning. On the other hand, Vygotsky argued that it actually facilitates cognitive development.

Work and play are not opposites but can be combined. Brown (2009) cites evidence from neuroscience that play stimulates nerve growth in the circuits of the brain where decisions are made and in the frontal cortex, which is linked to cognition. Lucas and

Claxton (2011) further argue that we need to think of intelligence as a function that involves emotional and moral dimensions as well as intellectual activity. Koops and Taggart (2010), however, question the wisdom of using play to meet educational targets. They worry that 'elements of play could be lost when it is a requirement or even hijacked for specific purposes' (*ibid*.: 58). This could be said to be a situation that confronts the teacher in the classroom. There are goals to be met, learning outcomes to be achieved and 'work' to be done. It is important not to let these demands obscure deeper aspects of learning and to remember that children of all ages need to engage in play. It is just that with older children we tend to view play as childish and secondary to work, despite the benefits it brings.

If play is seen to be important in a child's development, how can we use this in teaching geography? One way to do this is through games and puzzles. Csikszentmihalyi (1997) argues that when children (and adults) are involved in a game and other purposeful activities they sometimes become so engrossed in it that they lose all sense of time. He uses the term 'flow' to describe this state of total engagement and goes on to argue that flow is strongly associated with creativity. It also provides optimal learning conditions and promotes our sense of confidence and well-being.

The use of games in geography has been seen as beneficial by Tidmarsh (2009) as they allow children to learn through co-operative experience rather than instruction and can allow them to have fun. Tidmarsh identifies four types of games that could be used in the geography context:

1   Simulations ranging from sophisticated multimedia programs to modelling in class which replicate reality and real-life situations.
2   Role play in which children take on the mantle of another person in a real-life context.
3   Educational games that have a set of rules and are often linked to a particular area of knowledge and often involve either competition and co-operation.
4   Simulation games that combine features of the other categories, incorporating rules as well as defined roles.

Being aware of different types of games is useful when it comes to planning a scheme of work. Games also have potential to assess children's progress and achievement. For example, having studied rivers, you might ask children to develop a 'consequences'-type game based around physical processes and the things people do. Younger children could construct a role play in which they pretend to be animals living along a riverbank. Both activities would reveal their level of understanding.

STARTER ACTIVITIES

The way a lesson begins will often affect the way children respond throughout the rest of the topic. Good starter activities can be the hook that pulls in the attention of children. When mixed with an element of fun, play and healthy competition, they can be strongly motivating. Gilbert (2002) cites research that shows that mental limbering-up makes for more effective learning. Starter activities can therefore be seen as exercising 'brain muscles' in the same way as an athlete limbers up for a race.

Gardner's (1991) idea of entry points is a useful reminder that children think and learn in different ways to adults and that there are different ways to engage them. Starter activities can include child-initiated activity, problem-solving, role play, questioning and discovery. Linking creativity with fun allows for a wealth of different activities that provide a stimulating way into the main body of a lesson. For example, try placing a dirty walking-boot on your desk without making any reference to it through the day. This will invite questioning, discussion, imagination, hypothesising, collaboration, frustration and fun. There is no real way of knowing how the children will react. The creative teacher will relish the different directions the children take and the interactions that follow before revealing that the boot is the clue to the work they are about to do on mountains.

Research suggests that a sense of fun, personal curiosity and desire to learn are important aspects of creative teaching (Cremin *et al.* 2009). It is also important to establish a classroom environment that is safe, open and emotionally supportive so that children feel free to indulge their natural curiosity. In this environment children will be prepared for the unexpected. A word puzzle on the board, picture clues on a slide show or a mini-test on previous knowledge can encourage the whole class to pool their thoughts and knowledge. The challenge for the teacher is to devise new activities and keep one step ahead of the game. The following sections outline some of the possibilities.

WORD GAMES

Word games work with a range of ages of children and help to build on and consolidate geographical vocabulary, thus assisting with general literacy skills. An added bonus is the fact that they are relatively easy to set up, many are downloadable from websites and, after a little practice, can be child-generated, which adds to motivation.

Jokes

Geographical jokes are a simple way to engage children and change their frame of mind (Figure 2.1).

Knock knock jokes	Jokes
Knock knock. Who's there? Alaska. Alaska who? Alaska later when I see her.	What is the fastest country in the world? Russia. What do Penguins wear on their heads? Ice caps.
Knock knock. Who's there? Francis. Francis who? France is a country in Europe.	What did the sea say to the shore? Nothing, it just waved.

■ **Figure 2.1** Geographical jokes are one example of word games

Word association

Word-association games or word chains can get children thinking about geographical vocabulary. Using the topic of weather as a stimulus, try taking the children on a journey across the world to places with different weather conditions. Each child has to think of a word that links with one previously used, such as: hot–desert–sahara–Africa–tropical–rain–Amazon–humid–monsoon–India–flooding–wet. This activity can develop in many different ways, allowing a range of geographical features to be explored and perhaps explained along the way, and can be challenging. All children should be encouraged to participate, either in small groups or as a class. Another option, still using the idea of connections or chains, is to ask children to think of the next word that begins with the last letter of the previous one. For example: street–traffic–cars–shop–parking–garage. You might show younger children linking pictures as clues with the words on an interactive whiteboard.

Anagrams

Mixing up the letters of a geographical term to make a puzzle allows children to investigate phonics and spelling skills as well as the vocabulary itself. Use this as an early morning starter before during or after teaching a specific topic. Children can make up their own anagrams to test their peers, such as tenrinnvoem, telicma, hewtera. A simple printed paragraph for early morning reading could also include a number of words jumbled up for children to solve. An alternative is to challenge the children to see how many words they can make using the letters of a long word or term such as precipitation or volcanic eruption. They get special praise for finding further geographical words.

Hidden countries

Look at this sentence: 'Using a webcam, Erica can adapt nice landscape pictures.' Now ask the children which three countries are buried in the letters. The answer is: 'America', 'Canada' and 'Iceland'. Once they have got the idea, children should be able to make up puzzles of their own.

Odd one out

Provide a set of words on any geographical topic and see if the children can guess the odd one out. For example: London, Paris, Northampton, Berlin, Washington. The simple answer is Northampton because it is not a capital, but children might have other ideas. For example, all the cities are in Europe apart from Washington; Paris has the shortest name; Berlin is the only city containing the letter 'b'. An alternative would be to use groups of photographs. If you put the photographs on a PowerPoint loop, the speed of the loop will be another challenge (Figure 2.2).

Definitions

Identify a range of geographical terms together with their definitions. You might take a theme such as coastal or river features and turn to a glossary for help. Write each term and each definition on a separate piece of paper, put them in a bag and mix them up. The children now have to match the word with the definition. These could then be fixed to a

Odd one out

			Answer
Sydney	Manchester	Norwich	Sydney (other two are in the UK)
River	Reservoir	Sea	Reservoir (other two are natural)
Hawaii	Canada	Alaska	Canada (other two are States of USA)
			Pyramids (other two in the UK) **Or** (other two older)
			Middle Symbol (windmill) (other two are places of worship)

▓ **Figure 2.2** An example of an odd-one-out quiz

display board with drawing pins or Blu-tack. They could also be used as a bingo or snap game. An alternative is simply to put the terms in the bag. One child then takes a word, keeping it carefully concealed, and the others have to guess what it is with yes/no questions as in 20 questions.

Call my bluff

Call my bluff is where children are given a new or strange geographical term and have to decide which is the correct definition out of three possibles. For example, is 'erosion' (a) listening carefully to the wind, (b) the wearing away of rock and soil, or (c) a European money system? This game can be extended by getting children to make up the answers and having fun with terminology.

Vocabulary power

Select a range of vocabulary associated with the topic being studied and ensure that the children understand their meaning. Now challenge the children to use these words in everyday conversation as much as possible during the day, even if out of context with the subject matter. For example, how many weather words can be used? Depression, pressure, cloud, rain, precipitation, snow, heat, temperature … great fun!

Dingbats

A dingbat is a kind of picture puzzle. Each picture represents a word, phrase or name, and the picture can often be supplemented with a couple of letters to assist in the guessing. Dingbats are easy to construct with place names like Liver-pool, Black-burn, Corn-wall and Fin-land. They can also be useful for geographical terms associated with a topic such as waterfall, river, source, mouth and rainbow (Figure 2.3).

 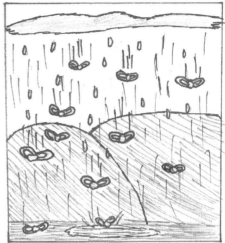

▨ **Figure 2.3** Dingbats for Washing-ton and rain-bow

Alphabet

Get the children to make a list of words or names relating to a theme beginning with each letter of the alphabet, starting with A and finishing with Z. You might focus on countries, cities, rivers, the local area and so on. This activity can be turned into a game in which groups compete against each other, perhaps to find as many examples as possible for a certain letter. An extension would be to allow children to take photos around the school that fit into the A to Z format. Maybe pupils can create their own booklet. *ABC UK* by James Dunn (2008) provides an inspiring model that they could emulate. Alphabet games can also be played, like 'I spy'. This could be done in the classroom, outside in the schools grounds or beyond, and encourages observational and language skills. It is a simple yet effective way of getting children to focus and be a little cheeky with their clues! Like so many other games it allows assessment of knowledge and children's ability to think creatively.

Crosswords

Crosswords don't have to be as difficult as the ones in *The Times*! Using simple clues and internet crossword creators (if required) makes using these word games accessible and fun for children. Crosswords also allow words to be seen in different contexts, mixed with others and in different orientations. Printed or displayed on a screen they make a good introduction to any geographical topic. Picture clues could also be used for differentiation. How about creating a giant wall-display crossword that develops over a week once the answers are discovered during lessons? A useful development is asking children to create their own crossword, which could be used to sum up their knowledge at the end of a topic. Crosswords often require a lot of thought to make them work. Providing a template and a list of suitable words is one way of supporting pupils who need help.

Word searches

Word searches seem to appeal to all ages of children as they hunt for hidden words or create puzzles for others. The obvious advantage of allowing children to create their word search is that they will know the answers (as long as the spellings are accurate). Their engagement comes in hiding the words among the letters. Again, this is a quick starter for an individual lesson or topic.

Acrostics

The acrostic format is a simple visual way to get children thinking around any geographical topic. If children illustrate their work it can make a very effective class display. One possible extension is to make pictures out of groups of words. For example, children might make a river shape out of a selection of words that describe river features (Figure 2.4).

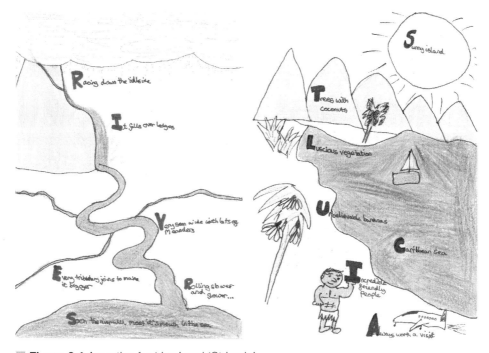

■ **Figure 2.4** Acrostics for 'river' and 'St Lucia'

STORIES AND POEMS

Children and adults like a good story and the anticipation that stories generate is a wonderful entry point for learning. Every story involves a place, either real or imagined, so the links to geography are immediately apparent. From the early years onwards, children listen to the tales about Red Riding Hood making her way through the forest to her grandmother's house, or how Jack climbed the beanstalk to enter the giant's house. They might find themselves going on a bear hunt in school, following the Gruffalo in the forest or joining the animals in *Handa's Surprise*. Older children might be engaged in Kensuke's kingdom, or travelling in the wonderworld of *The Lion, the Witch and the Wardrobe*. Once we realise the potential, we are able to use the stories that are read every day in every classroom to enhance geographical thinking.

Stories specific to locations can be linked to a piece of work or topic. With younger children, learning about the seaside can be enriched by picture-books such as *Sneakers the Seaside Cat* (Margaret Wise Brown), *Paddington: A Day at the Seaside* (Michael Bond) or *The Lighthouse Keeper* (Ronda and David Armitage). When studying a distant place, a well-chosen story can set the scene by describing the physical setting and the lives of the people who live there. Studying the environment can make much more sense if accompanied by a story.

Children can be very good at telling stories so the culmination of a unit of work might be in children creating their own. They could focus on everyday events such as a seaside holiday or family life in rural Kenya or take a theme such as waves fighting a battle against cliffs or the story of the gods of the storms. The imaginative possibilities are huge. How about street life around the school from a cat's point of view? There are obvious links between stories and role play/drama exercises, which might ultimately lead to a production, perhaps for a school assembly.

Using ICT to assist in visualising the story can also be motivating. Visualisers can magnify text and illustrations in a book, though there is often nothing better than firing up children's own visualisations through their thoughts and imagination. Photographs and video allow children to tell a story calling on their IT skills and IT 'apps' that allow movies and animations to be created are easily available. Even very young children are adept at producing animations using plasticine models or soft toys either to tell their own version of established stories such as *Little Red Riding Hood* and *The Hare and the Tortoise* or to make up their own creations. 'Publishing' these films through school websites or more public forums like Facebook and You Tube can provide a sense of celebration for children although you need to be aware of safeguarding issues. There is also the option of getting children to simply tell their story in the old-fashioned way.

Finally, it is worth remembering that you don't even need a book! Making up a story on the hoof requires confidence but it allows you to seize the moment, personalise experiences and include references to the children's locality. Photographs and images can provide a degree of scaffolding and will support stories on subjects as varied as the story of a raindrop, city life in New York, an island home, the pebble in the stream, the holiday journey or *Barnaby Bear at the Seaside*. As you gain experience your verbal artistry will develop. Why not encourage children to make up and tell their own stories in the same way?

Riddles

Riddles are statements that can have double meanings and are written to solve a puzzle. They allow children to investigate words and their meanings. Here are some examples:

> I am tall and I often wear a snow cap. Who am I? (Mountain)
> I am big and powerful and salty too. Who am I? (Ocean)
> What has five eyes and is lying on the water? (The Mississippi River)
> What stays in the corner, but travels around the world? (A stamp)

Limericks

Children take great delight in limericks. Limericks often include place names, which give them immediate geographical appeal. There is also good scope for making up your own to include local place names or to describe geographical processes (Figure 2.5).

There was an old man of Peru
Who dreamt he was eating his shoe.
He woke in the night
With a terrible fright
And found it was perfectly true.

There was a young lady from Niger
Who smiled as she rode on a tiger.
After the ride
She was inside
And the smile was on the face of the tiger.

■ **Figure 2.5** Examples of limericks that include place names

Haikus

Another poetic device is the haiku – a poetic form that originates from Japan. The simplest haikus have just three lines of five, seven and five syllables. They can focus on small details such as a pebble, leaf or speck of dust. The last line is sometimes a question or larger thought. Haikus provide a clear structure for children to follow and are a great way of getting children out of their classroom. Here are two examples that explore the environment:

Sand scatters the beach
Waves crash on the sandy shore
Blue water shimmers

Spring is in the air
Flowers are blooming sky high
Children are laughing

MUSIC

Music can conjure up a wide range of emotions and images. It can transport the child to a place associated with the sounds or take them on an imaginary journey. It can also widen their understanding of different cultures. Why not try to find a piece of music associated with your next geography topic? If the topic involves a distant locality, use music from that region to bring the place alive. For example, when studying a small area of the UK like the island of Coll in Scotland with young children, listening to fiddle and pipe music is an evocative way to introduce a cultural dimension. Similarly, the sound of samba music will help to develop children's images of Brazil for older children. Linking the music to movement and dance within PE adds a different dimension, and can be a lot of fun! Another approach is to devise a quiz to see if pupils can recognise musical styles from around the world. You might also select songs and tunes that refer to geographical events. You will find that a surprisingly large number refer to the weather. Perhaps children can compose their own music to represent weather, earthquakes, rivers, mountains, cities, countryside, coasts and so on?

There is nothing quite like getting children to sing songs themselves. Singing local and global songs can bring in languages and different rhythms. There are a number of very good websites available to assist in finding the songs, so you don't have to be an expert. Why not create your own songs about the locality, perhaps after a field trail? Consider sound effects that might be appropriate. What sounds best represent your locality? Getting children to record the sounds of their locality and edit the results using IT not only incorporates a range of skills but also has the opportunity to stimulate senses and include children with very varied abilities. What might it be like to be in the streets of New York or the wilds of Antarctica? What does the Amazon rainforest sound like? Consider using these sounds in a music/image presentation?

Let's take a break!

Remember to take a break in a lesson. This can have the effect of allowing you as the teacher to reflect on the feedback the children have given you and analyse the overall progress of the work. It will also give the children a physical and mental break and allows everyone to 'recharge their batteries'. Why not accompany the break with a blast of high-energy music that encourages everyone to move round, or calming music that serves to refresh? Ask children to get into a huddle to discuss their progress or talk to a partner about what they have learnt so far.

EXPLORING IMAGES

Every picture tells a story. Watching a video clip of polar bears in the Arctic or water toppling over the edge of the Angel Falls in Venezuela can evoke a powerful sense of awe and wonder. Images help to transport children imaginatively and to match their learning to the real world. This makes them a powerful teaching resource, particularly when learning about distant places in geography. However, as with reading, children need to be guided in the interpretation of what they see. Mackintosh (2010) reminds us that children tend to focus on details rather than whole scenes and that they do not always draw the conclusions you expect.

Photo packs and videos

Photo packs have traditionally been used in primary schools to examine a wide range of geography topics. While they can undoubtedly help pupils learn about places, they quickly become dated. An alternative is to use images from the web or to create a locality pack based on your own experiences. (Children could create their own photo pack in the same way.) Commercially produced educational videos are another way of bringing places alive, but be prepared to use the pause button rather than just viewing. The same also applies to websites. The internet provides a vast amount of visual information; it is important to examine material critically then deciding how to use it creatively.

Single pictures

Using the single picture for any topic is a good way of encouraging children to ask questions. Get them to focus on the foreground and background, speculate about the motives of the photographer and consider what lies outside the frame. Try placing a silhouette of the child or group of children in the picture. What is it like being there? What can they see and how do they feel? Use cut-out speech bubbles to decide what conversations the people in the picture might be having. You could also challenge the children to create a freeze frame of the picture they are examining? Can they find a way to represent a mountain, road, building or another person who lives in a distant place? Take a photograph of the freeze frame and compare it with original. Another way to use a single picture is to imagine what the landscape might look like in the future. Using tracing paper can help children devise how a landscape may change? Finally, you might want to use aerial photographs and images from Google Earth show different angles on places either familiar or unfamiliar. A simple game is to list all the places children can recognise and name on an image of the local area.

Photograph game

Use a photograph of somewhere famous to play a 'Where is this place?' game. Project an image onto the interactive whiteboard that only shows a small part of the picture. Get the children to guess the location. Gradually reveal other areas, getting the children to guess at each point until they get the right answer. Appropriate world landmarks include the Eiffel Tower, Houses of Parliament, Sydney Harbour Bridge and so forth. Again, children can make their own (Figure 2.6).

■ **Figure 2.6** Reveal picture of the leaning tower of Pisa

FUN WITH MAPS

Maps are an integral part of geography, and children tend to enjoy using and making them. Beginning a topic with maps can help them to locate and visualise their subsequent learning. This can apply to a local or distant place study as well as work on geographical features and processes. Children benefit from seeing many forms of map, so try to present them with examples that go well beyond the conventional Ordnance Survey and atlas formats. Increased development of IT applications like Google Earth allows children to *instantly* explore their world from the abstract 'birds eye' of view; to 'go' to the places they may be talking about or examine the physical features like oceans, mountains, volcanoes, deserts that they are studying or simply studying their own environment from above. Google Street View, for instance, allows each child to explore their neighbourhood.

Globes

Simply getting children to handle a large, plastic, inflatable globe engenders fun and encourages them to find out more about the world. You can focus their attention by asking questions. For example, can they find a country in Africa beginning with the letter Z, locate a small European country, identify the seas and oceans surrounding India or name a mountain range in each continent? Once engaged, children will soon want to devise questions of their own. As an extension you might decide to make a papier-mâché globe using a balloon as the base. Children can paint their globes to show land and sea and add small drawings of fish, boats and other items.

Atlases

Children's atlas skills can be enhanced using quiz cards. The questions can focus on a location, place or country and can be differentiated according to the age and ability of your pupils. At their simplest, the questions might just involve a page number or refer to an entry in the index. It is quite easy also to link questions to create a journey around the world using the atlas. Why not go on a journey around the world using Google Earth? Pretend with younger children to be seated on a plane and fly to places they name. Children can be the pilot and navigator and take everyone on a round the world journey to Disneyland, Australia, the South Pole and then back home again to land in the street next to the school.

Flags

Flags are colourful emblems that serve to symbolise and identify different countries. Get the children to look at different designs, comparing their similarities and differences. Try playing a 'guess the flag' game as a quick-fire end-of-day activity (or at any time), using cards or the interactive whiteboard. Flags can also be used as an introduction to learning about the different countries that are competing in a sporting event or linked together in groups as in the Commonwealth or European Union. Use atlases to help children find out more.

Puzzle pieces

Cut up a photocopied map from an atlas, geographical textbook or suitable website. The children then have to reassemble it. This activity is particularly effective at consolidating their understanding of countries and can be adapted for a range of abilities.

Ordnance Survey maps

There are lots of different ways of introducing children to Ordnance Survey maps. One approach is to ask them to do a name search of the local area. (The popular 1:50,000 or 1:25,000 scale maps work well.) How many places can they find that include geographical words such as water, street, hill, ford or sand? Rather than scanning the whole map you might get pupils to focus on a block of a dozen or so grid squares. This initial focusing exercise will almost inevitably raise questions about symbols and other map conventions, paving the way for future work.

Map symbols

You can develop children's understanding of map symbols by playing matching games. To do this you will need a set of around 30 cards in which each symbol appears twice. You can make the cards yourself, download them from the internet (use the Ordnance Survey website) or get children to make their own. Remember, there is no reason why children have to follow the conventional symbols. Devising their own symbols, for example landmarks around the school site, will involve them creatively and is likely to lead to lots of discussion.

Maps from memory

Getting the children to draw a map from memory is good for recognition and memory skills. Give them a distinctive map to look at for a specified period of time, say one minute, then ask them to draw what they have seen. You can differentiate this activity by using simpler or more complex maps and varying the time exposure.

Back-to-back mapping

In order to do back-to-back mapping you need to sit the children in pairs facing away from each other. One child describes a route taken, perhaps on the way to school, or in the locality or school grounds. The other tries to draw a map of the route (using a clipboard). The roles can then be reversed.

Maps of imaginary places

Do you remember creating your own treasure island map when you were young? Perhaps you made it look old by burning the edges and staining with tea or coffee. Why not make a large Treasure Island map covered with clues, riddles, instructions and pictures for a wall display? The links with literacy and stories are obvious and you need to be flexible enough in your planning to allow children to follow their own enthusiasms.

Monster map

Create a monster three-dimensional map of the locality in the school hall or playground using lots of cardboard boxes. There will be plenty of discussion as to where local roads end and begin. Add models of local landmarks using more boxes, then fix photographs of local scenes at appropriate places. A smaller, more permanent version of the map could be made with modelling clay or plasticine, then painted, decorated and celebrated. Remember to take photographs as memories and to inspire classes in the future.

Map corner

Have a map corner where children can find their own maps and set up map displays. They might select something from a newspaper or magazine or want to show where they have been for the weekend or on holiday. Remember to give children time to discuss their contributions. A map box may also be a good idea for children to look through in any spare moment.

GAMES

Quizzes

Children enjoy playing quizzes in whatever subject, so why not incorporate this into a geography topic, perhaps at the beginning as well as the end of a unit of work? Introduce an element of teamwork as well as a motive, perhaps a prize or a special concession. Try to organise questions to include all ability groups and emphasise participation rather than being correct all the time. Revising for a class quiz is more motivating than revising for a test. Try giving the quiz a theme, such as 'continents', or devise 'true or false' questions. Alternatively, you might focus on photographs or facts and figures.

Puzzle questions

Open and inviting questions are integral to eliciting wider thinking. Why not consider using a 'thunk'. A thunk, as Gilbert (2007: 3) explains, is a 'beguiling, simple-looking question about everyday life that stops you in your tracks and helps you to start looking at the world in a new light'. Examples of geographical thunks could be:

What does the back of a rainbow look like?
Can you step on water?
Can you touch the wind?
If I go somewhere by sat nav, who directed me there?
Are you manmade or natural?
If the water in a river changes all the time, what or where is the river?
Is a wooden table still a tree?
Can you always walk on the same beach?
Can you weigh the sky? Would it be heavier on a cloudy day?

Board and card games

Children enjoy board games and many of these can have a geographical perspective. Monopoly is a particularly good example, but others like Mouse Trap, Cluedo, Romans, Labyrinth, Battleships and Snakes and Ladders involve maps, real places, imagined, journeys and spatial representation in some form or another. Why not apply the format of these commercially produced games to geographical settings? Can children think how to use Snakes and Ladders, for example, to illustrate processes of coastal erosion and deposition? Could Monopoly be used to envisage the locality in the future? Card games have similar potential. Popular games such as Snap and Top Trumps can be used for capital cities, countries, flags and landmarks. Making and using games in this way has considerable potential as formative or summative assessment at the end of a unit of work.

Information technology games

The increased availability of video games means that with many school children spending a lot of leisure time playing with them at home. Robertson (2014) sees these as entertaining, enjoyable and beneficial to children in many ways. 'They educate, provide space for creativity and offer healthy social interaction.' But he also warns that 'the best examples are highly moreish and children will push boundaries to play for increasing lengths of time'.

Many of these games can be said to support Read and MacFarlane (2000) identification of three dimensions of fun: expectation, engagement and endurability. Using them in the classroom to enhance geography can provide stimulation, new information and challenge. Numerous games are available across a number of platforms ranging from simple word and picture quizzes introduced by Barnaby Bear for early years, to simulation games like Minecraft which is very strongly landscape based. The introduction of computer programming into Key Stages 1 and 2 curriculum has opened up opportunities for children to create their own gaming and control simulations, relating their learning to the application of IT in everyday life. Furthermore, simple programming of robotic roamers can assist the learning of location, directions, distances and scale, and collaborative use of these can lead to imaginative simulations and activities, especially with younger aged children. The key is to decide how and when these games can best enhance learning.

CONCLUSION

The ideas presented in this chapter could not possibly be comprehensive. They do however indicate some of the ways in which children can learn about geography in imaginative ways. More importantly, they suggest an ethos or a way of approaching learning which appeals to children and engages their enthusiasm. In an educational environment where learning is dominated by targets and assessment, it is all too easy to overlook how having fun can motivate children and improve their attainment. It can also serve to enhance their creativity and problem-solving skills. As Brown (2009) argues, creative activities can enrich pupils' learning.

You may not want to use these ideas exactly as they have been presented. They are intended to serve as frameworks and strategies that can be adapted to fit the needs of the individual class and children. They can also be child-led and child-initiated. Giving pupils greater responsibility for their learning and encouraging their intrinsic interest and motivation is an excellent way of bringing lessons to life.

Many primary school teachers are rather tentative and uncertain in their approach to geography teaching. Quizzes, games and imaginative starter activities are excellent ways to build up confidence, are easy to organise and can be extended or curtailed according to circumstances. An added advantage is that they appeal to different learning styles and ways of thinking. Stimulating children's curiosity and harnessing their enthusiasm makes it much easier to develop topics and themes in subsequent lessons. It is important not to be too serious. Having fun while pursuing educational objectives appeals to all those who are young at heart. That includes the teacher and learning assistants as well as the pupils themselves!

REFERENCES AND FURTHER READING

Brown, S. (2009) *Play: How it Shapes the Brain, Opens the Imagination and Invigorates the Soul*. New York: Penguin.

Catling, S. and Martin, F. (2011) Contesting powerful knowledge: the primary geography curriculum as an articulation between academic and children's (ethno-) geographies. *Curriculum Journal* 27(3): 317–35.

Catling, S. and Willy, T. (2009) *Teaching Primary Geography*. Exeter: Learning Matters.

Cremin, T., Barnes, J. and Scoffham, S. (2009) *Creative Teaching for Tomorrow*. Deal: Future Creative.

Csikszentmihalyi, M. (1981) Some paradoxes in the definition of play. In A. T. Cheska (ed.), *Play as Context*, pp. 14–26. West Point, NY: Leisure Press.

Csikszentmihalyi, M. (1997) *Creativity: Flow and the Psychology of Discovery and Invention*. New York: HarperCollins.

Csikszentmihalyi, M. (2000) *Beyond Boredom and Anxiety: Experiencing Flow in Work and Play*. San Francisco, CA: Jossey-Bass.

DfE (2013) *Geography Programmes of Study: Key Stages 1 and 2*. London: Crown.

Dobson, F. (2004) *Getting Serious about Play: A Review of Children's Play*. London: DCMS.

Dunn, J. (2008) *ABC UK*. London: Frances Lincoln.

Gardner, H. (1991) *Unschooled Mind: How Children Think and How Schools Should Teach*. New York: Basic Books.

Gilbert, I. (2002) *Essential Motivation in the Classroom*. London: Falmer.

Gilbert, I. (2007) *The Little Book of Thunks*. Carmarthen: Crown House.

Hyder, T. (2005) *War, Conflict and Play*. Maidenhead: Open University Press.

Koops, L. and Taggart, C. (2010) Learning through play: extending an early childhood music education approach to undergraduate and graduate music education. *Journal of Music Teacher Education* 20: 55–66.

Kratus, J. (1997) The roles of work and play in music education. Paper presented at the Philosophy of Music Education International Symposium III, Los Angeles. Available at www.researchgate.net/publication/280742192_The_Roles_of_Work_and_Play_in_Music_Education (accessed 15 April 2016).

Lucas, B. and Claxton, G. (2011) *New Kinds of Smart*. Maidenhead: Open University Press.

Mackintosh, M. (2010) Using photographs, diagrams and sketches. In S. Scoffham (ed.), *Primary Geography Handbook*, pp. 120–33. Sheffield: Geographical Association.

Martin, F. (2008a) Knowledge bases for effective teaching: beginning teachers development as teachers of primary geography. *International Research in Geographical and Environmental Education* 17(1): 13–39.

Martin, F. (2008b) Ethnogeography: towards a liberatory geography education. *Children's Geographies* 6(4): 437–50.

Moran, J. (2008) *Queuing for Beginners: The Story of Daily Life from Breakfast to Bedtime.* London: Profile.

Read, J. C. and MacFarlane, S. J. (2000) Endurability, engagement and expectations: measuring children's fun. *Journal of Service Research* 1(3): 196–214.

Robertson, A. (2014) Is my child spending too much time playing video games? *The Guardian* (5 June). Available at www.theguardian.com/technology/2014/jun/05/is-my-child-spending-too-much-time-playing-video-games (accessed 8 January 2016)

Russ, S. (2004) *Play in Child Development and Psychotherapy: Toward Empirically Supported Practice.* Mahwah, NJ: Lawrence Erlbaum.

Scoffham, S. (2007) Geography and creativity: an overview. Available at www.geography.org.uk/ (accessed 12 January 2016).

Tidmarsh, C. (2009) Using games in geography. Available at http://geography.org.uk/download/GA_PRGTIPTidmarshActivities.pdf (accessed 12 January 2016).

Vandenberg, B. (1986) Play theory. In G. Fein and M. Rivkin (eds), *The Young Child at Play*, pp. 17–22. Washington, DC: NAEYC.

Whitehead, D (2012) *The Importance of Play.* Available at www.importanceofplay.eu/IMG/pdf/dr_david_whitebread_-_the_importance_of_play.pdf (accessed 11 November 2015)

Wood, E. (2009) Play and playfulness in the Early Years Foundation Stage. In A. Wilson (ed.), *Creativity in Primary Education*, pp. 47–57. Exeter: Learning Matters.

CHAPTER 3

ENGAGING WITH THE WORLD THROUGH PICTURE-BOOKS

Anne M. Dolan

Picture-books are well placed for developing critical and philosophical thinking. This chapter builds upon contemporary research about picture-books and makes a case for their use in the geography classroom. Regularly used in literacy lessons, picture-books offer an opportunity to support creative geography teaching, since many feature a range of geographical ideas and locations. By connecting geographical ideas to children's personal experience, picture-books can accommodate different learning styles and help to promote creative and critical thinking. They also provide children with a range of windows through which they can view the world. Conversely, a variety of different geographical perspectives can be filtered into the world of the child through the virtual lens of picture-books. The creative potential of geography teaching through picture-books is substantial. The degree to which this potential can be achieved lies in the skill and the perceptions of creativity held by the primary school teacher.

PICTURE-BOOKS IN THE CLASSROOM

Typically, a picture-book is about 32 pages long with a balance between text and illustrations. In the better-quality picture-books the relationship between text and illustrations is tightly interconnected, complementary and seamless. This ensures that pupils 'read' both the words and the pictures. It is this relationship between pictures and words – this 'inter-animation', as Lewis (2001) calls it – that makes picture-books so special.

The influence of the teacher is paramount in guiding how the child interacts with the picture-book. Arizpe and Styles (2003) underline the importance of teaching children to deconstruct pictures. Their research confirms that 'children can become more visually literate and operate at a much higher level if they are taught how to look' (*ibid.*: 249). Roche's (2014) model of critical thinking and book talk helps teachers to develop children's visual literacy and critical thinking by focusing on the pictures as well as the text. Hence, the challenge for the primary teacher is to interrogate images from picture story-books in a manner that promotes enquiry-based learning and creative thinking, and develops skills of critical visual literacy (Figure 3.1).

Picture-books can bring the world into the classroom in a manner that makes sense to young children and enlarge their ideas about places at a range of scales from the local

■ **Figure 3.1** Through their drawings, children interpret and make sense of storybooks in different ways

to the distant. However, one of the greatest advantages of using picture-books in geography teaching is their potential to engage children imaginatively and creatively with abstract concepts such as interaction, movement, pattern and change. Responding to picture-books includes an analysis of illustrations and text, discussions about different places, and presentations based on 'What happens next?' This can prompt children to think about alternatives and relationships. Questions about how different characters might feel or respond can take their thinking further. There may also be opportunities to draw maps and plans to show the places that are mentioned in the story.

Picture-books feature in all preschool and early childhood classrooms. While often associated exclusively with younger children, many are appropriate for older children, adolescents and even adults. For example, although Anthony Browne's *Zoo* (2002) appeals to children at Key Stage 1, its anti-zoo message can more usefully be explored in depth across the curriculum at Key Stage 2. Indeed, it could be argued that because picture-books draw on previous experiences of people and places, they can be particularly effective in promoting creativity with older children. Nonetheless, they tend to be used less frequently at Key Stage 2 as other literary forms such as the novel take centre-stage. Furthermore, many early years and Key Stage 1 teachers see them as exclusively their jurisdiction.

Teachers need to ensure that they select high-quality picture-books for their teaching. Unfortunately, many primary teachers feel less than confident in their ability to select contemporary literature for children and tend to rely on the books they themselves enjoyed as children. In a survey of 1,200 teachers, the United Kingdom Literacy Association (UKLA) found that there was evidence that teachers relied on a narrow

authors and, in particular, had a very limited selection of poetry
nin *et al.* 2008). Hopefully, the ideas outlined in the following
uggestions that will encourage the use of a larger repertoire.

ENVIRONMENTS

eography that are most successfully presented through a
ories that focus on transport, communication, weather and the
in which children are engaged on a regular basis (e.g. shopping)
or through which the children can reflect on what they already know.

Skills

A range of map skills can be introduced to children creatively through picture-books. While some of the examples in this chapter feature maps as part of the narrative, others focus specifically on map skills. *There's a Map on My Lap* (Rabe 2002), *Follow That Map!* (Ritchie 2009) and *Mapping Penny's World* (Leedy 2003) are useful for introducing children to scale, perspective, bird's eye view, direction and symbols. Children can extend their map skills by creating their own maps in response to journeys depicted in picture-books. *The Once Upon a Time Map Book* (Hennessy 2010) allows children to explore traditional stories such as Jack and the Beanstalk, The Wizard of Oz, Peter Pan, Alice in Wonderland, Snow White and the Seven Dwarfs and Aladdin through maps. *Zoom* (1995) and *Re-Zoom* (1998) by Istvan Banyai are provocative wordless picture-books, with illustrations that slowly zoom out as though the viewer steps back from the previous pages. These are fantastic books for exploring perspective. Each frame yields to a progressively bigger view so that the net effect of moving through its expanding viewpoint is to loosen our imaginations about what we think is the ultimate environment.

Place

Place has a very special resonance in picture-books in that all stories need to be set in some kind of place, be it real or imaginary. The territory in which the story unfolds is more than just a decorative backdrop; it is, in many instances, the influencing frame of the story. The manner in which the place is depicted is governed by an array of artistic techniques employed by the illustrator. Therefore, place and setting in picture-books together provide fundamental aspects of the picture-book experience, hence underlying the immense geographical potential of using picture-books in the geography lesson. The classic Australian picture-book *My Place* (Wheatley 2008) represents the stories of children who live in one place over 200 years. Each child tells the story for every decade as the story moves from the present, back to the arrival of the first settlers. In print for twenty years, Walker Books has republished the book in a special twentieth anniversary edition which brings the history up to 2008. The story is also told pictorially through maps which represent the narrators' view of their place. The differences from map to map are surprising and moving.

Picture-books bring a range of global locations into the classroom from Africa and Asia to America and the Antarctic. Armed with a globe and a map of the world, children can virtually travel around the world. Take Peru, for example. The recent reprinting of the famous picture-book *Paddington* (Bond 2014) and the release of the movie of the same name has reignited our interest in the story about the famous stowaway from 'Darkest Peru'. The bear is discovered by the Brown family and named after Paddington Station, the railway station in London where he is discovered. I have always been amused with the term 'Darkest Peru' which is a contradiction in terms. Apparently Bond wanted his character to have travelled from 'Darkest Africa' but his agent advised him that there are no bears in Africa. But how can this image of 'Darkest Peru' be unpackaged in a primary classroom?

Children can be introduced to alternative images of Peru through picture-books. In *Up and Down the Andes: A Peruvian Festival Tale* (Krebs 2008) children travel using different modes of transport to the city of Cusco for the Inti Raymi Festival 'a majestic Inca festival held each year on June 24 to honor the Sun God'. With vivid illustrations and rhyming text the book communicates the vibrancy and colour of Peru.

> The mountains edge the western coast
> They parallel the sea
> And up and down the Andes
> There are children just like me

The book also includes helpful background information about the history of the festival, a brief history of Peru, a profile of its people and the story of Machu Picchu. *Enrique's Day: From Dawn to Dusk in a Peruvian City* (Farjado 2002) is based on the day of a life of a typical Peruvian boy Enrique in the Andean city of Ayacucho. Farjado is a photographer who studied in Lima and her photographs are fantastic visual resources for any primary teacher interested in Peru.

Going on a journey

Children's journeys provide a rich source for primary geography. Picture-books can extend children's experiences of journeys through story, illustrations, maps and virtual experiences. For young children several counting stories are available which are set in a variety of geographical locations. Readers can join Arusha, Mosi, Tumpe and their Maasai friends as they set out on a counting journey through the grasslands of Tanzania, *We all Went on Safari* (Krebs 2005). Along the way, the children encounter all sorts of animals including elephants, lions and monkeys, while counting from one to ten in both English and Swahili. The lively rhyming text is accompanied by an illustrated guide to counting in Swahili, a map, notes about each of the animals, and interesting facts about Tanzania and the Maasai people. *My Granny Went to Market* (Blackstone 2006) is a colourful rhyming story. Children are invited to join Granny and count with her from one to ten as she flies around the world on an unforgettable shopping trip:

▓ Istanbul: one carpet
▓ Thailand: two cats
▓ Mexico: three masks
▓ China: four lanterns
▓ Switzerland: five cowbells
▓ Africa: six drums
▓ Russia: seven nesting dolls
▓ Australia: eight boomerangs

▨   Japan: nine kites

▨   Peru: ten llamas.

Two notable picture-books deal with the heroic era of expeditions to the Antarctic. *Shackleton's Journey* (Grill 2014) is a visual masterpiece. It details Shackleton's preparations for the epic journey on the ship *Endurance* including the early stages of the journey, the experience of the men as the ship was surrounded by ice and their efforts to survive and travel to safety. *Tom Crean's Rabbit: A True Story from Scott's Last Voyage* (Hooper 2005) is based on the diaries of men who sailed to the South Pole on board the *Terra Nova* in 1910 and tells the story of an Irish man's expedition from the perspective of his pet rabbit. The wonderful illustrations from both of these books capture the splendour of the Antarctic landscape and additional notes provide supplementary information for teachers (see Figure 3.2).

In more abstract terms, the beautiful wordless picture-book *Journey* (Becker 2014) follows the adventures of a young girl who escapes the boredom of her lived reality to

▨ **Figure 3.2** Inspired by *Shackleton's Journey*, children at Egloskerry Primary School, Cornwall created an artwork of the *Endurance* and its crew stranded in the ice

Source: photo courtesy of Emma Kerr: great grand-daughter of Alexander Kerr, second engineer, the *Endurance*.

find a magical world – in which she can control her destiny with her imagination. The journey itself is intensified through the use of colour. In the beginning we meet the young girl sitting on steps with her red scooter (the only coloured item on the page). After attempting to find someone to play with her, she retires to her drab bedroom presented in sepia tones. Elements of excitement are conveyed through the map on the wall, the hot air balloon hanging from the ceiling and the rumpled sail-boat-covered sheets. With her red marker she draws a doorway on her bedroom wall and escapes into a world of colour, mystique and excitement. She creates a boat, a balloon and a flying carpet that carry her on a spectacular journey. This picture-book can inspire children to plan and communicate their own journeys around the world.

The physical landscape

Picture-books can demonstrate creatively the beauty and uniqueness of the physical world. In Michael Foreman's *One World* (2004) the self-contained environment of the rock pool is used as a metaphor for the beauty and diversity of our oceans. Similarly, the text in Liz Garton Scanlon's *All the World* (2009) flows from one page to the next with a thoughtful tone that makes the reader pause to let the words sink in. The story follows the family's day beginning with a morning on the beach and their daily routine until the evening, which is spent with family and friends. The words are simple but convey the idea that each moment is special and should be relished. A further message is that we each have a place in this world and that we are all connected. Beautifully illustrated, the book is inclusive in that it shows pictures of the young, the elderly and people from different cultures. Many of the double-page illustrations capture entire landscapes, evoking the sounds of waves against a rocky shore, or a pond in a rainstorm at dusk.

A River (Martin 2015) is a story which is told in the first person. It begins with a question, an open invitation to imagine a bigger world. 'Sometimes I imagine myself floating along the river … Where will it take me?' The story then transports the readers on an imaginative journey from the city to the sea, from cityscapes to farmlands and from wild jungles to mangroves. The illustrations are stunning and carry gentle messages about respecting nature. In addition to this environmental perspective, the illustrations include clues which relate back to the child's bedroom and are bound to provide ample opportunities for visual literacy. *Rivertime* (Balla 2015) is about ten-year-old Clancy, who is taken on a canoe trip along the Glenelg River in Australia. Initially he is unimpressed with mosquitoes and lack of access to his mobile devices. Gradually he is seduced by the power of nature and his outdoor adventures. Laid out in carton strips, the central message about the value of spending time in outdoor environments is persuasive.

Of course the best way to learn about our physical landscape is to take children outdoors. *Stanley's Stick* (Hegley 2012) provides inspiration to take an ordinary stick for an extraordinary adventure. In this picture-book we see Stanley's stick as it becomes a whistle, a banana, a match and a dinosaur (among other things). It also reminds us of the fragile and transient nature of childhood.

INTRODUCING A GLOBAL PERSPECTIVE

Picture-books include a variety of stories and illustrations from a range of different ethnic groups and cultures around the world (Dolan 2014). The beauty of the illustrations and the quality of the stories provide a strong visible statement that affirms the importance of valuing diversity. Increasingly, picture-books also deal with a range of complex geographical issues including interdependence, development, globalisation, justice and unequal distribution of resources in a manner that is accessible for young children.

Take for example the story of women involved in development – stories which have remained untold and uncelebrated for too long. There are a number of picture-books about the life of Wangari Maathai who was the first African woman to win the Nobel Peace Prize (in 2004). Wangari's personal story from veterinary medicine to the foundation of the 'green belt movement' to halting deforestation in Kenya is inspirational. Wangari grew up in the shadow of Mount Kenya listening to the stories about the people and land around her. As a young girl she was taught by her tribal elders about the significance of caring for the natural environment and, especially, trees. When the trees were removed, the foundation of a community was also destroyed. Wangari carried this message into adulthood. Planting trees, one by one, she became involved in local community issues. When local women came to her for help with their families she told them to do the same. Soon the countryside was filled with trees. Kenya was strong once more. Wangari had changed her country 'tree by tree'.

Mama Miti (Napoli 2010) tells Wangari's story, aided by Kadir Nelson's stunning collage illustrations. *Seeds of Change* (Cullerton Johnson 2010), *Wangari's Trees of Peace* (Winter 2008) and *Planting the Trees of Kenya* (Nivola 2008) are other picture-books about her life. The books highlight the importance of trees in a global context. Their aesthetic value is presented through the beautiful illustrations and the delicate relationship between humans and nature is carefully considered. These books demonstrate the potential of picture storybooks to introduce children to complex global geographical concepts in a way that makes sense to children.

Refugees and asylum seekers

The negative news reports about legal and illegal immigrants mean that the reasons why asylum-seekers seek refuge are often misunderstood. Many people do not realise how much suffering asylum-seekers, and especially children, have been through. Mary Hoffman's *The Colour of Home* (2002) tells, in simple language, the story of Hassan, a refugee from Somalia, who has witnessed things no child should ever see. When he arrives in England his life is so different that it is very difficult for him to respond to friendliness from his new classmates. His imaginative teacher invites him to paint a picture, and in this way Hassan is at last able to communicate the terrible things that happened to his family in Somalia when his home was burnt and his uncle was shot. Slowly, through the picture, his teacher and classmates begin to understand his story and why he must try to build a new life a long way from home. The clever use of colour – bright and happy for his home, red and black for anger and war, various tones of grey for his sadness and loss – explains Hassan's moods and feelings where words would fail. Towards the end of the story, colour and hope begins to return to Hassan's life.

Another perspective on asylum-seekers is provided by Ben Morley. His book *The Silence Seeker* (2009) tells the story of two boys, Joe and the boy next door who is seeking asylum. When Joe hears his new friend is seeking asylum, he misunderstands the term and believes he wants 'silence' instead. The book tells of their quest for peaceful and quiet places in the midst of a noisy city. *My Two Blankets* (Kobald 2014) takes a different approach and describes how a little girl arrives in a new country, and creates a safe place for herself under an 'old blanket' made out of memories and thoughts of home. As time goes on, and with the friendship of another young girl, she begins to weave a new blanket, one of friendship and a renewed sense of belonging. This book encourages discussion about refugees, immigration and change but it also urges us as readers to consider the implications of our actions on ourselves and on others. The blanket is a wonderful metaphor which can provide rich ground for classroom discussions and responses through drama, art and critical thinking.

In another picture-book *How I Learned Geography* (Shulevitz 2009), a boy and his family are living in poverty in Turkestan (modern-day Kazakhstan). Having fled from war in their troubled homeland, food is scarce, so when the boy's father brings home a map instead of bread for supper, the boy is at first furious. His mood changes, however, when the map is hung on the wall and it floods their cheerless room with colour. As the boy studies its every detail, he is transported to exotic places without ever leaving the room, and he eventually comes to realise that the map feeds him in a way that bread never could. This story, which is based on the author's memories of World War II, captures some of the key challenges in teaching geography. It stimulates the child's interest, takes the child on a journey and makes abstract concepts accessible.

CONSIDERING ENVIRONMENTAL ISSUES

Many picture storybooks deal with environmental issues sensitively, constructively and creatively. *The Curious Garden* (Brown 2009), for example, is a magical story about a boy's dream and how the efforts of one small person can help change the world. Gradually the city is transformed as other citizens follow Liam's example and take up gardening. The illustrations present a veritable feast for the eyes, as the reader encounters the indomitable will of this little garden to go beyond the boundaries of the railway tracks and its bridge, to every little nook and corner of a dreary city, livening up its landscape, and spreading its curiosities and happiness to the local environment and the local community. This book focuses on the impact of people on the physical environment in a positive manner through gardening. This central message could be creatively reinforced by setting up a school garden.

The Promise (Davies 2014) highlights the concept of interdependence by demonstrating our inextricable links to the environment. It celebrates the power we have to transform our world. Under difficult circumstances, a young girl is forced to steal. An old lady only allows her to take her bag on the condition that she will plant its contents. Expecting to find money, the girl sees acorns 'so green, so perfect … I held a forest in my arms, and my heart was changed.' She keeps her promise and plants the acorns wherever she can, beside roads, on roundabouts, at traffic lights, in parks, behind factories, at bus stops. And the city changes, trees grow, people talk and laugh and they start planting. This is reflected in the illustrations through bold reds and blues, yellows and oranges, greens and purples in perfect harmony.

This positive message of the power of citizens is reinforced by Jeannie Baker. In *Belonging* (2004), this Australian author/illustrator interrogates the theme of urban renewal through a series of scenes viewed through the same window over a period of several years. With the turning of every page, the years pass and gradual changes can be deduced. An alienating city street gradually becomes a place to call home. As little baby Tracy grows older, she begins to set about rescuing the street with the help of her neighbours. Together, children and adults plant grass, trees and bushes in the empty spaces. They paint murals over old graffiti. They stop the cars. Everything begins to blossom.

Belonging explores the re-greening of the city: the role of community, the empowerment of people and the significance of children, family and neighbourhood in changing their urban environment. The streets gradually become places for safe children's play, community activity and environments for nature and wonder. This is a positive book about urban renewal that shows that each individual can make a difference. It demonstrates the complex concept of interdependence in a thought-provoking, challenging manner that children and teachers can use as a basis for further discussion and interrogation.

Recycling

There is a range of excellent books that deal with the issue of recycling and positive actions to care for our environment. In *George Saves the World by Lunchtime* (Readman 2006), the main character is determined to save the world by lunchtime but he's not quite sure how. Grandpa suggests they start by recycling his yoghurt container, putting his banana peel in the compost pile and hanging the washing to dry in the sun. On his bike, George discovers many more ways he can help save the world. A trip to the recycling bank, charity shop and local farmer's market shows how recycling and reusing materials can make a difference. George even gets a favourite toy fixed!

Two books that deal with recycling on a micro-level, both by Alison Inches, are *The Adventures of An Aluminum Can* (2009) and *The Adventure of a Plastic Bottle* (2009). These stories are told from the point of view of the plastic bottle and the aluminium can whereby children can share their journeys through a diary. The plastic bottle goes on a journey from the refinery plant to the manufacturing line to the store shelf to a rubbish bin, and finally to a recycling plant where it emerges into its new life … as a fleece jacket.

STRATEGIES FOR RESPONDING TO PICTURE-BOOKS

Children have their own innate curiosity, inherent creativity and problem-solving skills. It is in the act of responding to the picture-book that the art of creativity and geographical enquiry lie. Responses can take many different forms: visual, aural, kinaesthetic, gestural and spatial, as well as more traditional modes such as oral and written expression. There is a wide range of media that can be used by teachers and children to present children's responses (e.g. role play, PowerPoint presentations, flash or multimedia presentations, blogs or websites, Claymation videos, soundscapes, films, plays, songs, poems, posters or advertisements). Some other strategies for promoting creative and critical engagement with picture-books include:

- discussing personal reactions to books;
- marking selections of text and illustrations with comments on post-it notes;
- writing questions beside text or illustrations, e.g. a question for a character, a question for the author or a question for the illustrator;
- using these questions to generate discussion;
- discussing the use of illustrations;
- trying to find alternative meanings for the illustrations;
- thinking of an alternative title for the book;
- writing the text and drawing an illustration for the next episode, i.e. What happens next?; and
- finding difficult or interesting words.

Anthony's Browne's *Zoo*: a case study

I have developed a five-point or five-finger approach for responding to picture-books which I offer here as a flexible framework (Figure 3.3). Anthony Browne's *Zoo* has been chosen to illustrate the framework. However, this can be adapted for all picture-books in response to the unique circumstances of each classroom.

Anthony Browne's book *Zoo* (2002) offers a very interesting twist on the traditional zoo visit story. Two brothers and their parents spend a day looking at the animals in the cages. They visit the elephant, giraffes, tiger, rhino, penguins, polar bear, baboons and orangutan and, finally, the gorilla. The images of the depressed captive animals provide ample opportunity for children to explore what it must be like to be in a confined area such as a cage within a zoo.

As the family walk around the zoo the personalities of family members emerge. Dad is bad-tempered, and the children are badly behaved because they are bored. Only the long-suffering mum seems to have any empathy for the fate of the animals. Anthony Browne uses the illustrations to make a powerful point. Is the family looking at the animals or is the family being observed by the animals? Winner of the Kate Greenaway Medal, this book is a fascinating examination of the relationship between humans and animals, and the role of zoos. Browne's sophisticated style, with its references to surrealism and his use of gorillas as interchangeable with humans, have made him one of the most intensely analysed and highly praised contemporary illustrators.

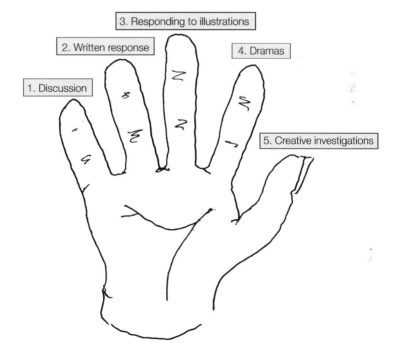

▨ **Figure 3.3** Five-point response strategy (five-finger strategy)

Applying the five-finger strategy to Anthony Browne's *Zoo*

1 Discussion: oral response
■ Initiate discussion about zoos. What do children think about zoos? Have the children ever visited a zoo? Ask them to talk about their trip, what they enjoyed or what they disliked.
■ Read the story *Zoo* with the class and explore why Anthony Browne may have written it.
■ Focus on the behaviour of the people in the zoo and discuss whether they behave well or not. Ask children to justify their opinions by referring to the text.
■ Debate the topic: zoos should be banned. Pair up students who then plan, present and contest points made by each other, drawing on and demonstrating their understanding and analysis of the issues developed through previous discussions.
■ After reading the book, make a list of arguments for and against zoos. This may be completed as concept or mind maps. Divide the class into two teams to debate the issues. For further ideas see Tony Buzan's (2003) work on mind maps.

2 Written response
■ Write a book review.
■ Write the story from the perspective of one character (e.g. mother, father, son, gorilla, etc.).
■ Write a thought bubble for each of the animals. Post-it notes in speech-bubble shapes can be used and stuck to the illustrations.
■ Write character profiles for Mum and Dad.
■ In *Zoo*, look at the pages where speech bubbles are used. Rewrite these as sentences using speech marks, then write them out again as reported speech. What effect does it have when you change the text in this way?
■ Write a diary entry for one day in the life of a keeper at London Zoo. Imagine you were looking after the tiger cub that had to be fed every two hours!
■ One of the animals has escaped from the zoo! Write a report for the local television news. This could be completed in groups and then videoed.
■ Give children pictures of zoo animals and ask them to write a caption for each one. This could be to advertise the good features of the zoo, a fact about the animal or a commentary about what the animal is doing.

3 Responding to illustrations
■ Examine the illustrations of the animals and the particular way that Anthony Browne has drawn them. How do the children feel about the animals? What do the illustrations convey about the animals?
■ Should animals be kept in zoos? Ask children to design a poster which shows how they feel about the issue.
■ Dreams: ask and talk about bad dreams the children have experienced. Draw and/or write about them.
■ Create your own poster/image of a zoo using framing, colours and other devices to make the viewer think positively or negatively about zoos. Write about your poster/image.
■ *Zoo* is a perfect book for examining inference in illustrations. How can we infer what the author thinks about zoos? What do the pictures tell us about Dad?
■ Examine the double-page spreads. Why are the animal pictures (right-hand pages) full-size while the humans are in small blocks on the left-hand side? Compare the words with the pictures. Discussion: Who is trapped? Who are the animals? Does the

author like people? Locate pictures of all the 'cages'; for example, Dad's jumper with 'bars'.

4 Drama: exploration of issues raised in the story
■ This book raises issues about keeping animals in a zoo. By focusing on the text and illustrations children can discuss the feelings of characters. This can be expanded using hot-seating and still images. Pictures from the story could be used to investigate the thoughts of the animals and their feelings about being in captivity. Divide the class into two groups for a debate about the pros and cons of zoos. The teacher can become a zoo inspector faced with the choice of leaving the zoo open or closing it down. The class forms a conscience alley to voice both sides of the argument, drawing on the discussion and written responses that have taken place earlier.

5 Creative investigation
■ Make a survey in school of those people who are for and against keeping animals in zoos. Display this as a graph, complete with relevant comments – 'I don't like zoos because the animals look unhappy' or 'I think zoos do a really good job of helping to look after animals that might otherwise be dead.'
■ Plan a trip to the zoo (this could be for real or hypothetical). The members of the class have to plan and organise the trip taking into consideration things like: health and safety, risk assessment, costs, supervision, transport, distance, food, itinerary, and expectations.

CONCLUSION

Picture storybooks help teachers and children to engage geographically and creatively with the world. Through this creative engagement children can learn to enlarge their perception, to see things from alternative points of view, to predict the future and to identify relationships in their immediate and global environments. With careful planning, primary geography teachers can use picture storybooks to promote a wide range of skills including creative thinking, information processing, reasoning, enquiry and evaluation. This chapter has highlighted a selection of picture-books for helping children to engage with geography. Teachers can introduce children to a range of contemporary issues through picture-books. Equally, picture-books provide a valuable mechanism for virtual journeys around the world.

REFERENCES

Arizpe, E. and Styles, M. (2003) *Children Reading Pictures: Interpreting Visual Texts.* London: RoutledgeFalmer.

Buzan, T. (2003) *Mind Maps.* London: HarperCollins.

Cremin, T., Mottram, M., Bearne, E. and Goodwin, P. (2008) Exploring teachers' knowledge of children's literature. *The Cambridge Journal of Education* 38(4): 449–64.

Dolan, A. (2014) *You, Me and Diversity: Picture-Books for Teaching Development and Intercultural Education.* London: Trentham Books/IOE Press.

Lewis, D. (2001) *Reading Contemporary Picturebooks Picturing Text.* London: Routledge.

Roche, M. (2014) *Developing Children's Critical Thinking Through Picture-Books: A Guide for Primary and Early Years Students and Teachers.* London: Taylor & Francis.

Children's picture-books

Balla, T. (2015) *Rivertime*. London: Allen & Unwin.
Banyai, I. (1995) *Zoom*. London: Puffin.
Banyai, I. (1998) *Re-Zoom*. London: Puffin.
Becker, A. (2014) *Journey*. London: Walker Books.
Blackstone, S. (2005) *My Granny Went to Market: A Round the World Counting Rhyme*. Oxford: Barefoot Books.
Davies, N. (2014) *The Promise*. Somerville, MA: Candlewick Press.
Hegley, J. (2012) *Stanley's Stick*. New York: Hachette Children's.
Hennessy, B.G. (2010) *The Once Upon a Time Map Book*. Somerville, MA: Candlewick Press.
Kobald, I. (2014) *My Two Blankets*. Richmond, VIC: Little Hare.
Leedy, L. (2003) *Mapping Penny's World*. New York: Owlet Paperbacks.
Martin, M. (2015) *A River*. Dorking: Templar Publishing.
Morley, B. (2009) *The Silence Seeker*. London: Tamarind.
Rabe, T. (2002) *There's a Map on My Lap! All about Maps*. London: Random House Books for Young Readers.
Ritchie, S. (2009) *Follow That Map! A First Look at Mapping Skills*. Toronto: Kids Can Press.
Shulevitz, U. (2009) *How I Learned Geography*. New York: Farrar, Straus & Giroux.
Wheatley, N. (2008) *My Place: 20th Anniversary Edition*. London: Walker Books.

Books about the environment

Baker, J. (2004) *Belonging*. London: Walker Books.
Bethel, E. (2008) *Michael Recycle*. Bath: Meadowside Children's Books.
Brown, P. (2009) *The Curious Garden*. New York: Little, Brown.
Browne, A. (2002) *Zoo*. New York: Farrar, Straus & Giroux.
Cullerton Johnson, J. (2010) *Seeds of Change*. New York: Lee & Low Books.
Foreman, M. (2004) *Our World: The World in Our Hands*. London: Andersen.
Garton Scanlon, L. (2009) *All the World*. New York: Beach Lane Books.
Hoffman, M. (2002) *The Colour of Home*. London: Frances Lincoln Children's Books.
Inches, A. (2009) *The Adventures of an Aluminum Can: A Story about Recycling*. New York: Little Green Books.
Inches, A. (2009) *The Adventures of a Plastic Bottle: A Story about Recycling*. New York: Little Green Books.
Napoli, D. (2010) *Mama Mia*. New York: Simon & Schuster.
Nivola, C. (2008) *Planting the Trees of Kenya: The Story of Wangari Maathai*. New York: Farrar, Straus Giroux.
Readman, J. (2006) *George Saves the World by Lunchtime*. London: Random House.
Cherry, L. (2000) *The Great Kapok Tree: A Tale of the Amazon Rain Forest*. Orlando, FL: Voyager Books.
Winter, J. (2008) *Wangari's Trees of Peace: A True Story from Africa*. Orlando, FL: Harcourt Children's Books.

Books about places around the world

AFRICA

Alalou, A. (2008) *The Butter Man*. Watertown, MA: Charlesbridge.
Chamberlin, M. and Chamberlin, R. (2006) *Mama Panya's Pancakes*. Oxford: Barefoot Books.
Cunnane, K. (2006) *For You Are a Kenyan Child*. New York: Atheneum Books for Young Readers.

Diakite, P. (2006) *I Lost My Tooth in Africa*. London: Scholastic.
Krebs, L. (2005) *We All Went on Safari: A Counting Journey through Tanzania*. Oxford: Barefoot Books.

ASIA

Ho, M. (2004) *Peek! A Thai Hide and Seek*. London: Walker Books.
Kwon, Y. (2007) *My Cat Copies Me*. Tulsa, OK: Kane Miller Book Publishers.
Choi, Y. (2010) *The Name Jar*. New York: Knopf Books for Young Readers.
Recorvits, H. (2000) *My Name is Yoon*. New York: Farrar, Straus & Giroux.

AUSTRALIA

Bancroft, B. (2011) *Why I Love Australia*. Richmond, VIC: Little Hare.
Bancroft, K. and Bancroft, B. (2000) *Big Rains Coming*. New York: Clarion Books.
Lester, A. (2005) *Are We There Yet?* Tulsa, OK: Kane Miller Book Publishers.
Harvey, R. (2010) *To the Top End: Our Trip Across Australia*. London: Allen & Unwin.

EUROPE

Banks, K. (2004) *The Cat Who Walked Across France*. New York: Farrar, Straus & Giroux.
Bond, M. (2014) *Paddington*. London: HarperCollins Children's Books.
Castaldo, N. (2005) *Pizza for the Queen*. New York: Holiday House.
Falcone, I. (2010) *Olivia Goes To Venice*. New York: Farrar, Straus & Giroux.
Fleming, C. (2001) *Gabriella's Song*. New York: Atheneum Books for Young Readers.
Sasek, M. (2004) *This is London*. New York: Universe.

NORTH AMERICA AND THE ARCTIC

Bania, M. (2004) *Kumak's Fish: A Tale from the Far North*. Portland, OR: Alaska Northwest Books.
Keller, L. (2002) *The Scrambled States of America*. New York: Square Fish.
Pattison, D. (2009) *The Journey of Oliver K. Woodman*. New York: HMH Books for Young Readers.
Pitcher, C. and Morris, J. (2007) *The Snow Whale*. London: Frances Lincoln Children's Books.
Priceman, M. (2013) *How to Make a Cherry Pie and See the USA*. New York: Dragonfly Books.
Levison, N. S. (2002) *North Pole South Pole*. New York: Holiday House.

SOUTH AMERICA AND THE ANTARCTIC

Farjado, S. (2002) *Enrique's Day: From Dawn to Dusk in a Peruvian City (A Child's Day)*. London: Frances Lincoln Children's Books.
Grill, W. (2014) *Shackleton's Journey*. London: Flying Eye Books.
Hooper, M. (2005) *Tom Crean's Rabbit: A True Story from Scott's Last Voyage*. London: Frances Lincoln Children's Books.
Krebs, L. (2008) *Up and Down the Andes: A Peruvian Festival Tale*. Oxford: Barefoot Books.
Mitchell, S. (2007) *The Rainforest Grew All Around*. Mount Pleasant, SC: Sylvan Dell Publishing.
Rand, G. (2005) *A Pen Pal for Max*. New York: Henry Holt & Company.
See also www.shackletoninschools.com

CHAPTER 4

PLAYFUL APPROACHES TO LEARNING OUT OF DOORS

Sharon Witt

Playful teaching and outdoor learning offer children and teachers opportunities to engage with the subject of geography in a creative manner. This chapter provides examples to demonstrate that playful learning opportunities that immerse children in their surroundings can provide children with valuable geographical experiences throughout the primary years. It also illustrates how promoting children's knowledge and understanding of their local landscapes encourages them to make connections to people and places on a global scale, while promoting their happiness and well-being.

PLAYFUL LEARNING IN MIDDLE CHILDHOOD

Although in recent years play has become increasingly associated with the early years curriculum, the need for play does not disappear as children mature. The definition of play is much contested and varies according to individual perspectives. While play in its purest sense is associated with children being in complete control with the freedom to explore independently, it is questionable whether this is truly possible within a curriculum that is planned and delivered by the teacher and constrained by time, resources and health and safety requirements. Moyles (2010: 21) suggests that within the classroom, playful learning can be defined as learning experiences that are child-led or adult-initiated or inspired when children engage in playful ways.

Research findings

This chapter focuses specifically on geographical outdoor play within 'middle childhood' (Sobel 2008), which broadly speaking includes children from five to twelve years old. Research suggests that during this developmental phase children experience the natural world in a highly evocative way producing a sense of connectedness which can remain with them throughout their adult life (Cobb 1959). Through seeing, smelling, tasting, hearing and feeling their surroundings children can connect and enter into dynamic, genuine, unique and profound relationships with nature. This first-hand experience can foster the children's curiosity, attentiveness, awaken wonder and enthusiasm. Exploration of places through play can create what Pyle (1993) calls 'places of initiation' where sensory and physical activities help children to communicate with the more than human world e.g. animals, plants, trees and rivers. Sobel (2008: 15) describes children's ability to become immersed in the physical world, yet remain unique and separate, as 'one of the core gifts of middle childhood' which can provide 'the foundation for an empathic relationship' with the earth.

It is widely recognised that play and playfulness have a key role in learning. Moyles (2010) argues that it is through this process that children acquire knowledge and insights into themselves and their world. Furthermore, as the Geographical Association contends, 'learning directly in the untidy real world outside the classroom' continues to be an essential component of a broad, rich geographical curriculum, which can motivate and engage children in their learning (Geographical Association 2009: 23). Despite this, there is evidence that opportunities for geographical fieldwork are diminishing (Ofsted 2011). There is clear evidence that children benefit from opportunities to explore their surroundings. A more recent report demonstrated a link between social deprivation and the opportunities that children have to experience the natural environment (Natural England 2015). Commentators also note that children's play is increasingly moving indoors and onto electronic screens (Sobel 2002: xi). This may bring benefits, but it has also been argued that children who have less direct contact with nature are liable to suffer from 'nature deficit disorder' (Louv 2011: 3). Meanwhile, research by Eureka Children's Museum in West Yorkshire found that over 80 per cent of children preferred outdoor play activities to using screens (Caswell and Warman 2014). It would therefore seem appropriate to draw on children's natural desires to explore, play and transform outdoor places in order to develop opportunities within geography, which are built on their personal interests and experiences.

Geography and outdoor play

Playful outdoor learning is a valuable vehicle for teaching and learning geography as it provides the children with opportunities to make meaning and develop understanding through enquiry and practical experience of the real world – all features of good-quality geography provision. Play allows teachers to promote a sense of fun and enjoyment and, therefore, enables them to focus on children's well-being and feelings about places, as well as their knowledge and understanding of the world (Figure 4.1). Planning a playful element within your geographical fieldwork invites the children to weave together reality and fantasy in order to provide affective responses to landscapes which can develop their sense of place, belonging and connectedness. I have decided to analyse approaches to outdoor play suitable for geographical learning using categories identified by Hughes (2002).

▨ *Free exploration.* Free exploration is where children are encouraged to explore a place for themselves in order to discover, investigate, examine and ask questions. This utilises their innate curiosity. In one class the teacher urged her children to 'leave no stone unturned' as she gave them freedom to explore a local woodland. In the feedback session one child remarked: 'I liked going down here. There is a ditch and I think it was once where a river was and it was a really deep ditch ... I like going down there because I like running from side to side.' As well as learning about landscape features this example also suggests that children enjoy the space and opportunities for movement in an unfamiliar outdoor space (Tovey 2007).

▨ **Figure 4.1** Playful opportunities for place-making can promote 'happy geographers'
Source: photo by Sharon Witt

▨   *Guided exploration.* Guided exploration occurs where children are guided by questions generated earlier, either by the class or by the teacher. Classic geographical enquiry questions include: What is this place like? How is this place connected to other places? How is this place changing? How does this place make you feel? What will this place be like in the future? Such questions encourage pupils to search for clues, collect data and draw conclusions. Contexts that are appropriate for guided exploration include: adventures, quests, journeys, voyages of discovery, treasure hunts, scavenger hunts and foraging for interesting/special objects.

▨   *Responding to stories.* One reception class inspired by the Winnie the Pooh story (Milne 1995) went on their own 'expotition to discover the North Pole' in their school grounds. On this walk the children developed their powers of observation through sensory exploration, used geographical vocabulary and shared their personal stories of the experience. The session ended, much to the delight of the children, when they found a broomstick with the words 'the North Pole' written on it. This was an imaginative and memorable lesson that excited and engaged the children both playfully and creatively.

■ *Close encounter play.* Close encounter play is where children immerse themselves in the environment. This type of play encourages teachers to use a 'slow pedagogical … approach' enabling children 'to pause or dwell in spaces for more than a fleeting moment', promoting the development of place attachments through stillness, silence and reflection (Payne and Wattchow 2009: 16). Cloud watching, watching waves or admiring a beautiful view provide suitable contexts. Close encounter play may also involve active engagement with the outdoors, such as rolling down a hill, puddle jumping or natural sculptures in the outdoors (sandcastles, mazes and mud pies). Such activities encourage children to use their senses to engage with the natural world and communicate their responses to the landscape in different ways.

■ *Creative play.* Creative play is where children are encouraged to change their surroundings through adaption, construction and transformation. This offers opportunities for place-making such as making dens and building shelters, yurts and tree-houses. Transformation of an environment may be temporary or permanent, reversible or irreversible, and can encourage children to consider their impact on their surroundings. The possibilities for these transformations are only limited by the children's imaginations. Shirley (2007: 10) neatly summarises the educational potential when he declares, 'We can … use the magic that is inherent in places' to foster genuine creativity within the geography curriculum.

■ *Imaginative play.* Imaginative play happens when children engage in fantasy play to help develop their understanding of the real world. This type of play can be full of important geographical content that is rich in meaning for the children. It allows them, through storytelling and folklore, to develop a connection to what William James (in Jenkinson 2001: 67) describes as 'the authentic tidings of invisible things', meaning the unseen forces of nature and the metaphysical world, which could be fairies, elves, giants, trolls and boggarts. McLerran (1991) details the true story of a group of children who constructed a magical imaginary town known as Roxaboxen in the desert around Yuma, Arizona. This fantastical world could be used as a stimulus for children to create their own special places. The classic story *Where the Wild Things Are* (Maurice Sendak) could also be used as a stimulus to inspire children to construct special places of their own.

■ *Simulations.* Simulations are where children use play to make sense of some real-life situations. For example, they might try to recreate the settlement of a rainforest community in order to develop an understanding of other people's lives and to consider problems that some indigenous communities are facing around the world. Playful learning can, therefore, provide children with the chance to 'put themselves in someone else's shoes and thus experience empathy with another point of view' (Walford 2007: 13). Creative teachers can also use playful learning to help children become involved in improving their local environment; it is therefore inclusive and participative. One teacher used the Planning for Real® approach where children use props to begin to make suggestions and plan improvements in their playground (Learning through Landscapes 2006). In this way, opportunities for play can encourage sites to become 'the canvas for the children's ideas' (*ibid.*: 1). A plan for changing an outdoor space using flowerpots, carpet squares, cones and other materials can been seen in Figure 4.2.

In order for playful learning to thrive, the environment needs to provide opportunities for children to manipulate, construct, observe, listen and touch their world. Geographical play

▨ **Figure 4.2** An example of using the Planning for Real® approach to create an outdoor
performance area
Source: photo by Sharon Witt; Planning for Real® approach created by MA (Ed)
students during a Learning through Landscapes course, University of Winchester

can therefore take place in the school grounds or during an educational visit in the locality
(e.g. a visit to the park). The Geographical Association reminds us that 'Geography in
schools … is concerned with perceptive and deep description of the real world
(Geographical Association 2009: 13). In addition to reading the landscape, we should be
encouraging our children to be 'authors' who are writing the landscape, as it is through
providing them with opportunities to create, imagine, reinvent and transform environments that children gain a deep sense of place (Tovey 2007: 55).

A playful approach to geography stands in contrast to traditional fieldwork, which
can be a highly structured, adult-led activity and may involve worksheets to record observations and data collected. This is not to suggest that experiential, exploratory playful
experiences are an alternative to fieldwork; they should be complementary. Placing the
learner at the centre of the learning process utilises their personal geographies to enhance
their knowledge and understanding of the world. Play enables children to develop their
geographical thinking through participative enquiry, deep and purposeful observation and

open-ended problem-solving. This provides children with the opportunity to shape their own environment by allowing them to express their ideas about the world in inventive and innovative ways.

A playful approach to learning within geography is underpinned by the theory of constructivism which highlights the way children learn actively through experiences. This helps them make sense of their world through existing and new ways of thinking (Roberts 2013). If we want our children to grow up caring about the environment and feeling empowered to change communities in the future, they need to have the opportunities that are afforded by playful activities in the outdoors. These activities allow them to experience and reflect upon the environment and enable them to develop an understanding of the dynamism and ever-changing world in which we live. As one 11-year-old stated: 'To respect nature – we learn it ourselves by being in such a nice place! By being in that place I want to look after it!'

PLACE-MAKING ACTIVITIES

Creative teachers recognise the potential that place-making activities can offer for children to achieve geographical outcomes through 'first-hand experience and practical work' (Richardson 2010: 303). Place is a key idea in geography, yet Ofsted (2011: 10) found the development of knowledge and understanding about geographical concepts, including place, to be 'very limited'. The potential for children to create places has been demonstrated by Barlow *et al.* (2010) who acknowledge that practical place-making can enhance a child's understanding of scale and engage children in meaningful map-making activities. Playful place-making activities in the outdoors have the potential to actively engage children to think geographically. Below are some suggestions for a range of contexts that might be used:

▨ *Creating a special place.* Children are free to explore the environment within given boundaries and utilise the natural resources in order to build a den.
▨ *Creating a shelter to camp in overnight.* Children are asked to build a bivouac or hammock to sleep in overnight. Research suggests that these spaces 'are 'owned' by their creators, safe, organised, secret and unique' (Sobel 2002: 96). This was evident with one group of children who said their shelter 'just felt really homely and the people in my bivvy used it like a bathroom. We hung our towels over a branch and brushed our teeth and had fun.'
▨ *A home for a bear.* This is an adaptation of the overnight camp idea where children are asked to construct a shelter for a teddy bear or a toy to spend a night outside. It requires the children to adapt their place-making skills to a smaller scale.
▨ *Enquiry headquarters.* Children create a base camp for forays and expeditions into an area when pursuing an enquiry. The HQ can be a place for storing equipment needed for the enquiry, e.g. maps, books, magnifying glasses, compasses and notepads. It can also be a place where first-hand and sensory experiences can be recorded, field sketches and notes created and observations and findings analysed. It can be designed to keep the geographical investigators sheltered and their findings secure until their conclusions are ready to be shared with the group.
▨ *Shelters from other cultures.* Children recreate shelters from other times and places such as a charcoal burner's hut from pre-twentieth-century England or an east-African boma.

▓   *Homelessness*. Children are asked to build shelters and consider a real issue such as homelessness.

The opportunity for children to engage in place-making activities can be identified at the beginning of a unit work. At this point it can provide an initial stimulus to hook the children's interest and engage them in a motivating activity. Alternatively, place-making can be used at the end of a topic/unit of work in order to provide an opportunity to extend and deepen children's relationship with a place. Place-making also promotes strong links across the curriculum. Construction techniques relate to design and technology, work on materials and forces are part of the science curriculum and teamwork and co-operation are elements of PSHE.

DEN-BUILDING

Den-building is a universal experience of childhood, which, according to Sobel (2002: 6), 'happens in both rural and urban settings around the globe'. Primary school children have a genuine interest in constructing their own places outdoors and they are often rich and motivating contexts for playful learning. Noddings (2003: 122) acknowledges the importance of enhancing 'the pleasure that pupils seem naturally to find in the places they love'. When one child was asked whether he would like to make dens as part of his geography lessons he announced with enthusiasm, 'Wow that would be amazing! If there was a vote for that, I would vote!'

Place-making in the outdoors provides children with the opportunity to engage both physically and cognitively with a landscape. It also allows children to understand and explore place and environmental geographies through their own personal experiences and viewpoints. Creative teachers, Sobel (2002) argues, should acknowledge the unique place-making desires of middle childhood and shape the curriculum to provide appropriate environmental experiences in school. Catling and Pickering (2010) develop this argument by saying that teachers should provide opportunities for children to create places in order to develop their higher-order thinking skills and to ensure depth of learning.

Den-building activities help children to develop their sense of competence and personal order. This was evident with a group of pupils who were asked to construct a special place; they were keen to add cushions, windows and doorways once the frame of their den was built. The activity allowed them to experience a sense of home-making and to operate as shapers and makers in what Sobel (2002: 110) calls 'small worlds'. The detailed research of American youngsters conducted by Hart (1979) reveals that the physical object of the den has great meaning for children. This individual and shared den-making experience creates a sense of place (albeit on a small scale) as the den has a 'particular location, a physical structure and even meanings' (Cresswell 2008: 134). Sobel (2002: 161) agrees that 'a sense of place is often born in children's special places.

Children's descriptions and feelings about the places they have constructed can be expressed in many different ways. Those that have particular relevance for geography include:

▓   conversations with the teacher and between children sharing observations and experiences that develop geographical language;
▓   creating and telling stories;
▓   maps and plans;

- scrapbooking responses to a place, which could include a colour palette, descriptive words, rubbings of textures, photographs or pictures;
- field sketches;
- postcards;
- estate agent details or advertisement;
- written descriptions of locations/settings;
- self-assessment or evaluation of the quality of the construction;
- photographs and videos;
- drama/role play.

Creative teachers who provide opportunities for den-building within their geography provision can help children build a deeper knowledge and understanding of local places. Den-building also relates directly to the world of work. One group of children who completed place-making activities in their school grounds made constant reference to real life when constructing their dens. Some of the children took a futures-orientated approach and viewed the activity as preparation for adulthood. One child enthusiastically declared, 'I am going to be really good at this because when I am older I want to be an architect.' The places the children created reflected their current understanding and their geographical imaginations. This is evident in the following conversation when one of the children said, 'Ours is like a block of flats. Now let's make a wig-wam.'

It is important for teachers to remember that children see their environments differently to adults. Research suggests that many adults care about the aesthetic quality of an environment, which is in contrast to children who value a landscape for the activity that is possible within it (Lindholm, in Kylin 2003). Children, especially those in urban areas, live and act in environments that have been planned and monitored by adults, yet they possess strong views about how they would like their places to be (O'Brien, in Catling 2011). Den-building can lead children to consider the quality of their own locality. In turn, this may eventually prompt them to participate in the affairs of their local communities (McKendrick, in Catling 2011). There are good reasons to conclude, along with Hart (1997), that active involvement in their local area can enhance children's self-esteem, help them adopt a more caring attitude to their school and neighbourhood and engender improved relationships.

IMAGINATION AND WELL-BEING

The provision of rich geographical outdoor play experiences can foster imaginative responses. These experiences provide a strong vehicle for children to express how they feel about themselves and the world. Catling and Willy (2009: 44) argue that children 'see places through two lenses': as real and imagined. As they play, investigate and transform spaces, children construct narratives based on the possibilities and potential of the environment. One teacher asked her Year 3 pupils to create a favourite place; they could base their work on places they had read about in books or upon their geographical knowledge. The children built a variety of places, including a desert and a football stadium. Once constructed, the children had an opportunity to visit each other's places and time to play and explore. This activity allowed children to describe places and to identify similarities and differences. Constructing places on a large scale encouraged them to generate questions and to use geographical vocabulary as they played in their imaginary worlds.

Research suggests that primary-age children really enjoy using their imaginations and can benefit in terms of being more thoughtful, open and creative (Scarlett *et al.* 2005). The following excerpts are from conversations of six-, seven- and eight-year-olds, recorded during a den-building activity. They demonstrate that these primary-age children are using their experiences to make stories that bring together their inner and outer worlds in language and space (Sobel 2002).

Child A: This is the time in the building process where we have the break!
Child C: Shall we have a cup of tea and a jam tart?
Child B: Egg sandwich anyone?
Child B: I want some toast and electric power.
Child A: Cor! Look at this! I'm a Viking, I am a Viking!

Creative geography teachers need to seek opportunities for children to use their imaginations through playful learning experiences. Inspired by Van Matre's 'earth education' approach in which children experience a series of immersion activities designed to develop their emotional attachment to a place, one school decided to answer the geographical question 'What is this place like?' by inviting classes of seven-, eight- and nine-year-old children to look for signs of elves on a woodland visit. Throughout the day, children were encouraged to explore the woods freely in order to develop a sense of place, to build houses to attract the elves to the wood and have moments to pause, be still and reflect. This imaginative work was built on woodland folklore and it was hoped that 'weaving a story, using clues and riddles, creating a special atmosphere, doing the unexpected' would 'enhance and intensify the magic of nature' (Van Matre 1990: 203).

The results were impressive. The teacher discovered that the children eagerly suspended their disbelief to engage with this fantastical experience. Recalling this event, one child said 'I remember thinking that I saw an elf … It had a bluebell hat on; it was a lady who had long hair on top and a green … grassy dress.' Another said, 'We knew we were like just pretending we were laughing about it. But it was like really fun! I learnt there are magical creatures. We got to use our imaginations – and when you don't use your imaginations you don't have much fun!' Imaginatively engaging in places can, as one child stated, 'enable you to see places in a different way'. It infuses children's experiences of place with wonder, beauty and enchantment and it truly involves teaching geography with a different view (Figure 4.3).

Working in outdoor settings can also contribute to our sense of well-being. 'There is something about the intrinsic nature of places,' Ballas and Tranmer (2008) declare, 'which can influence happiness and well-being.' This becomes evident when teachers provide children with opportunities to engage playfully in the outdoors. These sensory, exploratory activities can promote insightful geographical experiences that contribute significantly to the children's developing knowledge of themselves and their world. This is beautifully summed up in the observations of an eleven-year-old girl:

I think it is something to do with when you look at them you can sort of tell how bluebells are sort of in creation. You are seeing it actually happening – you see the place for real and it gives you a view that photos can't show because you are looking at it from every angle. You just notice things when you are doing an activity. Like when you are playing hide and seek you see how … plants grow to the light or there are lots of oddly shaped brambles growing, weaving through things.

■ **Figure 4.3** Looking for signs of elves in Captain Phillimore's Woods, Hampshire. Captain Phillimore left the use of the woods to Swanmore CE (Aided) Primary School as a legacy in his will
Source: photo by Sharon Witt

As Tovey states (2007: 31), 'we must allow children the opportunity to develop an intimate relationship with nature to understand but more importantly to feel the interconnectedness of all living things and to see their own place in the world'. Furthermore, it is important to remember that teaching geography creatively is an emotional process that engages the child holistically. The senses, imagination and feelings are all involved.

Direct and sensuous experiences can provide children with intense feelings of connectedness with nature. Kaplan and Talbot (1983: 135) describe this as 'a sense of union with something that is lasting and … of enormous importance'. Sobel (2008: 17) describes middle childhood as offering a 'window of opportunity' to develop children's transcendent experiences in nature and foster their sense of awe and wonder at the mysteries of the world. It is through this holistic approach to geography that links can be made to a spiritual dimension within the curriculum, including RE. Spiritual experiences are described by Peterson, Lexmond, Hallgarten and Kerr (2014) as 'moments of aliveness, rapture and homecoming that make the world feel viscerally meaningful'. Such moments can be inspired by children's encounters with the natural world whether through mindful reflective engagements in moments of solitude or through engagement in play. For example, following playful encounters on a residential visit to Swanage, children were given the opportunity to sit quietly in a picturesque spot looking out to sea. One girl wrote the poem below, which demonstrated a humble sense of the vastness of the world and a connection to this (the same girl drew the drawing shown in Figure 4.4).

The sea call

They stared into nothingness
Blue down to blue
The sea and the sky,
Nothing could part
The waves rolling and tumbling,
to lay out at their feet
They stared together,
the sea calling them,
whispering … whispering …

▧ **Figure 4.4** The Sea Call: one child's poetic response to playful place encounters

THE ROLE OF THE TEACHER

The value of playful activity is sometimes underestimated, and its validity as a learning tool questioned. Not all teachers and schools will be comfortable with this experiential, explorative approach, particularly given the demands of an overcrowded, assessment-driven curriculum. The creative teacher who adopts playful pedagogies thus needs to be clear about the geographical learning that may result. Through modelling 'a spirit of playfulness', creative teachers can champion an open-ended, exploratory approach to primary geography. Catling (2014: 367) suggests that such 'pedagogical flexibility' can help provide 'participatory and open contexts' in which to develop children's contributions.' Teachers can work alongside children to design, construct, produce and invent in order to promote new ideas and consider innovative ways of viewing the world. Yet the role of the creative teacher must be more than just a geographical playmate as they need to ensure, as Moyles (2010: 21) points out, that 'tasks are planned and presented in an enjoyable and meaningful way and links are made to the required curriculum and assessment procedures'. The challenge for teachers is to try to free up their planning to work with 'emergent purposes' rather than detailed learning outcomes. The ultimate prize must be to create 'spaces for growth' where learning from the children's exploration, ideas and interests can inform geographical curriculum-making (Clarke *et al.* 2006: 408).

Observing how children occupy spaces provides insights into what they consider important. However, this can be problematic as one of the reasons that children like to create places is so that they can escape the control of adults and feel free, uncontrolled and independent. There is an innate tension between children's natural desire to build a secret den away from adults, and health and safety concerns. When children at one school decided to seek a site for their den on the other side of the school field in the dwindling light of a winter afternoon, the teacher was quick to negotiate boundaries. This example demonstrates that playful geographical activities in the outdoors can only ever place the children in what Ba (in Catling 2011) describes as the role of 'supervised explorers'. They are monitored by teachers and other adults, rather than being the 'independent explorers' they naturally aspire to be. Does this limitation, then, change the real essence of playful learning – a freedom to explore? This needs to be carefully considered, but it is important to acknowledge that playful approaches, even when circumscribed, can place the individual child at the centre of high-quality, sensorial geographical experience, providing them with agency and ownership of their learning.

CONCLUSION

Working out of doors offers children the potential for powerful learning experiences. Within a broad and rich geography curriculum where play is valued, children have the opportunity to engage deeply with local places and consider geographical ideas of scale, interconnectedness and environmental change. Play is a strong vehicle for children's geographical learning as it 'empowers a child to be in tune with the whole self and the creative self' (Martin, in Moyles 2010: 109). Creative teachers recognise that high-quality outdoor play can enhance children's emotional well-being, while also deepening their understanding of a complex and dynamic earth. Playful learning provides primary-age children with opportunities to explore, manipulate, construct and respond to their surroundings, enabling them to build on and extend their personal geographies and celebrate the wonder of places while creating a lasting sense of stewardship for their world.

REFERENCES AND FURTHER READING

Ballas, D. and Tranmer, M. (2008) Happy places or happy people? A multi-level modelling approach to the analysis of happiness and well-being. Research paper. Available at www.iser.essex.ac.uk/research/publications/511692 (accessed 8 January 2016).

Barlow, A., Whittle, J. and Potts, R. (2010) Messy maps and messy spaces. *Primary Geography* 73: 14–15.

Caswell, R. and Warman, T. (2014) *Play for Today – A Report into the Importance and Relevance of Play for Children and Parents in the UK*. Halifax: Eureka Children's Museum.

Catling, S. (2011) Children's geographies in the primary school. In G. Butt (ed.), *Geography, Education and the Future*, pp. 15–29. London: Continuum.

Catling, S. (2014) Giving younger children voice in primary geography: empowering pedagogy – a personal perspective. *International Research in Geographical and Environmental Education* 23(4): 350–72.

Catling, S. and Pickering, S. (2010) Mess, mess, glorious mess. *Primary Geographer* (Autumn): 16–17.

Catling, S. and Willy, T. (2009) *Teaching Primary Geography*. Exeter: Learning Matters.

Clarke, H., Egan, B., Fletcher, L. and Ryan, C. (2006) Creating case studies of practice through appreciative inquiry. *Educational Action Research* 4(3): 407–22.

Cobb, E. (1959) The ecology of imagination in childhood: work in progress. *Daedalus* 88(3): 537–48.

Cresswell, T. (2008) Place encountering geography as philosophy. *Geography* 93(3): 132–9.

Geographical Association (2009) *A Different View: A Manifesto for the Geographical Association*. Sheffield: Geographical Association.

Gleave, J. and Cole-Hamilton, I. (2012) *Make Time to Play -A Literature Review on the Effects of a Lack of Play on Children's Lives*. London: Play England. Available at www.playengland.org.uk/media/371031/a-world-without-play-literature-review-2012.pdf (accessed 15 April 2016).

Hart, R. (1979) *Children's Experience of Place*. New York: Irvington Publishers.

Hart, R. (1997) *Children's Participation: The Theory and Practice of Involving Young Citizens in Community Development and Environmental Care*. London: Earthscan.

Hughes, B. (2002) *A Playworker's Taxonomy of Play Types* (2nd edn). London: PlayLink.

Jenkinson, S. (2001) *The Genius of Play: Celebrating the Spirit of Childhood*. Stroud: Hawthorn.

Kaplan, S. and Talbot, J. F. (1983) Psychological benefits of a wilderness experience. In I. Altman and J. F. Wohlwill (eds), *Behavior and the Natural Environment*, pp. 163–203. New York: Plenum.

Kylin, M. (2003) Children's dens. *Children, Youth and Environments* 13(1): 30–55.

Learning through Landscapes (2006) *Early Years Outdoors Planning for Real for Real Groundnotes*. Winchester: Learning through Landscapes.

Louv, R. (2011) *The Nature Principle: Human Restoration and the End of Nature Deficit Disorder*. Chapel Hill, NC: Algonquin Books.

McLerran, A. (1991) *Roxaboxen*. New York: HarperCollins.

Milne, A. A. (1995) *Winnie the Pooh: The Complete Collection of Stories and Poems*. Godalming: The Book People.

Moyles, J. (2010) *Thinking about Play: Developing a Reflective Approach*. Maidenhead: Open University Press.

Natural England (2015) *Monitor of Engagement with the Natural Environment: A Pilot for an Indicator of Visits to the Natural Environment by Children – Interim Findings from Year 1 (March 2013 to February 2014)*. London: Natural England. Available at http://bit.ly/1NhrXxD (accessed 5 September 2015).

Noddings, N. (2003) *Happiness and Education*. Cambridge: Cambridge University Press.

Ofsted (2011) *Learning to Make a World of Difference*. London: Ofsted.

Osborne, M. D. and Brady, D. J. (2010) Constructing a space for developing a rich understanding of science through play. *Journal of Curriculum Studies* 33(5): 511–24.

Payne, P. G. and Wattchow, B. (2009) Phenomenological deconstruction, slow pedagogy, and the corporeal turn in wild environmental/outdoor education. *Canadian Journal of Environmental Education* 14: 15–32.

Peterson, A., Lexmond, J., Hallgarten, J. and Kerr, D. (2014) *Schools with Soul: A New Approach to Spiritual, Moral, Social and Cultural Education*. London: RSA Action and Research Centre.

Pyle, R. (1993) *The Thunder Trees: Lessons from an Urban Wildland*. Boston, MA: Houghton Mifflin.

Rawding, C. (2007) *Reading Our Landscapes: Understanding Changing Geographies*. London: Chris Kington Publishing.

Richardson, P. (2010) Fieldwork and outdoor learning. S. Scoffham (ed.), *Primary Geography Handbook*, pp. 134–47. Sheffield: Geographical Association.

Roberts, M. (2013) *Geography Through Enquiry*, Sheffield: Geographical Association.

Scarlett, W. G., Naudeau, S. Salonius-Pasternak, D. and Ponte, I. (2005) *Children's Play*. London: Sage.

Shirley, I. (2007) Exploring the great outdoors. R. Austin (ed.), *Letting the Outside In: Developing Teaching and Learning Beyond the Early Years Classroom*, pp. 1–11. Stoke-on-Trent: Trentham.

Sobel, D. (2002) *Children's Special Places: Exploring the Role of Forts, Dens and Bush Houses in Middle Childhood*. Detroit, MI: Wayne State University Press.

Sobel, D. (2008) *Childhood and Nature: Design Principles for Educators*. Portland ME: Stenhouse Publishers

Tovey, H. (2007) *Playing Outdoors: Spaces and Places Risk and Challenge*. Maidenhead: Open University Press.

Van Matre, S. (1990) *Earth Education: A New Beginning*. Greenville, WV: Institute for Earth Education.

Walford, R. (2007) *Using Games in School Geography*. London: Chris Kington Publishers.

Websites and further reading

▩   *50 Things to Do before You Are 11¾:* www.50things.org.uk
▩   *Children and Nature Network:* www.childrenandnature.org/about
▩   *Council for Learning Outside the Classroom:* www.lotc.org.uk
▩   *I'm a Teacher Get Me Outside Here!* http://creativestarlearning.co.uk
▩   *Jan White Natural Play:* https://janwhitenaturalplay.wordpress.com/natural-play-philosophy-approach
▩   *Learning through Landscapes:* www.ltl.org.uk
▩   *Love Outdoor Play:* http://loveoutdoorplay.net
▩   *Mission Explore:* www.missionexplore.net
▩   *The Geography Collective:* https://thegeographycollective.wordpress.com
▩   *Wildtime for Schools:* http://schools.projectwildthing.com

CHAPTER 5

MENTAL MAPS
Learning about places around the world

Simon Catling

This chapter provides a rationale for and creative approaches to developing place knowledge from local to global scales. It outlines formal and informal approaches to learning locational knowledge using activities to adapt for the youngest to oldest primary children. Teaching and learning locational knowledge should be enjoyable, but it is vital to understand its importance to us. It is about more than just naming and locating countries and capital cities.

INTRODUCTION: MEETING LOCATION

The car sticker proclaimed:

WITHOUT GEOGRAPHY YOU ARE NOWHERE!

Its clear message is that geography is partly about place *location*. The old adage states that geography is 'about maps'. Inferring that if you 'know your geography' you can locate places on maps. Location means knowing *where* you are. Geography uses maps because they help in several ways. They locate places. They help us see and understand *what* is where, the features and *spatial patterns* in places, such a suburb's or village's area, a national park landscape, where various leisure activities occur, and global patterns for cities or volcanoes. Maps provide the basis for our awareness and appreciation at different scales of *locational knowledge*. This is part of the core information essential in helping us make sense of the world and being able to find places and know where they are, perhaps because we want to visit them or they are in the news.

Locational knowledge is vital for children in placing themselves and their geographical studies in local, national, continental and global contexts. Studying the many aspects of geography, at whichever scale, misses something essential if we do not know where features, places and events occur and how they relate spatially to each other. Digital technologies support this. Mobile phones are programmed to locate us; they use global positioning systems to pinpoint our location and movements very accurately. They provide us also with maps and other locational information to help us find our way. Location is everywhere!

LOCATION: WHERE IN THE WORLD?

Developing your own mental map begins locally and grows outwards. Try this activity with children:

■   *Where do you live?* Write your address. Start with your name on the first line, your home on the next line and Planet Earth on the last, as in Figure 5.1.

This engaging activity answers the question 'Where am I?'. A key part of being who we are lies in knowing *where* we are. This involves recognising 'I live in Newcastle' or 'Edinburgh', to affirm that we *belong* somewhere socially and can say, 'I'm a Geordie' or 'I'm Scottish'. Where we are from and where we live, locally and nationally, are important to us. Belonging is vital to our self-esteem and identity.

> Barnaby Bear,
> The Geographical Association,
> 160, Solly Street,
> Sheffield,
> South Yorkshire,
> S1 4BF,
> England,
> The United Kingdom,
> Europe,
> Planet Earth.

■ **Figure 5.1** Barnaby Bear's address tells us where to find him

Places matter; knowing where our place is matters. Saying 'I'm Welsh' helps to define us. Try not having a nationality! But if you don't know where or what Wales is, this statement means little. We need a sense of what our 'place' is and how it relates to its surroundings. Being from Wales is not the same as being from England, Argentina or Vietnam. We position ourselves relative to other people and other places. Our address represents this distinctiveness – it represents our *whereness* in the world. Barnaby Bear's address matters; he belongs at the Geographical Association!

We can write Barnaby Bear's address succinctly, as 'Barnaby Bear, 160, S1 4BF, UK', because we have developed coding systems which enable us to state locations with precision. In the UK our postcode does this; in the USA it is the zip code. To this code we simply add our home number and nation's name. Global positioning systems (GPS) locate us using links to satellite images and maps. When driving to unfamiliar destinations more and more people rely now on GPS links using a postcode to lead to their destination – though sometimes a route seems not quite as accurate as it should be!

Addresses are invaluable. Almost all of us have or want one, permanent or transient. Addresses place us in the world. With young children we can learn our addresses to know where we live in case of an emergency. Addresses help us think about the places we live in. By sharing addresses and talking about them, we can understand more about 'our place'. With older primary children we can investigate the nature and uses of addresses and discuss their importance for everyone. The activities in Figure 5.2 initiate this.

Send a postcard map
Children can send a postcard map to a friend or to a link or partner school. Have them include their own postal address so the recipient knows who sent it and can reply. You could add a cross to show a little more precisely where you live.
　　The map locates you and your 'cross' says 'This is where I'm from'. It gives the receiver a view – maps are very useful for this – of where 'your place' is. She or he can then use it to look up where you live on a national map or a world map to see where you are located. This is the nature of an address.

Make address maps
Create a series of maps of your address or of the place you sent your postcard to. Include:

- a local vicinity map to show the building and street;
- a town or local area map to show the place lived at;
- a national map to show where in the country;
- a continental map to show where the country is;
- a world map to show where the continent is.

These maps help to develop a sense of where we are in the world.

▨ **Figure 5.2** Creative activities to explore the meaning of an address

LOCATIONAL KNOWLEDGE IN THE GEOGRAPHY CURRICULUM

Locational knowledge is an aspect of the geography curriculum in very many countries, including in the UK (see Appendix, pp. 232–4). The features usually referred to include:

- the seven continents and five oceans;
- major continental rivers, deserts, mountains and the larger seas;
- major countries and cities;
- various natural and human environments and regions;
- places in the news;
- places studied.

There are many similarities between countries, even when these requirements are briefly stated or given in greater detail, particularly for primary age children to develop local area and national and global mental maps. To have a useful local mental map children need to know the whereabouts of and relationships between:

- *sites*, such as their own home and street;
- *pathways*, such as the road pattern in their area;

■ *nodes*, such as the main intersections, or street corners;

■ *landmarks*, such as key features like churches, parks and hills;

■ *personal landmarks* such as alleyways, play areas and friends' homes.

These elements enable children to locate themselves and understand the spatial relationships of their own places and others they visit or get to know (Lynch 1960). As they build their experience and skills, they learn to apply these to understand other places that they visit (Kitchen and Blades 2002).

Learning locational knowledge about our home country and continent contributes to building global mental maps (Downs and Stea 1977; Gould and White 1986). Children's mental maps are enhanced by their experiences of places and their encounters with national and world maps (Wiegand 2006). Teaching enhances children's locational knowledge (Ofsted 2011) by studying the locality and a good range of other places around the world and by using maps and atlases in geographical enquiries and investigations imaginatively and creatively, such as by using various of the ideas included here.

The purpose of locational knowledge teaching in the UK is to enable children to develop their mental maps of their local place, nationally and the world. They should develop each of these as they progress through their primary geography studies. Mental maps help children recall readily where key features and places are. Figure 5.3 outlines opportunities to introduce and enhance children's local, UK and global mental maps. It refers to the locational knowledge helpful for younger and older primary age children to develop. There is no specific sequence for doing this. It is a matter of continuous exposure and experience investigating places at all scales, during which children constantly use maps, globes and atlases to locate and find out about places at different scales.

WHAT RESEARCH TELLS US

Teaching locational knowledge builds on children's curiosity and interest in where places are and what's there. Children come to school with the capacity to locate themselves and navigate their immediate environment, learning this at home as soon as they can move about. Young children learn the features of and ways around school quickly: its landmarks, routes and areas. Their local *mental maps* include their home, local streets and familiar nearby features and places (Matthews 1992). Children develop discrete mental maps of particular places elsewhere from their experiences. They can draw these, however primitively. As their experience increases during their primary years, their maps become more accurate and detailed, though not necessarily perfect (Figure 5.4)! Children learn about places beyond their direct experience indirectly through the web, television programmes, computer games, information books and stories. They develop a sense of the world map through exposure to world maps, globes and atlases (Figure 5.5). Their knowledge is augmented by informal interactions with family, friends, classmates and others (Reynolds 2005; Reynolds and Vinterek 2016). Although their image of the world becomes more extensive, it is liable to be partial and large areas will remain 'unknown' to them if left to their own devices (Wiegand 2006). Using maps vitally extends their knowledge.

Research into the maps that young children draw from memory shows their knowledge is built up of discrete 'chunks' of information. Local maps show specific features of interest to younger children, perhaps with roads or pathways linking some elements, but are rarely accurate (Matthews 1992). When they draw world maps they draw discrete and

For 4/5 to 7/8 year olds

Introducing locational knowledge	Points to consider
Pupils investigate their local area: ■ the locations, types and uses of some features and places; ■ where it is in relation to other nearby places and in the United Kingdom.	Pupils use simple local maps, and aerial and ground feature photographs and fieldwork. They draw their own maps and make models, sharing their local knowledge to support each others' developing mental maps and sense of place.
Pupils name, locate and find out about: ■ The British Isles and Europe; ■ the UK's countries and capitals; ■ the world's continents and oceans.	Pupils use globes, atlases, British Isles and world wall maps, and jigsaw and other fun maps, in formal and informal activities to learn the shapes, names and locations of the world's continents and oceans, and the UK's countries and capital cities. They name some of the Earth's major physical features and find out information about some aspects of the UK.

For 7/8 to 11/12 year olds

Extending locational knowledge	Points to consider
Pupils investigate locally and elsewhere: ■ to extend their knowledge of places and features; ■ to know the types of links with other places.	Pupils access local primary and secondary sources, including local maps and aerial and ground photographs, and use fieldwork about: what happens there, how land and buildings are used, how goods reach them, and journeys that can be made in and out of the area. They draw plans, sketch maps and make models.
Pupils name, locate and investigate: ■ counties and cities in the UK, Europe, and across the world; ■ types of environments, features and natural and human regions; ■ places in the news, and met and studied in geography and history topics.	Pupils use maps, atlases, digital maps and written and pictorial information sources to find out about environments and regions, and aspects of the character and physical and human geography of places studied at various scales. They create their own world map books from their studies.
Pupils are introduced to: ■ latitude and longitude, the Equator, the Tropics, the prime meridian, the polar regions, the northern and southern hemispheres, and seasons; ■ the Earth's rotation, day and night, and time zones.	Pupils investigate the significance (for whom) of latitude and longitude, the relationship of the globe and hemispheres, and time zones; and the connections between Earth's rotation and tilt and day and night and seasons. They make appropriate links with the science curriculum.

▓ **Figure 5.3** Locational knowledge for the primary years

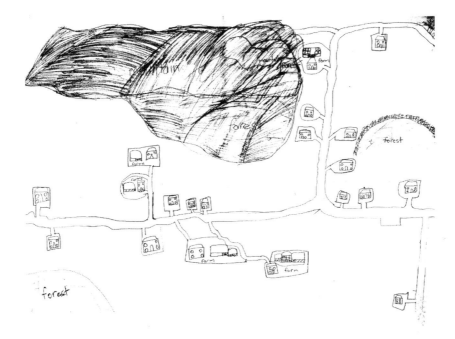

■ **Figure 5.4** Roads, homes and hills are key features in this local area map, drawn by a ten-year-old from memory

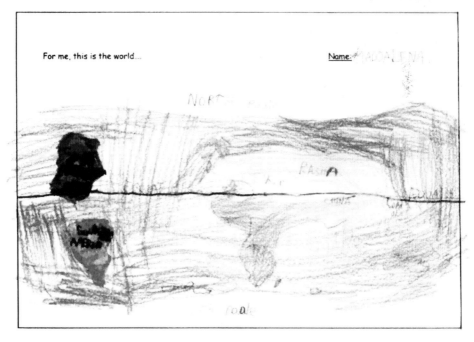

■ **Figure 5.5** Africa and North and South America are key features in this map of the world, drawn by a seven-year-old from memory

unconnected places, more likely randomly on the page (Wiegand 2006; Scoffham 2017). Knowing where places are involves understanding 'class inclusion' or 'nested hierarchy', when one place lies inside another and within yet another, like a set of Russian dolls or an address (Harwood and McShane 1996) as in Figure 5.1. Young children quite reasonably have difficulty with nested hierarchy relationships, so tend to see Sheffield, England and Europe as separate places. It takes time to understand the relationships, but this develops during their primary years and seems to be understood by the end of it.

Experience of their local area and of finding out about their own country and other parts of the world helps children develop their understanding, as does regular exposure to national, continental and world maps (Kitchen and Blades 2002; Barrett *et al.* 2006). For the youngest children, this must involve going out and about round school, visiting local places, playing with soft toy globes and maps on playmats, and nurturing their interest through investigations using atlases and exploring websites. For older primary children learning gains through a focus on enquiries in the local area and other localities in national or global settings, engaging them with large-scale maps and developing atlas skills. There is not an age when children can or must begin to learn locational knowledge; it is a matter of encouraging and refining the mapping and locational skills they need and of bringing increasing rigour to their growing understanding.

EXPLORING AND LEARNING ABOUT LOCATION

How do we help children to enhance, embed – and enjoy – locational knowledge? Left to chance the development of local, national and global mental maps is haphazard. While children undoubtedly construct their own 'personalised' mental maps, it is vital as citizens that their maps have shared characteristics. After all, the key features of the Earth – such as the continents and oceans – are the basis for everyone's mental map of the world, just as the key features and patterns of a locality and the nation make up its form and character. Which characteristics to select should be debated!

Investigating through fieldwork

Getting out and about is key to building young children's mental maps of their local area. When starting school, children bring some sense of places locally. Fieldwork helps extend this, fostering local knowledge and meaning as much as locational awareness. Locality-based books can be a way into investigations. *A World of Your Own* (Carlin 2014) and *My Place* (Wheatley and Rawlins 2008) can stimulate finding out about the local area through fieldwork and appreciating how places change while key sites remain. Figure 5.6 offers some pointers for this.

Children often draw the route to school or the area around their school or home. When doing this, ask them to take their maps home with them to check their route or area and what they included. Usually they will improve them and redraw them. Make comparisons with street, Ordnance Survey or other local maps to see how their maps are similar or different. Why is this?

Developing mental maps

Stories can foster children's mental maps. Picture-books offer a way to think about what places are like, what is there and how the different features and parts of an area relate to

Being 'out and about'

With Foundation Stage, Reception and Year 1 children, visits to selected places in and around the nursery or school help focus their attention on what is there and what the place is like.

- Observing and naming what is on the left, right, ahead, and in the corner helps develop children's spatial vocabulary.
- Walk round a route, asking the children to note the 'landmarks' they see. Stop to work out where their base is 'from here'. Talk about which ways they can go back to their starting point.
- Devise similar activities to develop early notions of location and direction for use at the local park, play area or shops.
- Introduce children to a simple map of the school's grounds to explore and find places. An aerial photograph of the grounds can be a great stimulus to observing and locating features.

During these activities observe and talk about the types of features children see, what they are used for and their spatial relationships with each other.

Fieldwork and local studies

With children from Year 2 onwards, local studies must involve the use of local maps.

- Use street maps during local investigations to help children identify their homes, key landmarks and favourite and less-liked places.
- Make journeys to develop their understanding of the connections between features and of routes around the area.
- Encourage children to map the land use in and discuss the character of the area, and look for evidence of changes that have occured.
- Building on fieldwork, children draw their own maps or make large floor maps with models to show parts of their area.
- Devise a leaflet for new families to the area, or a poster that shows where a new development is planned. This creative challenge helps children clarify their understanding of the layout of the area and its key features.

■ **Figure 5.6** Local fieldwork helps to develop children's mental maps

each other. Use the text and pictures to help children to map the layout of an area, building a sense of what is where, as in 'What's this place like' (Figure 5.7). Developing children's local mental maps involves them imagining an overhead view. Stories such as *Lucy in the City* (Dillemuth 2016), in which a character finds her way home, help children see such a view, reflect on their experiences of places and extend their mental maps.

It is informative to compare children's mental maps to see what they have in common and the ways in which they are unique. 'My world, your world' (Figure 5.7) encourages children to think about familiar and unfamiliar places. It involves identifying places that have meaning or interest for them and it relates to developing their sense of identity and belonging. They have to use maps and atlases to check their knowledge. The linked activity, 'My map, my gap', takes an alternative perspective and asks children to reflect on their current knowledge, as a personally focused or shared activity. Its purpose is to examine the extent of their locational awareness and identify parts of the world of which they are unaware, so that these can be investigated. The final activity (Figure 5.7) encourages children to identify significant places locally and globally and to explain why we should all know about them.

What's this place like?

Use picture-storybooks such as *We're Going on a Bear Hunt* (Rosen and Oxenbury, 1993, Walker Books), *The Journey Home from Grandpa's* (Lumly and Fatus, 2006, Barefoot Books), or *Binki's Big Adventure* (Blackwell and Nankivell, 2011, Avenue Publishing) create models, pictures and maps to show the locations of the features and places that are mentioned. Children can work individually or in groups on a story to devise their own maps of the places and then compare them. Why have they created different maps of these imagined places? Can they agree what a 'true' map might be?

My world, your world

This activity focuses on 'what I know' and 'what interests me', as well as on what is common or shared. Each child either draws from memory a local map, national map or a world map or adds information to a blank map. By their map they list places they want to include but cannot locate. In groups, they compare which places they have included, identifying those they have in common and those that are individual; they explain their choices.

My map, my gap

Children name and list places they know, perhaps making their own maps to record them. On a local, UK or world wall map use pins to locate places they know, where relatives live, which they have visited, that they hear about in the news, where they would like to visit, and which they have come across for other reasons. Link the places by a thread to pictures and/or information about them.

Periodically discuss the pattern of the locations and features marked. Where are most pins located, and where are the gaps? Why do some areas on the map have no pins? Talk about what and why we know about some places yet nothing about others. Plan ways to investigate the 'gaps on the map'. Take digital photographs of the maps from time to time to show how information builds up. Does the pattern change, say, across the year?

Why should I know there?

Encourage children to consider which features and places all children should know about, and which might be included individually to personalize maps. Focus on the local area, nationally or world map knowledge, as an individual or group activity. Children might focus on 'Where should new people to our area know about?' or 'What are the places in the UK/world we should know about?' Have the children:

- identify places they think everyone should know; debate and agree reasons to include them; create a map showing these places;
- propose/develop ways to help each other learn where the places are on the maps and how they show their learning;
- develop criteria to choose places they want to add because they have a personal interest or meaning.

Essentially you are considering why which places are significant to children, and what 'significance' means (Catling and Taylor, 2006).

▦ **Figure 5.7** Four ways to investigate 'my world' knowledge

Encountering the wider world

While children cannot readily explore the wider world, it can come to them. Globes, world wall maps and atlases are essential resources. From the earliest age children can search for continents, oceans and countries, and later for cities, rivers, mountains, deserts and other human and physical geography features. These searches can be refined, refocused and become more detailed with age and with the types of globes and atlases available. Google Earth, Google Maps and other internet sources can be used. Figure 5.8 suggests activities to adapt for children of all ages.

Exploring the world

A large world map provides opportunities for children to undertake a variety of enjoyable and creative activities that enhance their locational knowledge. Such activities can be undertaken using large-size maps of the British Isles and the continents.

Using a large floor map such as MaxiMap
With groups, or a class, ask children to point to and stand on named parts of the world (Figure 5.9). These might be continents or oceans, countries, mountains or deserts. Can children trace the line of a river or label a major city? Ask them about places they may not know or are uncertain of, so that they must use the atlas to find them and locate them on the world map. Have children drive a toy car, sail a boat or fly from one location to another.

Linking the globe and world map
Using large world floor maps or wall maps with a globe, children identify features and places on the globe and point them out on the world map. For young children these might be the continents and oceans. For older children they may be major cities or physical features. Have an atlas available for reference.

Labeling features and places
Lay a world wall map on a table. Children use a set of cards naming features and places, turned over one at a time, to label places, using an atlas as necessary. They might use transport toys to show journeys across countries, continents and oceans. Once they understand, groups of children can arrange this activity – but they need to know where the places they include are! They must prepare with suitable maps, globes and atlases.

Everyday products from around the world
Where in the world are various products grown or made? Consider daily foods, toys and goods, and television programmes watched. Locate and highlight their place or country of origin on a wall map. A good stimulus is the picture-book *The World Came to My Place Today* (Readman and Roberts, 2002, Eden Project Books).

World environments
As a class exercise, ask children to draw plants and creatures to place on a world or continental wall map. Show the children clips from wildlife films to extend their knowledge and fuel their enthusiasm. Use this stimulus to investigate the world's biomes, vegetation belts and environmental regions. Name them and locate them on maps. Find out about some of the threats to different creatures and habitats. What are people doing to threaten and to help preserve biodiversity?

■ **Figure 5.8** Activities to help children learn about the world

▤ **Figure 5.9** Children using a Maximap to explore the world map
Source: photo by Steph Pamplin

Many storybooks have a global dimension. *One World Together* (Anholt and Anholt 2014) and *Babar's World Tour* (de Brunhoff 2005) involve journeys through which children encounter different places. *Sidney and the Seven Seas* (Patterson and Jones 2013) introduces countries and places to find on a world map or in an atlas, while *Atlas of Adventures* (Williams and Letherland 2014) invites children to discover different events in places across the continents. These are enjoyable reads to use to find out where places are and what they are like. Children can develop their own stories involving local, national and world journeys. They might tell these orally, using a globe, an atlas or a map, or make their own illustrated book for others to read.

'Up' in the world map

Which way is 'up' on the Earth? Figure 5.10 shows two world maps. We 'know' the view in Map A: north is at the top; Europe and Africa are central. Looking at a globe, we see north at the top; magnetic north is the point of reference. When viewed from space, the Earth can be seen from any angle. An engaging way to challenge the 'correct' view in Map A is to use the 'upside-down' world map in Map B. Figure 5.11 outlines an approach to discuss and investigate these different perspective.

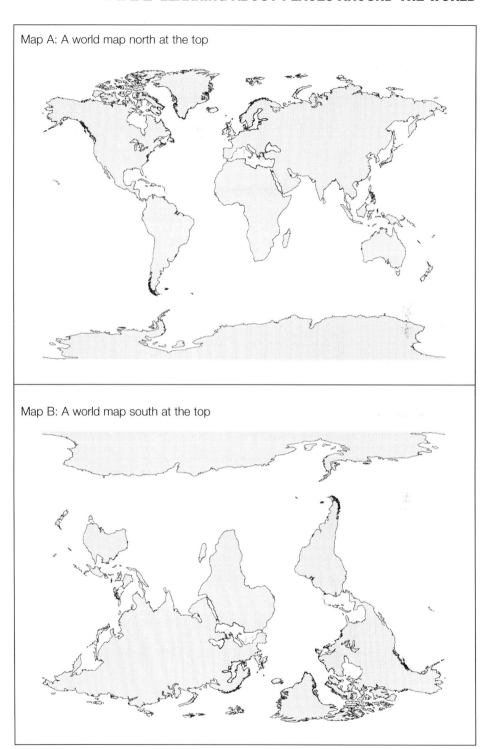

Map A: A world map north at the top

Map B: A world map south at the top

■ **Figure 5.10** Which of these world maps is the 'right way up'?

Which way is up? Does it matter?
Give the children two copies of the world map, one with 'north' marked at the top, and the other with 'south' at the top. Discuss which one the children feel more comfortable with and why? Ask what appears 'strange' about the other one? Invite them to name the continents and oceans on the south-on-top map without turning it round. Investigate these questions:

■ Does it matter whether north or south is at the top?
■ When and why did people start drawing world maps with north at the top?
■ Why might people have wanted to put east at the top before magnetic compasses were invented?
■ Find a 'Pacific-centred' world map. How does this look different to a Europe/Africa-centred map?
■ Use Oxfam World Maps. How many different ways is the world map drawn? Which do you most like and which do you like least? Which fascinates you most? Explain why.

▨ **Figure 5.11** Re-orientating the world map can be a highly creative process

FURTHER ADVENTURES IN LOCATIONAL KNOWLEDGE

Many other approaches to developing locational knowledge can be included in or alongside geography topics. The activities in Figure 5.12 use investigations, problem-solving and enquiry approaches, and are for class activities, a map club or homework.

What's going on where – and why?
Use broadcasts, papers or websites to keep up-to-date with news reports locally and globally. Mark places mentioned on maps of the local area, British Isles, Europe and the world. Have different children write a brief summary, make a drawing or print off a captioned photograph to pin on or by the map. Discuss why it helps to know where events happen. Over time note the places referred to more often and discuss why they are significant.

Atlas addicts
Encourage children to check the location of places they encounter but do not know. Use local street, national road and world atlases. From time to time, ask children about:

■ which places they know the locations of;
■ how they have discovered where these places are;
■ what sort of places they are;
■ the locations of the oddest, strangest or nicest places they have found;
■ what fascinates them about using atlases and finding out about places.

▨ **Figure 5.12** Ten engaging ways to develop locational awareness

Atlas investigation
Use atlases in finding out where places are to develop children's map skills (Richardson & Richardson, 2016). They could:

■ use the contents and index pages to find particular maps and places;
■ learn to read alpha-numeric grids or longitude and latitude to locate places;
■ find out the longitude and latitude of key features such as the Equator, the Tropics, Arctic and Antarctic Circles, and the Prime meridian;
■ use map keys to see how symbols show different features, including point features (like cities), line features (like rivers) or area features (like countries);
■ interpret the symbols to describe how the atlas map portrays an area;
■ use compass directions to say which direction places are from/to each other;
■ use scales to measure distances;
■ appreciate how atlas maps relate to the globe by comparing continent shapes and sizes.

Atlas quiz
Children enjoy quizzes. Create questions for groups to say where places are and what they know about them. Following several quizzes, teams of children can set the questions. Provide children with atlas quiz questions to investigate as homework; in the class quiz they must recall the answers, not using an atlas.

Country factfile
Provide a cut out or an outline drawn shape of a country to identify. Children create a factfile for that country about such things as the capital city, other cities, main physical features, language(s), neighbouring countries, main industries, farm products, habitats, tourism and environmental concerns. They draw a map of the country. They add its national flag, population, the range of things its people do, where they live and how, its links with the UK, and what it is well-known for. Use this approach to investigate counties in the UK or states in countries such as the USA and Brazil.

What's the time?
We know what 'our' time is, but what is it elsewhere? Introduce time zones through books like *At the Same Moment Around the World* (Perrin, 2011, Chronicle Books). This can generate discussion about longitude, the Prime (Greenwich) Meridian and the International Date Line, using a globe and an atlas, linked to the Earth's rotation. Investigate where it is nighttime when it is daylight in the UK, using city centre webcams which you have checked, for cities like Buenos Aires, Argentina; Los Angeles, USA; Cape Town, South Africa; Delhi, India and Sydney, Australia.

Map and picture postcards
Make a collection with the children of postcard maps and photographs showing different places in the UK and around the world. There are many types of postcard maps: world and country maps, satellite photographs of continents and Earth, regions in a country, and urban areas. Postcards show landscapes, national parks, coasts, tourist resorts, towns and villages. These are named; when someone receives a postcard they know where it shows. Use atlases to locate the places postcards show. Use postcard maps and pictures to identify some aspects of these places (Catling and Baker, 2011).

■ **Figure 5.12** continued

Google Earth
Use Google Earth to see satellite views of the Earth. Zoom in to see where places are and what they look like from 'above'. On a world map mark places you have looked at; include a variety of places. *Looking Down* (Jenkins, 1995) shows views scaling down from space to a microbe! Use Google Maps to view maps showing the same areas as in the satellite photos. How are the areas mapped? Discuss why particular features and places are included and named? What do the names of features and places tell you?

Create your own globe
Children can make their own globes. Blow up a (almost circular) balloon, cover it in papier-mâché and let it dry. Use a commercial globe to help draw on the continents and major islands of the Earth. Colour the land green and the sea blue. Use other colours to show major mountain areas, deserts, forests and so forth. Add the largest cities, lakes and some major rivers. Children select other features to add to 'personalize' their globe.

Add a map to your school playground
School playgrounds provide large open-ground spaces on which to paint a local, British Isles, Europe and/or world map. This can be done commercially, or children and parents can chalk out the maps on a grid layout for accuracy and then use 'road' paint. Decide whether to use an equal area map or a Mercator map. Include a compass rose: align the maps with North pointing in the right direction!

Use playground maps for various activities: name places; add features using coloured chalks; use planes, ships and vehicles to make journeys; stand at a named site and point to it on a globe; see how far you can move only on land; consider distances between places; and locate features and places studied in topics. Children enjoy having such maps on their playground and will create their own games.

Paint a British Isles, Europe or world map on a suitable wall for children to look at. This might show some physical features and/or countries and cities.

▨ **Figure 5.12** continued

CONCLUSION: HAPPY MAPPING LEARNING LOCATIONS

Knowing where places are in the locality or around the world can be enhancing, even useful! Such learning happens when children can explore places and use maps, globes and atlases from their earliest years. This requires thoughtful planning. One of the pleasures for children in locating places lies in getting to know where they are and finding out what is there. It involves developing increasingly effective map-reading skills and building ever more sophisticated mental maps. Objectives include that ensuring children have fun with maps and that they value maps and atlases. Celebrate their world awareness. Figure 5.13 identifies how to create such happy mappers.

Enjoying mapping and locating places comes about through children:

■ having local maps, road atlases, globes and atlases in class to pick up and explore, as well as to use in their investigations and projects;
■ learning the skills of map reading;
■ realising that maps and atlases matter for our daily lives;
■ being able to go and look up places when they hear about them to find out more, because there is map or an atlas to hand;
■ gaining pleasure from poring over a map just because it looks fascinating, there is much to see and it sparks imagination;
■ realising it's fun to know stuff about the world;
■ recognizing, sharing, valuing and extending their local to global mental maps.

For this to happen, ensure that:

■ there are atlases and maps of all sorts easily accessible in the classroom;
■ there is a globe (or two or three);
■ children know they can look at maps when they need and wish to;
■ you include map skills and place learning in geography, other subjects and cross-curricular topics;
■ the children see you looking at maps and know you value them – and the world;
■ you celebrate your own and their knowledge of places locally and globally.

▨ **Figure 5.13** Creating happy mappers

REFERENCES

Anholt, C. and Anholt, L. (2014) *One World Together*. London: Frances Lincoln.

Barrett, M., Lyons, E. and Bourchier-Sutton, A. (2006) Children's knowledge of countries. In C. Spencer and M. Blades (eds), *Children and their Environments*, pp. 57–72. Cambridge: Cambridge University Press.

Carlin, L. (2014) *A World of Your Own*. London: Phaidon.

Catling, S. (2002) *Placing Places*. Sheffield: Geographical Association.

Catling, S. and Baker, P. (2011) Wish you were here? Exploring postcard maps. *Primary Geography* 75: 12–13.

Catling, S. and Taylor, L. (2006) Thinking about geographical significance. *Primary Geography* 61: 35–7.

De Brunhoff, J. (2005) *Babar's World Tour*. New York: Abrams Publishers.

Dillemuth, J. (2016) *Lucy in the City*. Washington, DC: Magination Press.

Downs, R. and Stea, D. (1977) *Maps in Minds*. New York: Harper & Row.

Gould, P. and White, R. (1986) *Mental Maps*. London: Routledge.

Harwood, D. and McShane, J. (1996) Young children's understanding of nested hierarchies on place relationship. *International Research in Geographical and Environmental Education* 5(1): 3–29.

Jenkins, S. (1995) *Looking Down*. New York: Hmh Books for Young Readers.

Kitchen, R. and Blades, M. (2002) *The Cognition of Geographic Space*. London: I. B. Tauris.

Lynch, K. (1960) *The Image of the City*. Cambridge, MA: MIT Press.

Matthews, H. (1992) *Making Sense of Place*. Hemel Hempstead: Harvester Wheatsheaf.

Ofsted (2011) *Geography: Learning to Make a World of Difference*. Manchester: Ofsted. Available at www.gov.uk/government/publications/geography-learning-to-make-a-world-of-difference (accessed 8 January 2016).

Patterson, E. and Jones, A. (2013) *Sidney and the Seven Seas*. Bath: North Parade Publishing.

Perrin, C. (2011) *At the Same Moment, Around the World*. San Francisco, CA: Chronicle Books.

Readman, J. and Roberts, L. H. (2002) *The World Came to My Place Today*. London: Eden Project Books.

Reynolds, R. (2005) *Where is That Place? Primary Children's Attitudes to and Knowledge of the World*. Proceedings of the AARE Conference. Available at http://hdl.handle.net/1959.13/35149 (accessed 8 January 2016).

Reynolds, R. and Vinterek, M. (2016) Geographical locational knowledge as an indicator of children's views of the world: research from Sweden and Australia. *International Research in Geographical and Environmental Education* 25(1): 68–83.

Richardson, P. and Richardson, T. (2016) *Everyday Guide to Map Skills*. Sheffield: Geographical Association.

Scoffham, S. (2017) Devising maps and atlases for schools. In A. Kent and P. Vujakovic (eds), *Routledge Handbook of Mapping and Cartography*. Abingdon: Routledge.

Wheatley, N. and Rawlins, D. (2008) *My Place*. London: Walker Books.

Wiegand, P. (2006) *Learning and Teaching with Maps*. Abingdon: Routledge.

Williams, R. and Letherland, L. (2014) *Atlas of Adventures*. London: Wide Eyed Editions.

Resources and websites

Primary Geography (the Geographical Association's magazine for primary school teachers) is an invaluable source of ideas for finding and learning about locational knowledge from local to global scales. Atlases for all primary ages are available from the major school atlas publishers: Oxford University Press, Collins and Philips. Globes of many varieties can be obtained from school suppliers. Look out for soft globes and inflatable globes that young children can hug, as well as for small and large globes on stands. Obtain globes that show the continents and oceans unnamed, as well as those that show the Earth's physical features, countries and major cities.

SOURCES FOR GLOBES, ATLASES, WALL AND FLOOR MAPS

- *Hope Education:* www.hope-education.co.uk
- *MaxiMap:* www.maximap.net
- *TTS:* www.tts-group.co.uk
- *Wildgoose:* www.wildgoose.ac

SOURCES FOR SCHOOL PLAYGROUND MAPS

- *Promain (school playground graphics):* www.promain.co.uk/School_Play_Ground_Graphics
- *Road Art:* www.roadartltd.co.uk/schools.html

ADVICE ON TEACHING LOCATIONAL KNOWLEDGE

- *Geographical Association:* www.geography.org.uk
- *Geography Expert Subject Advisory Group:* https://geognc.wordpress.com/

MAP WEBSITES

- *Google Earth:* www.google.com/earth
- *Google Maps:* www.maps.google.co.uk
- *National Geographic Map Machine:* http://maps.nationalgeographic.com/map-machine
- *Ordnance Survey Mapzone:* www.ordnancesurvey.co.uk/mapzone
- *Oxfam Mapping Our World:* www.oxfam.org.uk/education/resources/mapping-our-world
- *Streetmap (UK):* www.streetmap.co.uk
- *Tiger Moon:* www.tigermoon.co.uk/geography
- *Worldmapper:* www.worldmapper.org

CHAPTER 6

REPRESENTING PLACES IN MAPS AND ART

Margaret Mackintosh

This chapter aims to excite teachers and pupils with different and innovative pictorial ways of representing and communicating geographical spatial information, ideas and concepts. The way that we view the world from different perspectives creates strong links with both ICT and art. These links are explored here with particular reference to ethnic paintings, Google Earth and the work of two European artists, Friedensreich Hundertwasser and David Hockney. The focus is on what some might call 'out-of-the-box' approaches, since more familiar ideas about using pictorial visual communication resources are published elsewhere, notably in the Geographical Association's Everyday Guides (series editor Julia Tanner), *Primary Geography Handbook* (Scoffham 2010) and *Learning and Teaching with Maps* (Wiegand 2006). The aim is to give some practical, geography-led but interdisciplinary examples of how to be creative with spatial representation and communication. It is hoped that, as a result, children will develop enthusiasm for and enjoyment in looking at, reading and making different types and styles of spatial representation and a love of maps.

LANDSCAPE AND ART

- 'It was good fun, creative and geographical.'
- 'I learnt to rely on other people, working in a team.'
- 'I consider it both art and geography because I used both sorts of techniques.'
- 'It was a good experience, fun, interesting and good inspiration – an art project with a geographical twist.'

What were these pupils talking about? What was the project? The pupils were commenting on a day's activity for a cluster of rural schools, 'Right or Left, Up or Down?', led by Kim Etchells, a practising artist and part-time tutor in north Devon. It was initially planned as an art project but the focus and potential was definitely geographical, so it is described here in some detail. In a fun, practical, creative and inspirational way it introduced and provided opportunities to develop many concepts and techniques essential to representing geographical spatial information in maps, photographs and diagrams. The power of the geography in Etchells's approach was most evident when the work of the cluster of participating schools was brought together in an exhibition in Great Torrington, north Devon. Organising a similar event in your school would make a powerful impact, which, if accompanied by a display of all sorts of formal and informal maps, oblique and vertical aerial views, photographs and postcards, would highlight in a geographical context the importance of visual literacy, sometimes referred to as graphicacy (Mackintosh 2010).

There were three elements to the activity day: (i) landscape through maps, (ii) landscape through models, and (iii) journeys. In preparation, a map of the area centred on each school had been greatly enlarged, and the roads, settlements and field boundaries copied on to white paper. This was stuck on cardboard and cut into 15cm squares. A limited but appropriate colour palette was chosen involving greens, reds and browns.

Landscape through maps

The day started with a talk about land use, pattern and texture in the landscape. Pupils were already familiar with Google Earth, which they had used to explore features of the landscape in their local area and beyond. Now they looked at photographs of, for example, the pattern made by the bushes in a tea plantation, and other vertical and oblique aerial views. They were shown landscape paintings by artists such as Hockney and Hundertwasser. The children were encouraged to talk about their own area and the characteristics of their environment, and to collect descriptive words. They were asked to consider the meaning of the term 'rural'.

Each child was then given one of the 15cm squares and a palette of ready-mix colours. They each painted their square using the colours in a (fairly!) controlled system, leaving the roads white and giving the landscape colour and texture to indicate possible land-use. Further squares were painted as time allowed and the whole was assembled to recreate a map of each school's region (Figure 6.1).

In future geographical work children would be expected to look for pattern and texture in landscape on a range of photographs and maps. Using a restricted palette and indicative land-use textures on their own map helped them to understand the need for a key and symbols. Further discussion and practical work would lead to an eventual understanding of the significance of the stylised conventions used in OS maps.

■ **Figure 6.1** This close-up of some of the squares of the map created by pupils at Clinton C of E Primary School, Merton, Okehampton, Devon shows road and field patterns and uses texturing to indicate land use
Source: photo by Margaret Mackintosh

Landscape through models

The next part of the day consisted of a 'leap of freedom'. Using the same-size squares of card as for the earlier map exercise, the children were put together in teams to construct a model landscape (Figure 6.2). The possibility of including a river or lake – blue paint added to the palette – caused excitement and the children spontaneously wanted to relate one piece or square to another and to where they lived.

▨ **Figure 6.2** Imagined landscapes by pupils from several participating schools in North Devon. Pupils created their model landscapes and appreciated the value of teamwork as they planned for adjacent squares to fit together
Source: photo by Margaret Mackintosh

In future geographical work, children would make drawings, diagrams and maps of the landscape in their models. Young pupils could also do this with model landscapes created in their sandtray and construct a model from a given landscape photograph. Older pupils could make models from maps and photographs and annotate photographs of their models to identify geographical features such as rivers, hills, routes and settlements. In doing this they would be exploring different ways of representing geographical information and beginning to appreciate the strengths and weaknesses of each. Children might also consider the need for a key, a scale and an indication of compass direction for the benefit of themselves and others, rather than because they had been told to include them by the teacher. In this way they will eventually begin to picture photographs and maps as three-dimensional 'models' by reconstructing or visualising the landscape represented. It is known that many children have difficulty interpreting the scale of geographical features they see in photographs (Lieben and Downs 1993). Creative teachers will provide fieldwork opportunities where children can see examples of streams, hills, cliffs and farms for themselves and bring photographs back to the classroom to relate to their models and maps. They may also get children to guess the distance to nearby landmarks during fieldwork and then check the distance on an Ordnance Survey map.

Landscape through journeys

The afternoon activities focused on journeys. Pupils visualised a real or imagined journey of their own, which they depicted using collage and drawing techniques in a four-page concertina book. They thought about mode of transport, reason for the journey, the terrain, speed, destination, what they could see along the way, the season and the weather, and other geographical aspects. As the work was centred on collage, the children focused on how to use colour as a mosaic, rather than on drawing pictures of landmarks (Mackintosh and Kent 2014).

To generate ideas pupils looked at how different artists have depicted routes and journeys. Hockney's landscape paintings such as 'Winter Tunnel with Snow', 'Roads and Cornfields' and 'Road across the Wolds' (see Plate A in colour plate section) provided a valuable stimulus. While some of Hockney's paintings depict hedge-lined tracks, others show a more elevated view over a road with the landscape and route disappearing into the distance. At times Hockney is more 'playful' with landscape, using photographs, as in his photo-collages and, more recently, an iPad. Following these inputs the children became more experimental, more open and playful themselves in their interpretation of their journey. Eavesdropping on conversation revealed the different scale of the journeys being portrayed, from transcontinental to a microscopic journey inside the human body.

The creative teacher might want to develop the visual communication of journeys in future geographical work. Children could look at some of the many ways of representing or communicating a journey pictorially. Young children could sequence photographs they had taken of landmarks seen on a class walk or journey. They could make a map of the journey, locate the landmarks on a large-scale map and look for them on Google Earth, using the satellite images and the facility Street View. Children might compile an album of photographs taken on a school residential visit and recreate the journey. They could look at journeys portrayed in art, in diagrams such as of the journey of a river or the London Underground, and in maps of many sorts, from pictorial oblique views to street maps and road and world atlases.

Map work is best not treated as an isolated and de-contextualised exercise but related to real situations and needs. We use a dictionary or a calculator when we require them but seem much less ready to refer a map or diagram to support our work. The creative teacher will find many opportunities to use maps in connection with journeys. Whenever the class is going on a long or short journey, for whatever subject, an appropriate map should be consulted beforehand, to plan the 'best' route, taking distance, time, safety, mode of transport and cost into consideration. After the journey the route will be confirmed by again looking at the map. If the route is coloured on the map, pupils will be able to see the distance, direction and shape of the journey related to their school. This will help them to construct their spatial understanding of the school's surroundings.

Some weeks after the end of the project, pupils were asked for their reactions and responses. They replied:

- 'I learned about all different parts of the place where I live, but in a fun way.'
- 'I liked making my own map of somewhere – I enjoyed it.'
- 'I thought it was very interesting and fun – I most enjoyed creating my own little environment, a mountain.'
- 'I learned that there are so many different views in Devon.'
- 'You learn about the environment and can draw the/your surroundings – it was geography and art.'

The combination of geography and art provides the focus for later sections of this chapter. As well as being informative, maps can be beautiful works of art in their own right. Paintings and photographs can also communicate geographical information. Used creatively, separately or in combination, they can help to encourage a lifelong love of maps and geography.

STARTING WITH PAINTINGS

Many paintings have a spatial, almost map-like feel to them. This section suggests a range of paintings and artists that can be used as starting points for more geographical work on maps, diagrams and visual communication. Each painting could be used to encourage an interest in and enthusiasm for different ways of representing the three-dimensional world in two dimensions, ultimately to foster a love of maps.

Quechan paintings

Paintings by indigenous artists often portray everyday life and scenes. This one, for example (see Figure 6.3, also Plate B in colour plate section), shows a busy scene from the high Andes with people busy harvesting crops from the fields and celebrating their harvest festival.

The volcano Cotopaxi dominates the skyline in the background. Cotopaxi can be seen from many parts of Ecuador and symbolises the spirit of the country. The picture was painted on sheepskin (why?) by a Quechan artist from Tigua in Ecuador. This painting

▨ **Figure 6.3** Communal life and landscape around the village of Tigua, Ecuador, with the volcano Cotopaxi dominating the scene. (Access 'Volcanism Blog' and search for 'tigua', or access images of 'art from tigua'.)
Source: photo © The Volcanism Blog

introduces rural life in an unfamiliar, rather naïve style. It invites its reinterpretation as a map, showing a mosaic of fields (how could cliffs and the volcano be shown?) and comparison with a GoogleEarth image of 'Tigua, Ecuador' (Mackintosh and Kent 2014; Kent and Mackintosh 2015b). Children might like to adopt this style in paintings of their own, perhaps showing cliffs and mountains from the UK in similar bright, clear, colours.

Dreamings

Aboriginal 'dreamings' are timeless, spiritual and private creation stories, but some are now depicted in paintings. This map, diagram, plan or painting (does it matter what we call it?) relates to the Papunya community in Australia's Northern Territories desert and was produced around 1990. It tells a story using traditional symbols. The Aboriginal artist Nita Rubuntja has written the story on the back of her painting (Figure 6.4).

Get the children to study the painting carefully but don't tell them the story yet. They could:

- tell their own interpretation or story of the painting;
- represent one of their own activities, journeys or personal stories in Aboriginal style for others to 'read';
- create an alternative mapping of either of the above options in their own personal style, rather than an Aboriginal style.

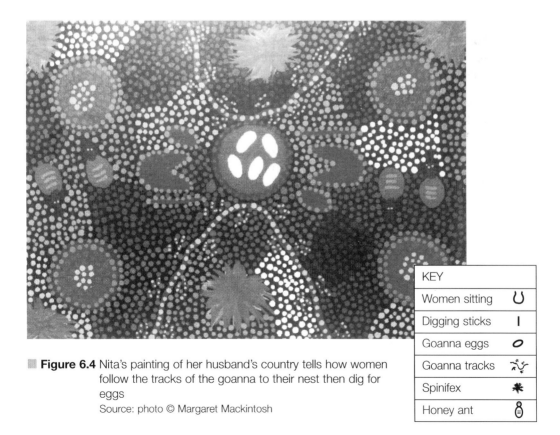

Figure 6.4 Nita's painting of her husband's country tells how women follow the tracks of the goanna to their nest then dig for eggs
Source: photo © Margaret Mackintosh

KEY	
Women sitting	∪
Digging sticks	I
Goanna eggs	O
Goanna tracks	ᕚ
Spinifex	✳
Honey ant	⚇

Some children in Sheffield did this, making mappings of the Meadowhall Shopping Centre inspired by Aboriginal symbols, as part of work on Australia (Collis 2011).

Once they know Nita's story, encourage children to interpret the painting creatively in a western-style drawing or map. Needing to know the meaning of the Aboriginal symbols to read or tell the painting's story could create a memorable bridge or link with later work on keys and symbols. Letting the children into the secret of Nita's story vividly illustrates why we need a key to explain the symbols that we use. A key is a necessity if maps and diagrams are to communicate spatial information effectively and be fully understood.

Hundertwasser

Friedensreich Hundertwasser was an architect, artist and environmentalist who used bright colours and organic forms to link humans and nature through his paintings, graphics and environmental posters. His works are a rich resource that cannot fail to interest and excite children and stimulate them to suggest their own interpretations. Some of the works are rural, others are urban, so will relate to schools in every setting. Some are from a street level (horizontal perspective), others are drawn from above (vertical perspective) and others are a combination of the two. Many of Hundertwasser's works make excellent starting points for exploring viewpoints. Here are a few you might like to try. Locate paintings 88, 125, 170, 241, 373, 433, 525 on the Hundertwasser website. Plates C and D show two Hundertwasser paintings: 'An Almost Circle' (175) and 'City Seen from beyond the Sun' (241).

Try to elicit the children's ideas about the paintings before giving them the title to encourage them to make their own interpretation. Once they know the title, 'City Seen from beyond the Sun' readily conjures up city streets circling a square city-centre piazza, park or even lake (it's painted blue), but children might have other ideas. 'An Almost Circle' (175) looks very much like a map. It could be seen as an inner ring road or other major road with blocks of buildings, but are there faces, is there a central park or does it represent something entirely different to a child? A creative approach encourages a range of responses – there isn't one right answer. There are also plenty of opportunities to encourage children to create similar paintings of their own. Some pupils might want to overpaint a photocopy from a Google Earth image, photograph or map. Others may decide to follow their own creative ideas (Figure 6.5).

Further geographical work would include using different types of map, considering colour and texture and exploring the need for scales, compass directions and keys. Asking younger pupils to use a given palette to paint the roads, buildings, water, fields and woods in appropriate colours would check their understanding of a blank map. Studying Hundertwasser's works and their own artistic creations would encourage recognition and understanding of pattern in both urban and rural environments. Depending on the stimulus used, children would be able to recognise the patterns made by motorways, streets, housing estates and more. Pupils could search for these in whatever maps, aerial photographs and satellite images they use in future geographical work. This would also serve to sensitise them to patterns, shapes and form and the way they are represented in more conventional maps.

■ **Figure 6.5** This ten-year-old's overpainting of an oblique aerial view of the Eden Project, Cornwall has some similarities to a Hundertwasser painting and emphasises the pattern of routeways in a map-like way
Source: painting by Alexander Mackintosh; photo © Margaret Mackintosh

Hockney

David Hockney's later work includes many magical paintings of landscapes and routes in the Yorkshire Wolds and other places (Plate A). Teachers can help children to identify the landscape features and land use, get them to 'walk into' the picture and imagine that they are travelling along the route. What would they hear, feel, see and smell around them? They could also create a map for someone else to use for the same journey. Elevated viewpoints increase the field of view and the complexity of the challenge.

Going further

The range of activities described will involve children looking at Aboriginal and other ethnic art, inspirational paintings, photographs, satellite images and maps in different and creative ways. The examples have focused on Hockney and Hundertwasser but there are many other artists and photographers whose work might also appeal to pupils and engage their imaginations, including Rousseau, Canaletto, Monet and Salgado (Mackintosh and Kent 2014). Developing pupils' interest in and enthusiasm for visual communication in many styles can establish the foundations for a lifelong love of maps, environments and geography. And, as Clayton (2016: 32) shows, 'art and environmental engagement can be used to develop pupils' geographical skills as well as key concepts and core knowledge'. As one child with learning difficulties commented when doing this sort of work while he learned geography without realising it: 'I can *do* pictures!'

STARTING WITH MAPS

Maps are informative and useful but they can also be wonderful works of art in their own right. Their essence and purpose is to represent a three-dimensional world in a two-dimensional format to communicate spatial information. Maps tell a story. Spatial thinkers are fascinated by this, but linear or sequential thinkers can find it challenging.

Maps, and also diagrams, tell a story that is represented, essentially, pictorially. Children need to be taught to read this pictorial story in much the same way as they are taught to read word stories. The term 'visual literacy' or, in a geographical sense, the word 'graphicacy' is often used to describe these skills. There are many different types, styles, perspectives and scales of maps, but in this section there is only room for a few cartographic styles, each fascinating in its own way, to be suggested as starting points. The message is to use as wide a range as you can.

It is easy to make people feel that maps are incomprehensible, and even to alienate them from maps for life. One explanation is that maps *per se*, and especially Ordnance Survey maps with their conventions, are sometimes taught to children too soon and in isolation rather than in a relevant context. Although some youngsters are able to complete the tasks associated with OS maps, their understanding is often limited. This negativity can be easily overcome by devising activities to foster and encourage children's innate love of, fascination for and curiosity about maps, especially if maps are used in association with other pictorial representations of places, spaces and environments.

Historical maps fascinate children both in content and style. The Hereford Mappa Mundi was drawn on vellum (calf skin) in about 1290 and is one of the cathedral's treasures. Hereford appears in the map alongside the River Wye, its location marked by a drawing of the cathedral. As the cathedral website says, this circular map:

> reflects the thinking of the medieval church with Jerusalem at the centre of the world. Superimposed on to the continents are drawings of the history of humankind and the marvels of the natural world. These 500 or so drawings include around 420 cities and towns, 15 Biblical events, 33 plants, animals, birds and strange creatures, 32 images of the peoples of the world and 8 pictures from classical mythology.

Start by encouraging children to marvel at the intrinsic beauty of the map and at the way it records the known world of its time. Help them to recognise the continents, rivers, places and other geographical features along with the fantasy creatures. An exciting challenge would be for pupils to try to draw a map of their own known world in a similar style. Some children might try to draw a local map while others might work on a more global scale, perhaps related to their travel experiences. The Mappa Mundi is drawn with Asia at the top and Europe at the bottom. Surprisingly it is orientated towards the east – the direction of Jerusalem. This decision, which seems surprising nowadays, provides an opportunity to introduce children to compass directions and the modern convention of orientating a map with north at the top.

■ **Figure A** 'Winter Tunnel with Snow' (March 2006) is one of a number of Hockney paintings that suggest routes and journeys. Oil on canvas 36" x 48".

Source: Copyright © David Hockney; Photo: Richard Schmidt

■ **Figure B** Communal life and landscape around the village of Tigua, Ecuador, with the volcano Cotopaxi dominating the scene. (Access 'Volcanism Blog' and search for 'tigua', or access images of 'art from tigua'.)

Source: photo © The Volcanism Blog

■ **Figure C** Hundertwasser's (1953) 175 An Almost Circle. Does this look like a map or aerial photograph of an urban area, or something very different?

Source: © Hundertwasser Archive, Vienna

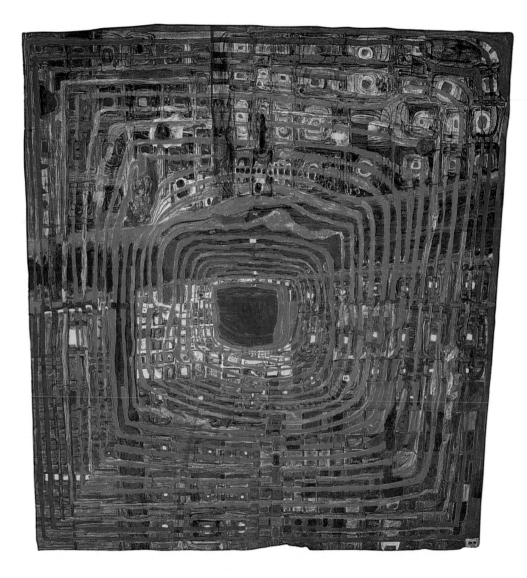

■ Figure D Hundertwasser's (1955) 'City Seen from Beyond the Sun' (241). Is this the street pattern of a city with buildings between, or something very different?

Source: © Hundertwasser Archive, Vienna

Whatever locality is being studied, encourage children to look at as wide a range of maps as possible, helping them appreciate that there is not just one way to map a place. Compare the content of the maps. What do they all show? What does only one include? Maps show different features depending on the purposes, interests and choices made by the cartographer. This means that maps of the same place can look different even when they are drawn accurately. Using appropriate websites (see references) and other sources such as libraries, seek out maps from different dates. Children often find John Speed's seventeenth-century maps intriguing as they use pictorial oblique views. Such maps provide a natural opportunity to link history and geography. You might also encourage children to become time detectives by looking at, say, four maps of the same area at different dates in the past. Early maps of Hull, for example, only show buildings within the city wall. Subsequent maps show how the moat has been turned into docks and that the town is beginning to spread. When the railway arrives, the town grows still further, especially to the north and west.

Be on the lookout for maps in the street that convey information for visitors as well as local people. There are many information boards with pictorial maps at industrial and coastal tourist spots. A good example is in Leeds where the 'waterfront heritage' area has recently been improved. These maps are ideal for primary children because they are designed to be engaging and identify key landmarks. In recent years, pictorial maps have become increasingly available from bookshops, tourist centres and in tourist brochures. These employ a range of perspectives from horizontal to vertical and make valuable links between overhead views and OS maps. Aerial photographs are an additional resource accessible to the full primary age range, especially those by Arthus-Bertrand and Burleigh (2002), Experience suggests that children love looking at these – they should be in every school library, as should a full range of road and world atlases.

MISSING MAPS

Have you ever read a novel and thought to yourself 'this book needs a map'? A good example of a book that needs one is *Half of a Yellow Sun* (Adichie 2006), which is a story about eastern Nigeria before and after the Biafran war. There are some books that do benefit from maps, including the Beast Quest series, Arthur Ransome books, Winnie the Pooh stories and the Katie Morag book series by Mairi Hedderwick (set on the Isle of Coll), although in some hardback library copies the dust jacket and date page are stuck down, obscuring the frontispiece map. The maps vary from rudimentary sketches to detailed pictorial representations but at least they communicate the spatial relationships of the places featured in the stories. Encourage children to visualise the setting and create maps to accompany stories they read. Roald Dahl's *Danny, Champion of the World* is good for this. It would be interesting to compare children's maps of Danny's environment with its representation in the 1989 film of the book. This requires them to think spatially and can help to indicate their understanding of place and story. The ability to visualise land- and townscapes is an essential skill in reading and interpreting a conventional map.

CONCLUSION

Creative approaches will inspire other teachers and children to develop and foster a love of graphicacy in its widest manifestations and lead to imaginative work by teachers and children within and beyond geography. The suggestions presented in this chapter are deliberately divergent and possibly 'outside the box' to encourage imaginative and creative thinking and teaching. As a step towards developing the confidence to use visual communication more creatively, try using different graphicacy forms in combination to help children make the link between the horizontal, oblique and vertical viewpoints summarised in Figure 6.6.

There are several important points to keep in mind:

▨ Use all sorts of maps and other geographical visual images as often as possible whenever the context is appropriate.

▨ Help children to read and interpret a wide range of two-dimensional representations of three-dimensional spaces, places and environments.

▨ Help children move from their everyday eye-level view of the world to the bird's-eye view of conventional maps by including images from the full range of horizontal to low- and high-angle oblique to vertical perspectives.

▨ Use a wide range of styles and scales of image, including globes.

▨ Include maps during fieldwork, and use photographs (from personal to satellite), drawings, diagrams, field sketches, paintings, maps of all sorts (pictorial, street, road atlas, OS, globes) in context to support and enhance geographical work.

▨ Aim to use different pictorial resources about a location in combination, rather than in a sequence. In combination, children can switch from one to another, can see the relationship between the photographic, satellite and pictorial, road and OS map representations and diagrams, so that clues from one representation can help under-standing of another.

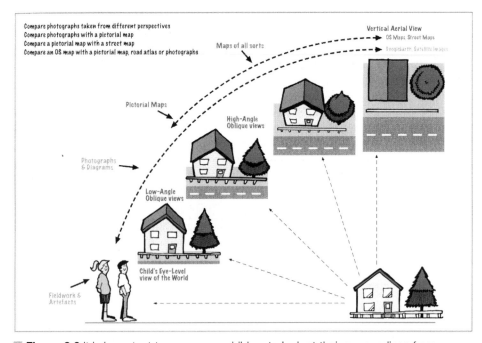

▨ **Figure 6.6** It is important to encourage children to look at their surroundings from different perspectives
Source: Scoffham (2010: 122)

But, most of all, through creative teaching and creative activities that encourage creative responses, foster an enthusiasm for landscapes, a fascination for places, spaces and environments and a love of maps.

REFERENCES

Adichie, C. (2006) *Half of a Yellow Sun*. New York: Alfred A. Knopf.

Arthus-Bertrand, Y. and Burleigh, R. (2002) *The Earth from the Air for Children*. London: Thames and Hudson.

Bridge, C. (2010) Mapwork skills. In S. Scoffham (ed.), *Primary Geography Handbook*, pp. 104–19. Sheffield: Geographical Association.

Clayton, J. (2016) Art and the locality. *Primary Geography* 89: 30–32.

Collis, S. (2011) Global mapping: looking at where I live with fresh eyes. *Primary Geographer* 75: 10–11.

Dahl, R. (1975) (2013), *Danny, Champion of the World*. London: Puffin.

Horner, T., Mackintosh, M., Kavanagh, P. and Kent, G. (2014) The art of perceiving landscapes. *Primary Geography* 83: 8–10.

Kent, G. and Mackintosh, M. (2015a) Art and geography: children's own places. *Primary Geography* 86: 26–7.

Kent, G. and Mackintosh, M. (2015b) Through other eyes. *Primary Geography* 87: 16–17.

Lieben, L. and Downs, R. (1993) Understanding person-space-map relations: cartographic and developmental perspectives. *Developmental Psychology* 29: 739–52.

Mackintosh, M. (2010) Using photographs, diagrams and sketches. In S. Scoffham (ed.), *Primary Geography Handbook*, pp. 120–33. Sheffield: Geographical Association.

Mackintosh, M. (2011) Graphicacy for life. *Primary Geographer* 75: 6–8.

Mackintosh, M. and Kent, G. (2014) *The Everyday Guide to Primary Geography: Art*. Sheffield: Geographical Association.

Rand, H. (2007) *Hundertwasser*. Cologne: Taschen.

Scoffham, S. (ed.) (2010) *Primary Geography Handbook*. Sheffield: Geography Association.

Stieff, B. (2008) *Hundertwasser for Kids*. London: Prestel.

Wiegand, P. (2006) *Learning and Teaching with Maps*. London: Routledge.

Websites

▨ *Aboriginal art:* www.thanguwa.com/symbols.htm

▨ *Ethnic art:* search for 'tigua' on https://volcanism.wordpress.com

▨ *Friedensreich Hundertwasser's paintings:* www.hundertwasser.com

▨ *David Hockney paintings:* enter the keywords 'David Hockney landscape paintings', 'photocollages' and 'iPad art' in a search engine

▨ *Mappa Mundi:* www.herefordcathedral.org/visit-us/mappa-mundi-1

▨ *Maps and plans:* www.google.com/earth/index.html; http://freepages.genealogy. rootsweb.ancestry.com/~genmaps; www.cassinimaps.co.uk

CHAPTER 7

LANDSCAPES AND SWEET GEOGRAPHY

Niki Whitburn

Rocks and soils are fundamental to life on Earth. They form the landscapes in which we live and provide nourishment for the plants on which we depend for food. Learning about rocks and soils can facilitate links between geography and other curriculum areas. An unusual way to introduce and develop this topic is to use food as an analogy. Children of all ages can relate to food, and using it in a creative way can enable them to build up their understanding of key geographical concepts. Food is also an area that links many parts of the curriculum, particularly when studying other countries and cultures. It was the Chinese philosopher Confucius who once said, 'I hear and I forget; I see and I remember; I do and I understand.' Bearing this in mind, the ideas presented here illustrate physical features and processes in a practical manner. They also provide a basis on which to develop and enhance the children's own creativity. Most can be delivered at various levels depending on the age and ability of your class.

LOOKING AT MINERALS (KEY STAGE 1)

Treasure chest

This is a sorting exercise, which can be turned into a game in which children create their own treasure chest of chosen 'jewels'.

AIMS

- To help children appreciate that there are different types of minerals.
- To enable children to develop and discuss their likes and dislikes and relate these to sorting criteria.

WARNING

Take care when handling any minerals, rocks or soils. Ensure normal health and safety rules are applied and hands are washed afterwards

RESOURCES

- Small boxes
- Silver foil or coloured paper
- Small mineral pieces of different colours and textures (or a mixture of liquorice allsorts, dolly mixtures or sweets)
- Large tray and several smaller trays or boxes

Small pieces of polished minerals can be obtained from gift shops, and could be mixed with other pieces of minerals found as chippings in order to obtain a mix of colours and types. Educational suppliers also have sets of minerals and gems (e.g. TTS – see websites at end of chapter).

Before the main activity the children could use the small boxes to make their own treasure chests and cover them with silver foil or decorated paper. Alternatively, they could be provided with pre-made ones.

THE CHALLENGE – THESE ARE MY TREASURES

Introduce the challenge to the children by showing them a large tray containing a good variety of mineral pieces. Discuss how they look and feel and ask the children what they like and don't like about them. The mineral pieces can then be placed in 'mines' (small trays or boxes) at various places in the room. The children decide what criteria they will use to collect their treasure (e.g. a certain colour, clear ones, smooth ones, rough ones). The miners (children) then tour the country (classroom) to find the ones they have chosen, placing them in their treasure chests. Once all the children have collected their treasure, small groups can discuss what they have chosen and why, and describe the difference between the various minerals (Figure 7.1). The ensuing discussion can help to develop the children's knowledge and understanding of minerals and rocks and may provoke questions, which, in turn, will lead them to search for answers as Cremin and Reedy (2015) argue.

EXTENSION

This activity can be progressive and lead into setting up a display table of unusual examples. Children will want to contribute their own specimens. Although you probably won't be able to identify these, the main teaching point is to draw attention to different minerals. Granite, for example, contains easily visible crystals of black mica and white/grey quartz. Shap granite also includes pink feldspar. This introduces the idea that rocks can be formed from several different minerals mixed together.

Rocks and minerals

We now come to the first analogy relating to food. Discuss with the children how biscuits can be very different depending on the ingredients. Get them to write down or produce a group list of as many different types of biscuit they can think of. Then discuss what the ingredients might be, e.g. chocolate chip biscuit has chocolate pieces added, fruit biscuit has sultanas, digestive has neither. Alternatively, with more able children, get them to write down their favourite biscuit and a list of what it is made of, then compare lists. All the above could be done using cakes rather than biscuits.

▨ **Figure 7.1** The 'treasure chest' on the left has coloured minerals and the one on the
right has sparkly minerals

AIMS

▨   To learn that rocks are made of minerals (treasure).
▨   To demonstrate that biscuits are different because they are made of different foods.
▨   To link this analogy to the composition and appearance of rocks.

WARNING

With all food activities, check for nut and other allergies. Ensure normal health and safety
rules are applied (e.g. hands are washed before and after and hair is tied back).

RESOURCES

Each child will need a biscuit or cake bar, a plate and lolly sticks or similar. The most suitable biscuits are those such as chocolate chip cookies, or fruit shortbreads. Alternatively,
health-food bars work just as well. Small cake bars containing fruit or chocolate chips
could also be used and may be easier for younger children to dissect. The activity works
best if more than one type of biscuit or cake bar is used.

THE CHALLENGE – MINING FOR TREASURE

Ask the children what they can see in the biscuits/cakes – chocolate chips, grains, fruit, sponge? The choc-chips or fruit represents the minerals that are valuable. Get them to break them up, or 'dissect' them, and sort them into the different components, so they end up with small piles of choc chip, grain, fruit, biscuit, sponge and so forth (Figure 7.2). Who has the most 'minerals' or which type of biscuit or cake bar has the most minerals? Ask the children questions to aid description and comparison such as:

▓　　Which component is the largest/smallest?
▓　　Do all the choc-chip ones have the same amounts of chocolate?
▓　　Do the fruit ones have more fruit than the chocolate in the choc-chip ones?
▓　　Do they think there is enough chocolate/fruit in the biscuits?
▓　　How would they alter them?

These questions could prompt children to design their own biscuits, which they might actually cook to see if they work. Remember that Robinson and Aronica (2015) suggest that creativity involves both play and taking risks.

▓ **Figure 7.2** Which biscuit is easier to break up?

EXTENSION

Explain that the choc-chips/fruit/grain is the mineral they want to find, the rest is the rock. Discussions could focus around the time it takes to 'mine' the mineral and the costs; how much money they could earn from the mineral; how much rock would have been wasted. Older or more able children could be given costs to enable them to calculate earnings.

Moving on

Work within Key Stage 1 forms an introduction to learning about the landscapes that are created by the rocks and soils around us. Within Key Stage 2, this can be developed further to enable the children to understand why the landscapes they see are like they are, and how they might have evolved. This can lead into questions relating to their surroundings and a deeper understanding of our physical world. Their imagination and creativity can be stimulated and they can be encouraged to develop their own expertise together with unusual ways to depict landscapes or demonstrate physical features and processes. As de Bono (2010) puts it, creativity goes beyond the obvious to generate novel solutions.

ROCKS AND THEIR PROPERTIES (KEY STAGE 2)

There are three main types of rocks. Igneous rocks are created from magma which comes to the surface in volcanic eruptions, or cools below the surface. Sedimentary rocks are formed from the remains of plants and creatures or sediments formed from eroded remains of previously formed rocks which build up over geological time. Rocks which have been buried back beneath the surface and have been changed by heat and / or pressure are called metamorphic rocks. You can help pupils relate to rocks and their properties to their own experiences using the analogy of food. Making biscuits and cakes, for example, illustrate how mixing different components together can result in a different end product with different properties. Using unusual media can help develop these skills. Some basic information may help to underpin your understanding.

Earth movements

Although we tend to think that the ground beneath our feet is solid and stable, it is actually constantly moving. Earthquakes and volcanic eruptions remind us of the huge forces deep inside the Earth which are released as the plates which make up the Earth's crust move towards, away or past each other at very slow rates. Where plates move apart, as in Iceland, these earth movements result in almost constant volcanic activity. Where two plates move towards each other layers of rock are pushed up to form folds, creating mountains such as the Andes, Alps and Himalayas.

Erosion

Rocks are worn away or eroded over very long periods of time by the action of ice, water, wind, sun and chemical processes. Rocks break down differently depending on their strength, hardness and/or internal 'glue'.

Transportation

Rocks that have been eroded are moved from one place to another by the wind, rivers, sea and other forces. Those that break down more easily are thus most likely to be transported.

Deposition

Material that has been transported is deposited in layers to create sedimentary rock. The layers that are at the bottom will, unless disturbed, be older than the layers on the top.

The following activities explore these processes through practical work and discussion. The activities are all based on small group work, usually in competition with each other.

Mountain biscuits

You can illustrate how the Andes and Alps were created by bending layers of different coloured plasticine to make mountains. An alternative is to use strips of at least two colours of fondant icing (or marzipan), which can be eaten afterwards.

1   Roll out four or five strips of the different colours about 7cm by 15cm and lay on top of each other, alternating the colours.
2   Place a solid object at either end, as high and wide as the layers. Push these towards each other to make folds in the icing.
3   The folds created can be compared to the folds of mountains in pictures. The down folds are synclines the up folds are anticlines.
4   Repeat several times to see if the folds are the same each time. Try using different amounts of pressure on the two ends. Sketch or photograph the results.
5   Cut the 'mountains' vertically and note the shapes formed.
6   Use these to top biscuits or cakes, keeping them in their unusual 'mountain' shapes.

A slightly simpler approach is to make peppermint creams in two colours (e.g. white and green). Roll these out and use them to make layers as above. After making the mountains, cut them into circles to make sweets. These will show various orientations of the two colours and thus the mountain folds.

Sandstone crispie cakes

One type of rock that can help children understand more about rocks and erosion is sandstone. Making crispie cakes is a favourite classroom activity which can help children understand more about the properties of rocks and why some erode more easily than others.

AIMS

▨   To demonstrate how sandstones are formed and particles bound together by a matrix (glue) using a food analogy.
▨   To challenge the pupils to create their own edible 'rocks' with different properties.

INTRODUCTION

Discuss how sandstones and other rocks are composed of loosely bound grains, held together by a matrix or glue, and many are highly susceptible to erosion. If possible, demonstrate this by rubbing away the corner of a small piece of sandstone. Show how easily individual crispies can be knocked off a crispie cake by way of comparison.

RESOURCES

- ▓ Plain cooking chocolate and crispies
- ▓ Saucepan (to melt the chocolate)
- ▓ Bowl (to mix the cakes in)
- ▓ Large spoon (to mix with) and two teaspoons
- ▓ Paper plates and paper cases
- ▓ Access to heat source (e.g. hot plate)

THE CHALLENGE – CREATING EROSION

Divide the pupils into groups. Their challenge is to make one crispie cake that is easy to erode but still holds together and one that is hard to erode but still has enough crispies to be called a crispie cake. Once pupils have made their cakes they present them to be tested. To ensure a reasonably fair test, each cake should be tested by the same adult. This adult might also decide which is the easiest and hardest to erode or the class could vote on it.

Each group reports back on how they decided what to do and what amount of each ingredient they used. Employ open-ended questions to aid this discussion and see that the children talk about what holds rocks like sandstone together and why some rocks erode more easily than others (Figure 7.3). This builds on the approach suggested by Johnson, Halocha and Chater (2007: 93), who remind us that 'in order to develop children's abilities to question, it is necessary to develop their curiosity and interest and provide a questioning environment'.

▓ **Figure 7.3** The crispie cake on the left was easier to 'erode', it had less chocolate matrix to hold it together

FACILITATING THE ACTIVITY

Depending on their age and abilities the children may need adult support. You could suggest that they change the amount of chocolate or crispies that are included. Draw up a plan and think about how to test their results. Older pupils can work more independently on planning and testing with adult supervision rather than support. Suggest that within each group children might like to divide into two groups and focus on one type of cake each. Alternatively, the challenge could be divided over two sessions, one for each type of cake. Emphasise to the children that they don't need to use all the chocolate or crispies. You may also decide to limit the number of paper cases as well as the amount of chocolate and crispies to create boundaries.

As with others in this chapter, this activity includes, or has the potential to develop, cross-curricular links. These include:

▨ *Science* – formation and properties of rocks and soils, and their subsequent uses; planning to solve challenges; changes of state.
▨ *Maths* – weighing and measuring.
▨ *Design technology* – cooking, planning, experimenting.
▨ *Literacy* – descriptive writing, vocabulary.
▨ *Art* – recording by sketch and drawing.
▨ *IT* – recording by photography.

What cross-curricular links can you make with the following activities?

Sedimentary layer biscuits

One idea that can be used to show how rocks can be eroded and deposited is to build a 'rockface' using various types of biscuit. A photograph of an actual layered eroding cliff would be a good starter. This can build into explanations relating to how the layers were deposited in different environments and are now being eroded differentially.

The activity can be facilitated as either a participatory demonstration or, preferably, a challenge, or challenge with adult support, depending on the age of the pupils, available assistance and resources. The rockface is constructed by using layers of different crushed biscuits mixed with melted fat (as in a cheesecake base). Suggested layers are:

1   choc-chip cookies;
2   digestives;
3   double choc-chip cookies;
4   fruit shortbreads (or similar).

AIMS

▨   To learn how different rocks can be deposited into and eroded from a rockface and have different strengths.
▨   To challenge pupils to create and investigate their own 'food' rockface to demonstrate erosion.

RESOURCES (FOR ONE FOUR-TIER ROCKFACE)

▨ One packet of each type of biscuit to be used
▨ 300g margarine
▨ Saucepan; mixing bowl, spoon
▨ Small, square or rectangular tin, minimum depth 12cm, preferably with removable sides (this makes it easier to remove the cliff face) or a margarine tub or similar that can be peeled away once set.

METHOD

Each layer needs approximately 175g biscuit and 75g margarine. Melt the margarine and then mix with the crushed biscuits. Press the mixture into the tin. Repeat this with further layers using different biscuits. Chill or allow to set. Remove from the tin so that all sides can be used to test for erosion (this is best done with the back of a knife). Try to ensure the layers are a good thickness (minimum 2cm) to aid investigation.

THE CHALLENGE – CREATING A CLIFF FACE

The level of this challenge will be different depending on the ages and abilities of the pupils. The older, more able children can be challenged with the whole of the activity, others may need to be introduced to it at different stages of its development. The challenge is to build a cliff that demonstrates how some layers erode more easily than others.

FACILITATING THE CHALLENGE AT DIFFERENT LEVELS

Pupils are told or shown how each layer is made and given the amounts to use plus necessary equipment. At whichever stage they are introduced to the challenge, they will need to predict which layer(s) will be easier to erode than others and decide how best they can demonstrate this (i.e. place one that is easier to erode between two that are harder to erode).

▨ *Level 1* (easiest) – As a class activity, pupils are given a fully built cliff of three or four layers such as choc-chip, digestive, double choc-chip, fruit shortbread. The pupils discuss which might be the easiest to erode and why. They then test them (see 'Method' above) and relate their findings back to the reasons they gave.
▨ *Level 2* (moderate) – In small groups or as a class activity, pupils are given a partially built cliff – two layers are ideal – and asked what type of layer to place on top and why. If the first layer is choc-chip, the second digestive, the best third layer is another choc-chip or similar as digestives are easier to erode. Using a fruit short-cake layer would place two that are easier to erode next to each other and possibly not demonstrate the erosional qualities so well.
▨ *Level 3* (hardest) – In small groups the pupils are given three (or four) different types of biscuits and asked to build a cliff that demonstrates different erosional layers. They will need to discuss how to make it a fair test, and in which order to build the layers. Once built, they will need to demonstrate the erosion and discuss why they built the layers as they did. They should then link their ideas back to the qualities of the original biscuits. Hint: if more 'glue' is added to the mix in the form of chocolate, the layers stick together very well.

Conglomerate cakes

Pupils sometimes bring rocks into school to see if you know what they are. These often contain a mixture of materials including concrete that has been manufactured by people. Rocks that are composed of pieces of other rocks are called conglomerates. These demonstrate how previously formed rocks can be broken down into fragments and then stuck back together in a new form. They are often found in riverbeds where components have been brought downstream, particularly in an estuary where there may be different river sources.

INTRODUCTION

This activity is for more able upper Key Stage 2 pupils, after studying rocks. Discuss how conglomerate rocks are formed, and allow the use of books and the internet to aid research if necessary. If possible, show them some examples of conglomerate rocks.

AIMS

▨ To demonstrate how many different types of rock can be deposited and re-formed within a matrix to create a new type of rock.
▨ To investigate how easily conglomerates can be broken down further.
▨ To show how cakes can be used to demonstrate erosion processes.

RESOURCES

▨ Plain chocolate cake covering
▨ Fruit and biscuit or fruit and nut or plain fruit chocolate bar
▨ Margarine
▨ Saucepan
▨ Heat source
▨ Large mixing bowl
▨ Large spoon
▨ Tinfoil

SUGGESTED INGREDIENTS FOR ROCKY LINKS

▨ Digestive biscuits – sandstone
▨ Glacé cherries – pink feldspar from granite
▨ Raisins – dark mica from granite
▨ Dates or sultanas – minerals
▨ Mini pink and yellow marshmallows – softer more pliable rocks
▨ Nuts – harder rocks; these could be included by using fruit and nut choc bar as part of a chocolate matrix

THE CHALLENGE – CREATING CONGLOMERATE

Divide the pupils into groups. Pupils are challenged to design and make their own conglomerate rock using different sorts of food to represent the different fragments of original rock. Provide a choice of chocolate or margarine – to use as a glue or 'matrix'.

Provide a choice of ingredients to represent the various rock components. Pupils then choose the appropriate components and the type of glue. This will involve them deciding what they want to create and what 'rocks' it should include: Once this is decided they need to work out amounts of 'matrix' in relation to 'rock fragments'.

Encourage the pupils to invent/create their own special conglomerate. They may also try to relate their cakes to some actual examples. The key idea is that they should argue about and discuss the properties of the 'rock' fragments that they select and why some might be smaller and smoother than others. When they slice their rock, what does it show? Are all parts of the 'rock' as easy to slice as others? Learning flourishes when children generate and seek to answer questions of this type. As Catling (2011: 189) reminds us, creativity can be thought of as a frame of mind which involves 'new insights, new perspectives, new alternatives and new possibilities'.

For guidance, here is a basic recipe for the conglomerate cake:

- Melt 200/250g plain chocolate cake covering, 200g fruit and biscuit milk chocolate bar (or fruit and nut or plain fruit or similar) and 50g margarine.
- Break 200g biscuits into small pieces (not crumbs).
- Chop 50g dates (or sultanas) and 50g cherries into irregular sizes and add to biscuits with 50g raisins; add 50g small marshmallows, or any mix of these amounting to approximately 200g.
- Stir well, then add melted chocolate and mix well together until all ingredients are coated.
- Place on tin foil and mould into the desired shape using the foil to help keep the shape. The mixture could be shaped into one large roll (or rock) or smaller ones.
- Chill, then slice.

FOSSILS

Fossils are often found in rocks, and provide us with evidence of plate tectonics. They are the remains or trace of a plant or animal which lived many years ago and can be used to date rocks, provide evidence of past environments and of evolution. Fossils come in many shapes and sizes. Children will probably be most familiar with the bivalve shell shape, found on many beaches. Those that are the easiest to make in the form of biscuits are ones that curl and can be made by piping the appropriate shape (ammonites). Others that can be piped are trilobites (like woodlice) and echinoids (like sea urchins). Access to fossil samples or pictures will aid making the correct shape.

AMMONITE BISCUITS

1   Make up a basic biscuit mixture (see below) and place in a piping bag with a plain half inch nozzle.
2   Pipe a coiled ammonite shape onto a greased baking tray, starting in the middle and working outwards without stopping. The coils should be touching. Make each biscuit about 2 to 3 inches in diameter (5–7 cm).
3   Mark the segment pattern that is found on the shell using a fork and pressing it down firmly into the biscuit, working along the coils from the inside outwards.
4   Cook for approximately 15 minutes at 375°F; 190°C; Gas 5. The biscuits will spread during cooking.

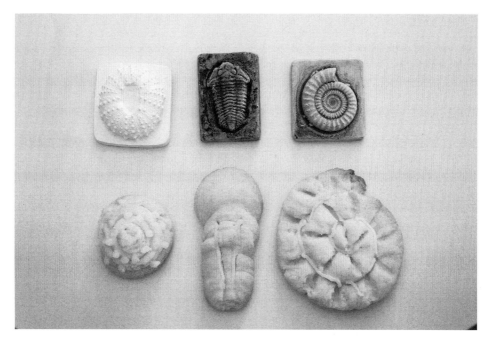

■ **Figure 7.4** Echinoid, trilobite, ammonite fossil biscuits

TRILOBITE BISCUITS

1   As above, but using a slightly larger nozzle, pipe the mixture into a straight line, trying to create the sections of the trilobite, particularly the head, by varying the pressure on the piping bag and thus the amount of mixture and width of line being piped.
2   Mark appropriate segments on the body as above.
3   After cooking pipe on eyes and enhance the segments.

ECHINOID (SEA URCHIN) BISCUITS

1   Again using a slightly larger nozzle, pipe a bun shape to create the round echinoid shape, squashing down slightly.
2   Mark segments and once cooked enhance these with piping.

BASIC BISCUIT RECIPE FOR GUIDANCE.

1   Cream 125g butter with 25g icing sugar, add a few drops of vanilla essence.
2   Gradually beat in 125g plain flour and ¼ level teaspoon of baking powder.

Extension

Two challenges:

▨ The children research fossils on the internet and then copy different fossils, working out how they can best form the appropriate shape.
▨ The children design their own fossil and then work out how to form it.

The combination of enquiry approaches that are developed in an environment where both pupils and teachers are encouraged to be creative can help develop more creative people (Johnson, Halocha and Chater 2007: 159).

SOILS (KEY STAGE 2)

The formation of soils is linked to the erosion of underlying rocks, and the type of soil is directly linked to the type of rock it is derived from. Soils consist of five elements: weathered fragments of rock, humus (dead plant and animal remains), living organisms, water, and air. The mixture of these five elements and the resulting soil type tends to limit the plants that will grow and food that can be produced. Some plants thrive in well-drained sandy soils, others like the moist environments that are associated with clay soils.

Soils also vary in their chemical composition depending on whether they are acid or alkaline. This is expressed as a pH number which ranges from strongly acidic (1) to strongly alkaline (14), with neutral point of 7. Peaty or sandy soils tend to be acidic as do waterlogged ones; chalk soils are alkaline. Peas, beans and cabbage grow well in alkaline soil but are averse to acidic soil. Potatoes prefer acidic soil either sandy or peaty.

The soil is closely related to the provision of food, and its type and quality are important worldwide. Crops rely on the correct type of soil being present, their maintenance and good use is essential in order to provide enough food for the world's population. Food security is a particular issue for developing countries where malnutrition remains a major problem. There are also important questions to do with land degradation and soil fertility which need to be addressed.

Will it grow?

Pupils can try growing different vegetables in different soils in order to see what happens. The food they produce could then be used in the school kitchen. Depending on resources and space, this is probably best done as a whole-class activity, with pupils looking after the plants in turn.

AIMS

▨ To investigate if a specific plant grows better in one type of soil.
▨ To see if other plants also prefer that same soil.

RESOURCES

▨ Different types of soil (e.g. one sandy acidic soil, one clay-ey, waterlogged soil, one chalky alkaline soil and one loam soil)

■ Some grow bags or large plant pots
■ Vegetable seeds (peas or beans) or cabbage seedlings (for a longer-term project try potatoes)

A variety of soils can be obtained from educational suppliers, garden centres or collected by pupils or staff from the local area or more distant places. You mix garden soil with sand, chalk or clay to create varieties of your own.

THE CHALLENGE – WHICH SOILS AND PLANTS DO WE WANT FOR OUR GARDEN?

The school is to develop a vegetable garden and wants to know which type of soil to use and which plants to grow. We have several types of soil samples and different vegetables. How can we find out what would be the best for us? Pupils should decide how to set up their experiment. The amount of support needed depends on their age and ability. Ideally, each type of soil should have samples of each type of seed/seedling; positioning and watering should be the same. Pupils could devise a rota to care for the plants and guidance or rules for doing so. Records should be kept of any differences, size and growth monitored, and a weekly update discussed in class. Digital cameras could be used to record changes. Once there are visible results they can decide why plants have developed as they have and produce a plan for their garden. If you are able to provide opportunities for pupils to develop their enquiries, you will also be putting them in an environment where they can begin to think about their own thinking and learning (Johnson, Halocha and Chater 2007: 158).

EXTENSION

Pupils could investigate the properties of the soils either beforehand or afterwards, looking at texture, colour, porosity and permeability. They should also establish their pH level using a simple testing kit. This may help them to decide why plants are growing well or not so well and what environment the plants prefer. You can also make links to sustainability by considering what keeps a soil healthy and productive. Worms are one obvious answer!

Artistic soils

Soils vary in colour and texture and some very interesting art work can be achieved by exploiting their properties. Soil colours differ from being almost black through dark brown, tan, red and gold to almost white in chalky areas. Textures can be from the very fine clay soils to coarser loams through to very coarse sandy soil. Pure sand can be used with glue to form a coarse texture. Soil can be mixed with very little water to make a thick painting material almost like a sludge in order to produce more solid shapes or with more water to make a colour wash that can be used in a background or any consistency between these two extremes, depending on what you want the pupils to achieve. You may decide to provide pupils with ready-made consistencies or allow them to make their own mixtures. Depending on age, ability and assistance available, it could be a good idea to let them practise a little first to explore the medium.

AIMS

▓ To understand that soils have many different colours and textures.

▓ To learn to use these colours and textures to produce a natural painting.

RESOURCES

▓ A selection of as many different coloured and textured soils as possible (ready-mixed, or not, depending on the situation)

▓ Pots for mixing soil and water

▓ A selection of different-sized paint brushes and sheets of paper (at least A4)

CHALLENGE – SOIL PAINTING

To produce a painting using only soils. You may wish to add further criteria such as making a link to a topic you are currently studying, or to restricting the focus to land-scapes or plants or creatures.

EXTENSION

You could enhance the work by getting the children to include other natural objects such as leaves and bark or food such as grains in their paintings. Upper Key Stage 2 could investigate why the soils are the colours they are – a result of original compounds and specific mixtures, such as red soils being linked to iron content. The links to history, cave paintings and Aboriginal art are particularly fruitful and an excellent way of extending the creative possibilities particularly by making use of the internet to find examples (Figure 7.5).

CONCLUSION

Some ideas suggested here may seem rather unusual in relation to physical geography. However, if children are to be creative they need to be given the opportunity to extend their ideas in a variety of ways. By approaching the teaching of physical geography creatively, teachers can enhance children's ability to bring their own ideas to activities, which can aid understanding and promote further investigation and creativity. Children need to be given the chance to take risks and become confident in doing so.

This chapter has provided some ideas to help develop creativity using analogies that children can relate to within their everyday lives. They are aimed at providing a stimulating starting point for practical activities that can be used flexibly within any curriculum, providing children with the opportunities they need to become truly creative.

ACKNOWLEDGEMENTS

Many of these activities have been developed by the ESTA primary team for use in workshops for physical geography (estaprimary@hotmail.co.uk).

REFERENCES AND FURTHER READING

Catling, S. (2011) Creativity in primary geography. In A. Wilson (ed.), *Creativity in Primary Education* (2nd edition), pp. 189–98. Exeter: Learning Matters.

Cremin, T. and Reedy, D. (2015) Developing creativity through talk. In R. Cremin with D. Reedy, E. Bearne and H. Dombey, *Teaching English Creatively*, pp. 11–24. Abingdon: Routledge.

De Bono, E. (2010) *Six Thinking Hats*. London: Penguin.

Johnson, J. Halocha, J. and Chater, M. (2007) *Developing Teaching Skills in the Primary School Classroom*. Maidenhead: Open University Press.

Robinson, K. and Aronica, L. (2015) *Creative Schools*. London: Allen Lane.

Websites

■ *Earth Science Teachers' Association (ESTA):* www.esta-uk.net
■ *fossils-facts-and-finds:* www.fossil-facts-and-finds.com
■ *Fossil Museum:* www.fossilmuseum.net
■ *How to make peppermint creams:* www.wikihow.com/Make-Peppermint-Creams
■ *Painting with Soil:* www.nrcs.usda.gov/wps/portal/nrcs/detail/soils/ref/?cid=nrcs142p2_054282
■ *TTS:* www.tts-group.co.uk

CHAPTER 8

CREATIVE APPROACHES TO LEARNING ABOUT THE PHYSICAL WORLD

Susan Pike

Physical geography focuses on processes and patterns in the natural environment. These include the atmosphere (air), hydrosphere (water), biosphere (plants and creatures), and geosphere (rocks). Such topics are the basis of geography and so tend to appear in some way within all primary geography curricula. Many ideas in physical geography can be complex but they also provide opportunities for children to learn in creative ways, as they are best approached through active engagement and practical enquiries. However, they cannot be taught in isolation, as all aspects of the physical world are affected by human activity.

This chapter outlines children's thinking, questions and misconceptions about the physical world, using the children's school, local natural environment, country and the wider world as the context for topics such as rocks and soil, weather and climate and earth and space. Within this chapter, ideas are suggested which show how children's conceptual understanding of the physical world can be developed, specifically:

- how to teach physical geography through enquiry;
- using the school grounds and locality to enhance learning in physical geography; and
- opportunities for children to learn together, in creative ways.

USING CHILDREN'S QUESTIONS IN PLANNING

Questions are one of the key ways primary children find out about the world. These may be questions they ask themselves or others. They may be spoken or simply thought about, with some children asking hundreds of questions each day! As teachers know, children have many questions to ask about the physical world. In fact, surveys of children's questions have found that many of their questions are geographical in nature. In relation to geographical questions, Scoffham (2013), in a study of children's spontaneous questions, found that earth in space attracted the most questions, followed by hazards (volcanoes, earthquakes and natural disasters), as shown in Figure 8.1.

Factual questions
- How big is our planet?
- How many continents are there?
- Is there a core in the middle of the Earth?

Process questions
- How was the Earth made?
- Why does it rain?
- Is there a way of stopping natural disasters?

Existential questions
- Why is there a sun and a moon?
- Why does the world turn round?
- Can you touch the clouds?

▨ **Figure 8.1** Some sample questions which children ask about physical geography
Source: Scoffham (2013)

These questions could be used as the basis of many geography lessons. However, it is essential for teachers to carefully consider the conceptual ideas they would like the children to learn as they work through the enquiry process. For example, children may ask questions such as:

- Where is the biggest volcano?
- Why do volcanoes explode?

These are important questions about physical processes but children should also be encouraged to think about the impact of volcanic eruptions, by asking questions such as:

- How do people react to volcanic eruptions?
- What are the problems and benefits of living near volcanoes?

Teachers may also want to steer their pupils into think more deeply about the differing impacts of volcanic eruptions and encourage them to ask questions such as:

- Why do some places have worse effects of volcanic eruptions than others?
- How do places recover after volcanic eruptions?

Once these types of questions are covered, children will have had the opportunity to think about the key ideas about volcanoes and their eruptions, the causes, effects and responses of volcanic eruptions. For all topics in physical geography it is important to think in terms of key concepts, as well as being open and responsive to children's own ideas (Pike 2016). Although the sequence 'know', 'would like to know' and 'learned' (commonly known as KWL) is popular in classrooms this sequence is quite restricting as it does not give children the opportunity to formulate and refine geographical enquiry questions. Careful use of children's questions in lessons on the physical world, for future planning, could include:

■ Having the children put their questions on scraps of paper, then grouping and collating the questions into geographical enquiry questions. These can then be displayed in the classroom and referred to as the topic is worked through;

■ Deciding which questions involve geographical enquiry, then creating a brainstorm of the children's questions which can be displayed on a flip chart or display board.

CHILDREN'S 'CREATIVE' IDEAS ABOUT THE WORLD

Teaching physical geography can be rather daunting, as teachers tend to rely on their own knowledge of a vast range of topics. Children also have alternative ideas or misconceptions about the world. These are often evident through the questions they ask. Some of the ways children may get mixed up are outlined in Figure 8.2. As can be seen from this list, many of these ideas do make sense – they just happen to be either misleading or completely wrong! The debates about children's misconceptions or alternative conceptions in geography are an important consideration when teaching physical geography. Wiegand (1993) summarises research which focused on children's meanings and definitions of words, their ability to recognise features in photographs, and associated pedagogical issues. He concluded that physical geography poses challenges for pupils since their 'own direct experience of the landscape and examination of photographs of features of the surface of the Earth can show similar-looking features that have different names and dissimilar features called by the same name' (*ibid.*: 91). For example:

■ Some features have different names even though they could be the same e.g. people have different perceptions of hills and mountains. People from the Lake District may not consider a chalk downland hill justifies the term!

■ Some features vary dramatically in size; for example, an island could be large like Greenland or relatively small such as Lundy Island or Portsea (the island that the city of Portsmouth lies on).

Clouds – Children sometimes think that clouds are made of water vapour or cotton wool. They actually consist of water and/or ice droplets.

Land – Younger children may think that land floats on water. It does not.

Lightning – Children may believe the saying 'lightning can never strike twice' in the same place. It can.

Magma – Children may think magma comes from the core of the Earth. In fact it comes from upper layers of the Earth.

Rivers – Children often believe rivers flow faster in upland than lowland areas. They are also sometimes taught this, but it is not always true.

Volcanoes – Children may think that volcanic eruptions produce large, steep sided cones. They may not.

Water Flow – Children may think that water flows only down slopes. There are places and occasions where this is incorrect, for example when water moves up through soils (a good example of this is watering plants from beneath!)

Wind – Children are often puzzled by the wind and sometimes suggest it is generated by turbines. It is actually the result of differences in air pressure.

▦ **Figure 8.2** Common misconceptions in physical geography

Furthermore, many of these terms are vernacular, so can vary from place to place. In one location a hill could be considered high but in another location a similar hill would be considered simply undulating ground! Generally, Dutch people may have very different ideas about hills than those from Japan!

If constructivist and creative teaching is embraced, then children's misconceptions are a great source for learning as their ideas are not seen as problematic but a starting point. Children can share their ideas, they can debate and argue about them and, with the support of the teacher, work out what is actually right or recognise that there may be more than one possible answer. However, we do need to check our facts before we teach about the physical world, for example by drawing on the vast amount of material online, including excellent video material to explain physical geography. We also need to read up on and check common misconceptions children may have by reading about these online, using websites such as the Geographical Association's.

RESEARCH EVIDENCE

The limited amount of research in physical geography in primary geography is varied and insightful. It includes the work of education theorists, research in teaching and learning and international comparative studies of children's learning. Piaget explored children's notions of physical phenomena. He suggested that children's early ideas have artificial characteristics, but as they grow older they develop more natural explanations (1929). Although his ideas have been challenged, experience suggests that children's descriptions and explanations of the physical world do become more accurate with age. In the 1990s the Science Process and Concept Exploration (SPACE) project (Russell *et al.* 1993; Osborne *et al.* 1994) explored children's ideas in Science but these included their learning about the nature and origin of soil, rock, underground and the structure of the Earth, weathering and weather. The pattern across these studies was consistent, that conceptual understanding increased with age. However, the study also found that interventions/teaching in child-centred, constructivist ways helped children to understand concepts they would otherwise not have grasped till later. As one study concluded:

> The picture that emerges from this study is one in which children's knowledge of astronomical events seems to be in a process of development across the age range. Additionally, in many instances, the intervention has had a positive effect in improving their knowledge and understanding.
>
> (Osborne *et al.* 1994: 121)

Harwood and Jackson (1993) used the SPACE methodology to investigate 9- to 11-year-old children's understanding of nine common vernacular physical landscape features. In demonstrating a correlation between children's direct experience of features and their level of understanding of geographical terms, they recognised an urgent need for a systematic and progressive approach to the teaching. Further research by Platten (1995a, 1995b) into 7-year-old children's understanding of geographical terms revealed that children construct their own meanings for features but found no significant differences between experiences and knowledge. The Trends in International Mathematics and Science Study (TIMSS) compared abilities of pupils in a range of countries (including England, Northern Ireland and the Republic of Ireland) in a range of subjects, including Earth Science (Eivers and Clerkin 2011, 2013). The percentages of children

aged 9 to 10 who were able to explain physical and human patterns and issues were relatively low:

- Only 42% of pupils we able to describe one advantage of farming along a river.
- Only 34% of pupils were able to describe one disadvantage of farming along a river.
- Only 27% of pupils were able to describe two things people can do to avoid wasting water.

These figures varied significantly between countries and the studies did not investigate why pupils may or may not understand particular concepts. However, it appears from the TIMSS research that pupils will have better understandings of physical geography where it consistently features in:

- curricula and geography resources;
- teacher education and professional development courses;
- other programmes and projects such as green schools and eco schools.

It also seems that children who live in rural areas are likely to have better ideas about physical geography, whereas those who live in urban areas are more likely to have an understanding of human processes (Pike 2011). This suggests that when children construct their own knowledge about their physical environment they tend to understand it better. Mackintosh offers a possible explanation. She argues that children may not understand concepts in physical geography because they are taught them, as the 'top-down, guess-what-teacher-knows models' which do not take account of how pupils construct their knowledge (Mackintosh 2005: 71). However, by working together creatively pupils can develop their knowledge and understanding of physical features, patterns and processes and incorporate them into their conceptual frameworks, Mackintosh argues that instead of concentrating on the terminology for features and processes, it is much more effective to give children experience of rivers, visiting sites from source to mouth in different places. Reflecting the findings of the TIMSS studies, she also points out that fieldwork is especially important for urban children who often see rivers in concrete channels or even underground pipes (*ibid.*). This is equally important for rural children who cannot access local rivers and streams due to land ownership and parental restrictions.

ENABLING CHILDREN TO CREATIVELY MAKE SENSE OF THE PHYSICAL WORLD

The above research findings show the importance of providing opportunities for children to develop their understanding of physical geography concepts. Overall, it is important to remember:

- Conceptual understanding needs to come before learning vocabulary and terms for physical features. (Catling and Willy 2009).
- Practical learning activities and fieldwork allow the children to build up their understanding together (Scoffham 2010; Pike 2016).
- Conceptual understanding should progress through the primary school years. For example, it is essential to start with the concept that water flows in early years

downhill before progress can be made in understanding river processes with older classes (Mackintosh 2005).

The following examples show how such understanding can be built up through creative teaching and learning:

Example 1 From questions to fieldwork – a trip to our river

The River Tolka is one of Dublin's three main rivers. It flows from a muddy field near Batterstown, County Meath through of the town of Dunboyne and follows the M3 motorway/dual carriageway through to Dublin city. For part of its route it flows through the suburb of Drumcondra and the river is an integral part of the landscape of this suburb of the city. A starting point for learning about this or any other river can be a collection of photographs of the river, old and new, high quality and not! The children can simply talk about the photographs together. Children in one school came up with the questions about the Tolka River (Figure 8.3).

■ How many parks does it go through?
■ When did the Tolka flood first?
■ Where were most of the floods based?
■ How many bridges are there across it?
■ What is the most polluted part of the river?
■ Is there fish in the Tolka?
■ What wildlife is here?
■ Were people killed in the flood?
■ Is the river dirty?
■ When did the river start?
■ How long was it flooded for?

■ Has anyone ever died in it?
■ How long did the floods last for?
■ How many times does the Tolka flood?
■ Has anyone died in the floods?
■ Has anyone been injured in the floods?
■ Does the Tolka flow into the sea?
■ How many different fish are there?
■ Are there any fish in the Tolka?
■ Has anyone ever made a living off it?
■ Does the river have fish?
■ How old is the river?

Figure 8.3 Some of the children's questions about the River Tolka (Drumcondra National School)

Although, on initial view, the questions seem somewhat random, they can be broadly grouped as shown in Figure 8.4. By doing this with the children, it is evident that the questions generally align well with curriculum requirements for learning about rivers.

These questions cover different aspects of physical and human geography. Ideally children could find out about their local river in different classes across primary school (Figure 8.5). Starting in the early years, they could play with water and come to realise that it moves down-hill and naturally meanders. In other classes children could learn about the processes and features of the river, about the changes people have made to the river and events along it (flooding). Children usually react favourably when they have to answer their questions through fieldwork. As one child said after a visit and follow-up work on the River Tolka: 'I loved it, we had good fun. We had fun but we also learned things. I always see the river but I had never really thought about it before.'

Features of the locality
■ How old is the river? (4)
■ How many parks does it go through?
■ How many bridges are there across it?
■ Does the River Tolka flow into the sea?
■ Has anyone ever made a living off it?

River processes, features and events
■ How many times does the Tolka flood? (2)
■ Where were most of the floods based?
■ How long did the floods last for? (2)
■ Did anyone get hurt / die in the floods? (5)

Environmental issues
■ Is the river dirty?
■ What is the most polluted part of the river?
■ What is the wildlife like?
■ Is there any / many different fish in the Tolka? (6)

▧ **Figure 8.4** Children's enquiry questions sorted into groups (Drumcondra National
School)

▧ **Figure 8.5** Investigating a local river (Drumcondra National School)

Example 2 Geography rocks! Learning about rocks

Teaching about rocks is a subject that can be difficult to envisage. Many of us have experiences of being bored learning about rocks and soils because they seemed sterile and dull! There are two simple things to remember when teaching this topic; one is to use real rocks and the other is to ask children their questions about rocks. It follows that the first stage of any work on rocks and/or soils must start with children and teachers collecting rocks and/or soils to investigate, examine and sort! From these types of activities children can then devise their questions. As Figure 8.6 shows, children have a lot of questions about rocks.

Key questions – from children
- How are rocks formed?
- What happens to rocks?
- How are rocks used?
- How do people benefit from rocks?
- Would people survive without rocks?
- How do rocks and soils affect people?
- Is there any bad use for rocks?
- Why is rock and roll called rock and roll?

Resources: photographs and maps of school, weather recording equipment, etc.

▨ **Figure 8.6** Children's questions about rocks (Newtown National School, Co. Waterford)

These questions can lead to some simple activities which in turn suggest a great range of answers. This shows how simple planning and the use of supporting resources can lead to many answers. Activities could include:

- Using images of amazing rocky sceneries across the world for children to talk about, such as:
  - The Lake District, Cumbria, England
  - The Grand Canyon, Arizona, USA
  - Giant's Causeway, Antrim Coast, Northern Ireland
  - Uluru / Ayer's Rock, Northern Territory, Australia
  - Cappadocia, Turkey
  - The Dolomites, Italy.
- Generating ideas through school fieldwork to find rocks and then examining / sorting rocks found.
- Getting children to ask 'random' questions when are then grouped into enquiry questions.
- Investigating possible rock experiments for homework using internet sites such as www.sciencekids.co.uk, www.esta-uk.net and www.youtube.com to find out possible ways to do them.

▨ Investigating the properties of rocks through experimentation. Chapter 7 has some fantastic ways to do this through 'sweet geography'.

▨ Organising fieldwork trips to local site where rocks have been used. For example, children in Newtown visited Kilmacthomas Workhouse and found much to their fascination that rocks had been used for the building as well as in the 'dead' room.

▨ Homework then fieldwork: changing nature of rocks in the locality – evidence of weathering and erosion in and around the school.

▨ Mystery Skype or Skype to geologist: schools can register on the Mystery site and link up with experts on all sorts of topics or can simply link up with schools around the world.

Homework could include bringing in rocks for a display table, making a survey on types of rocks in and about homes, or questioning people about rocks – how used, last time used and so forth. Throughout this series of lessons the learning can be directed by the pupils, resulting in high levels of intrinsic motivation. Rocks and soils is a topic that can be transformed through this type of planning, or 'non-planning'! Furthermore, work on rocks helps children understand other topics in geography such as 'people and work' and develops their ideas about the sustainability of extracting and using rocks, gravels and metal ores for building and production (Figure 8.7).

▨ **Figure 8.7** Investigating rocks in the locality (Newtown National School).

Example 3 Learning about climates near and far

The differences between weather and climate can confuse children and teachers. However, this is a topic of great importance due to the impacts of climate change across the world. Children can build up their understanding of weather and climate by starting with familiar places, such as the school or a local park. A very sensible way to do this is to investigate micro climates in their surroundings, by answering the question: What is the weather like in our school? Here is a sequence you might like to follow:

■ Look at and talk about maps and aerial photographs of the school. Working in pairs get pupils to discuss where the warmest and coldest places might be. Now discuss other aspects of weather in the school such as temperature, wind and sunshine.

■ The teacher should note the topics the children identify.

■ The children then devise questions about the school climate and weather. The teacher can encourage the children to focus on temperature and wind, for example:
  – Where are the coldest places? Where are the warmest? Why are they different?
  – Where are the windiest places? Where are the calmest? Why?

■ Children take part in fieldwork to investigate differing micro-climates around the school grounds, measuring winds, light and temperatures. In each place they should:
  – Note where they are on an outline/base map of the school
  – Describe what they can see around them
  – Measure the temperature using a thermometer
  – Measure the wind using and bought or made anemometer
  – Set up rain gauges to measure the rainfall over a number of days.

■ With the support of the teacher, in each place pupils should also consider why the climate is as they found it.

■ Children can map their findings on plans of the school. Encouraged by the teacher they can decide how to present their findings. For example, they might use colour coding for temperature and arrows of varying size for the wind.

As a follow up, or possibly in another school year, children can investigate climates around the world, building on their conceptual understanding of the influences on climate from the above activities.

Example 4 Finding out about biomes through climate and weather

A biome is a very large community of plants and animals where similar soils and climate enable particular forms of life to thrive. Basically the Earth's land areas divide into four main biomes – forests, grasslands, deserts and tundra. There are also biomes in the seas and oceans such as coral reefs. These major areas divide naturally into smaller units each with their own qualities and characteristics. As children learn about world climate and weather, there will be plenty of opportunities for them to develop their understanding of related plants and creatures. This will gradually extend their understanding at a global scale and lead them to appreciate the connections between different forms of life and the conditions that supports them.

By carrying out these activities, children will learn more about the weather and the differences between climates and biomes at a global scale. This is still liable to be challenging for pupils given the generalisations involved. However, if they have developed ideas about weather patterns and sequences through practical activities they will be able to relate what they learn to their own experience. To specifically look at climates and their associated biomes, children could:

▨ Generate ideas by bringing in global weather forecasts/records from newspapers/internet searches. Children could then decide on a suitable colour code and record temperatures in different locations on a large world map. They might do the same on a globe – the bigger the better. Challenge the children to come up with explanations as to why temperatures vary across the world.

▨ Start an enquiry by sorting photographs and maps of different places according to their vegetation. Use the photographs of differing biomes to generate questions.

▨ Collate data on climates and biomes by investigating places in the news and find out about the climates there and the natural landscapes. Younger classes could also send a mascot to people living in different biomes around the world. Classes/schools could aim for the mascot to get to every type of climates zone or biome in a year!

▨ Use activities such as 'living graphs' to help build up an understanding of life in different climate zones. In this activity a climate graph has information on slips of paper which the children have to place on the graph. This helps them gain a sense of place for these distant places. Using a local climate graph provides a helpful frame of reference for children. For example, the uniformity of daily climates in the tropical rainforest are understood by slips of paper not referring to changing seasons! Older children who have researched particular climate zones could make up living graphs for other groups in their class.

▨ **Figure 8.8** Setting up school grounds for outdoor learning about the physical world (St Colmcille's National School)

▨   Arrange postcards of places around the world showing different climates or biomes around a world map. Children and teachers can use other images for the 'missing' places, such as the rainforest or tundra that people may not visit. Children can also investigate what biomes make the best or most exciting holiday destinations.

▨   Children should investigate biomes in their school grounds and locality, before they look at unfamiliar places. Many schools explore natural biomes by growing flowers and other plants. St Colmcille's National School in Westmeanth, Ireland has taken their studies a stage further. As well as creating imaginary habitats (Figure 8.8) the school plans to devise a woodland walk in an area near to the school.

▨   Children can also make a contrasting biome in their classroom, for example the NASA website shows ideas for making a mini desert, as well as other biomes. For a rainforest all that is needed are plastic bottles, soil, gravel, plants, a knife and packaging tape.

▨   Children could investigate human lives in different biomes. There are excellent resources online to do this, such as clips on YouTube. The BBC programmes, such as Human Planet are also very effective at showing the impact of climates and biomes on people's lives as well as the connections and interactions between people and their biomes.

Furthermore, children can research different climates and biomes in context as they learn about particular countries in the world and so build up their understanding over time. Throughout the school year when investigating a contrasting locality, look up the weather forecast for the locality in question. Children can consider if it is experiencing typical weather conditions.

CONCLUSION

Topics and themes in physical geography provide opportunities for children to learn about their surroundings through fieldwork and creative interactions. They can focus on different environments ranging from the school grounds to local streams, rivers and rocks asking and answering questions which they themselves have generated. Research indicates that children construct knowledge of the physical world over time. Where teachers help children engage with physical phenomena their understanding of geography improves. However, when children are just taught about the physical world, the learning opportunities are much more limited. Quite simply children benefit from quality experiences in the physical world. So we need to tell children less and let them do more fieldwork! However there is a danger that practical geographical activities will be lost among the pressures of school curricula.

The formative nature of learning in and about the physical environment provides children with experiences that often stay with them well beyond their primary schools days. As our world comes under ever increasing strain and shocks from human activity, it is essential that children learn about the physical processes and the way that they are changing. At the same time children need the conceptual frameworks to understand the complex processes which shape our physical environment. Learning about interactions in their school grounds and immediate locality provides them with frameworks and references points for understanding unfamiliar places in the wider world. The chapters elsewhere in this book provide many other ways to help children build up a good understanding of the physical world. Interacting with their surroundings, with each other and with adults through play and structured enquiries can lay the foundations for a life-long interest in geography.

REFERENCES

Catling, S. and Willy, T. (2009) *Teaching Primary Geography*. Exeter: Learning Matters.

Eivers, E. and Clerkin, A. (2011) *PIRLS and TIMSS 2011: Reading, Mathematics and Science Outcomes for Ireland.* Dublin: Educational Research Centre.

Eivers, E. and Clerkin, A. (2013) *National Schools, International Contexts: Beyond the PIRLS and TIMSS Test Results*. Dublin: Educational Research Centre. Available at http://static.rasset.ie/documents/news/national-schools-international-contexts.pdf (accessed 28 October 2015).

Harwood, D. and Jackson, P. (1993) Why did they build this hill so steep? *International Research in Geographical and Environmental Education* 2(2): 64–79.

Mackintosh, M. (2005) Children's understanding of rivers. *International Research in Geographical and Environmental Education*, 14(4): 316–22.

Osborne, J., Wadsworth, P., Black, P. and Meadows, J. (1994) *Primary SPACE Research Reports: The Earth in Space*. Liverpool: Liverpool University Press.

Piaget, J. (1929) *The Child's Conception of the World*. London: Routledge and Kegan Paul.

Pike, S. (2016) *Learning Primary Geography: Ideas and Inspirations from Classrooms*. Abingdon: Routledge.

Platten, L. (1995a) Talking geography: an investigation into young children's understanding of geographical terms part 1. *International Journal of Early Years Education* 3(1): 74–92.

Platten, L. (1995b) Talking geography: an investigation into young children's understanding of geographical terms part 2. *International Journal of Early Years Education* 3(3): 69–84.

Russell, T., Bell, D., Longden, K. and McGuigan, L. (1993) *Primary SPACE Research Reports: Rocks, Soils and Weather*. Liverpool: Liverpool University Press. Available at www.nuffieldfoundation.org/primary-science-and-space/rocks-soils-and-weather (accessed 28 October 2015).

Scoffham, S. (ed.) (1998) *Primary Sources: Research Findings in Primary Geography*. Sheffield: Geographical Association.

Scoffham, S. (2013) A question of research. *Primary Geography* 80(1): 16–17.

Warwick, P. (1987) How do children see geographical pictures? *Teaching Geography* 12(2): 118–19.

Wiegand, P. (1993) *Children and Primary Geography*. London: Cassell.

RESOURCES

The best resources for learning physical geography are the school, its buildings and grounds as well as the immediate local environment. There are a number of websites that are very helpful for developing teacher knowledge in physical geography many of which contain very useful films and images.

▨ The *Guardian* newspaper updates information and photographs about volcanoes as they erupt: www.theguardian.com/world/volcanoes. The site has good coverage of such events.

▨ The National Oceanic and Atmospheric Administration has a wealth of material on physical features and events, including an image of the day, each day: www.nnvl.noaa.gov.

▨ eSchool Today is a Ghanaian website outlining some key content in physical geography: www.eschooltoday.com.

▨ The various BBC sites for geography have plenty of videos and information for teachers and children: www.bbc.co.uk/education/subjects/zbkw2hv.

▨ A great book for helping to understand children's misconceptions is Jane Dove's 2005 book *Immaculate Misconceptions*, published by the Geographical Association.

CHAPTER 9

GEOGRAPHY AND HISTORY IN THE LOCAL AREA

Anthony Barlow

This chapter recounts my experiences of developing a cross-curricular study of a small village in northern England for children in Key Stage 2. The enquiry-led approach to teaching geography and history which I adopted can be applied to other locations. The case study suggests that enquiry *through* fieldwork enhances pupils' creativity and agency, enables teachers to 'make' a curriculum in response to pupil needs and, in so doing, build on pupils' affective responses to place including giving time for observation, imagination and collaboration.

PRINCIPLES

> Younger children's daily lives are lived in their home localities … Neighbourhoods provide their home, schooling and community – key elements of their local attachment and identity. They are the sites of friendships and acquaintances, of early and later play and social activities … Neighbourhoods are places of smells and textures …
>
> (Catling 2011: 16)

The geography curriculum for junior-school age children outlined in the Programme of Study for England (DfE 2013a) encourages teachers to move their gaze 'beyond the local area'. However, as Catling describes above, most primary children live in close proximity to their schools and the local area is an important part of their geographical identity. While there is an obvious need for study of places *beyond*, which take pupils away from their immediate human and physical worlds, the case study in this chapter shows the value of spending time re-examining local areas for pupils aged 7–11 with a geography and history lens. Situating geographical learning in what pupils see around them and focusing on which is familiar, similar and known is said by Martin (2006) to be 'everyday geography'. At its core this everyday approach has relevance to pupils in contrast to a (possibly) more exclusive, reified knowledge beyond themselves, of an 'other' (or others) that is unknown and different to them. What the study shows is these local connections need to be made so meaningful links can be forged to the wider, interconnected world whether it is close by or further afield.

THE IMPORTANCE OF A SENSE OF PLACE (AND TIME)

A sense of place (and time) is created through an area's history, physical landscape and human community. Tuan (1975) argues that all places are both human constructions and highly localised 'centres of meaning'. This idea also applies to pupils that we teach: they develop their own meanings, knowledge and understanding of places. It follows that the subjective element – the pupil voice – should not surprise us and should not be ignored. At the same time we need to recognise the validity of pupils' own identity and knowledge as Pollard points out:

> From a teacher perspective we need to acknowledge that children probably know a lot more than we think they know. If only we could tap into the funds of knowledge that are sustained in the social practices of families, communities and networks, then pupils' learning might become much more authentic, flexible and sustained.
>
> (Pollard 2014: 63)

An *authentic* historical–geographical, place–time approach allows us to include both past, present and future perspectives. It is also a useful way of starting to develop pupils beyond their everyday geographies through imagined histories and geographies, what I call a *'then, now and maybe?'* approach. Such approaches are necessarily collaborative (teacher and pupil; pupil and pupil) and need an appropriate pedagogy for success. This is where the enquiry approach comes in. For reasons of space I will focus on geographical enquiry here, however, it should be noted that enquiry is also highlighted as a way of *doing* history. The Programme of Study states that pupils should 'understand the methods of historical enquiry, including how evidence is used rigorously to make historical claims, and discern how and why contrasting arguments and interpretations of the past have been constructed' (DfE 2013b: 1).

GEOGRAPHICAL ENQUIRY

Geographical knowledge is not something that is fixed. Local definitions (and re-definitions) of the world through an enquiry-led process of planning and teaching are important. Roberts (2013b) suggests, geographical enquiry has four characteristics. Enquiry should be question-driven and is an investigative approach to knowledge and knowledge construction. Secondly, it should be supported by evidence and pupils need to study sources of geographical information. Thirdly, Roberts believes that enquiry should provide opportunities for pupils to make sense of geographical information for themselves. Finally, if pupils are to make sense not only of the evidence but of a sequence of learning as a whole, they need to reflect on what they have learned (*ibid.*: 9–10).

Enquiry-led teaching exemplifies a model of 'curriculum making' (Lambert 2011) where the teacher is empowered and has agency. For me, such curriculum making meant my teaching gained *authenticity* as I considered pupils' own knowledge which then led into what I highlight as a range of (small 'c') creative outcomes. Margaret Roberts (2003) devised a much imitated model for geographical enquiry which I too used as the basis for my planned sequence of learning. The model outlines her four stages:

- *creating a need to know*;
- *using data*;

▩   *making sense*; and
▩   *reflecting on learning* (Figure 9.1).

Enquiry-led learning as a pedagogy for geography has a long history and has sometimes been referred to as 'discovery learning' or 'teaching through thinking skills'. Perhaps most notably, the notion of enquiry can be traced to the writings of Dewey in the 1930s and his 'frameworks for reflection' which encourage learners to reflect on the process of learning. For the past two decades enquiry learning has dominated geographical education in England partly due to the emphasis it is given in the National Curriculum. However, this is now under challenge, not least because it is not mentioned directly in the latest version of the Programme of Study.

While, at worst, enquiry can become little more than unstructured open-ended activities (Rawling 2008) the best enquires are both negotiated and guided. In my experience, pupils need an appropriate level of support to ask geographical questions. This helps them to structure and develop their thinking so they can explore their environment as active agents commenting, assessing and even influencing the world around them. Pickford, Jackson and Garner (2013) suggest three stages of developing progression in enquiry skills, starting with focused enquiries for the younger children which are carefully controlled by the teacher. These are followed by framed enquiries and ultimately facilitated enquiries as pupils' independence and autonomy develops.

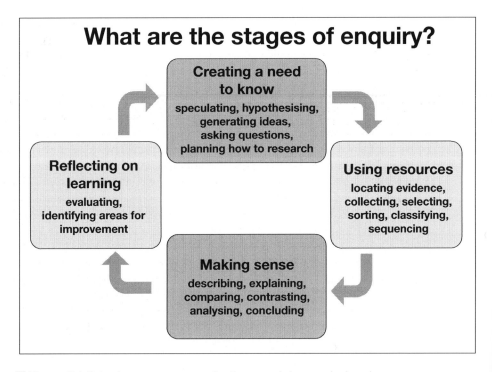

What are the stages of enquiry?

Creating a need to know
speculating, hypothesising, generating ideas, asking questions, planning how to research

Using resources
locating evidence, collecting, selecting, sorting, classifying, sequencing

Making sense
describing, explaining, comparing, contrasting, analysing, concluding

Reflecting on learning
evaluating, identifying areas for improvement

▩ **Figure 9.1** Roberts proposes a concise framework for enquiry learning
Source: adapted from Roberts (2003: 44)

Enquiry process stage 1: creating a need to know

Enquiry gives pupils a chance to connect with the natural and built environment around them, developing deep not just surface level recall and learning. It's no surprise, therefore, that fieldwork is so strongly associated with enquiry. Creating some excitement and a 'need to know' are important for success when an enquiry begins and starting with some outdoor experience is often a good way to do this. While in my study most pupils lived within two miles of the school and near the local village, their knowledge of official map locations appeared poor. It was only through the stimulus of photos that I realised that their everyday knowledge was actually quite varied and detailed; it just wasn't what was represented on an Ordnance Survey map. They knew where they could (and couldn't) play outside, where they walked the dog, who they visited regularly (e.g. 'grandmas') and many had excellent knowledge of the best retail parks and football grounds! This meant I could identify the places they knew and could relate these to a local map. We then simply stood in the playground and talked about what we could see, where things were in relation to each other and how far they were. This elicited positional and directional language: 'What is over/up there?', 'Where is North, South?' and 'How far is …?' etc.). What I hadn't realised was how much of a stimulus for wonder that the 80 metre high former bleach-works' chimney would be to get them enquiring *where, why, what* and *how*!

The tall chimney (something I used to call Grandad's Chimney as a child) was just the landmark to get us started thinking about the village of Barrow Bridge and stands at the entrance to the village. Seek out these landmarks when doing enquiries and learn about them in detail; their significance should not be underestimated. In this case the chimney commemorates just one of the big Victorian personalities, Mr. Ainsworth, whose bleach works changed the quiet valley's geography of the area for ever. This gave us the impetus to form many other questions (Figure 9.2) about the various families whose actions changed this village on the outskirts of Bolton over time. However, while the village began as a site-specific centre for cotton spinning and weaving centred around a small brook, decline came fast in the Twentieth Century and by 1910 the hamlet was largely abandoned. Much of the evidence for the bleach works and spinning mills has been lost and the shadow the West Pennine moors has again come upon the valley. The valley quickly reforested after having been stripped of its vegetation and its upper course is once again became wild, overgrown and impassable.

Our first fieldtrip to the site focused on human geography: *Why did people move to and settle in the valley just one mile from our school?* Figure 9.3 indicates the range of initial responses. My focus as the teacher was on the built environment (stone houses, extant mill, field-boundary walls, the Victorian post box), something that would give a sense of time past and a place very different to the gentrified suburb of today. Put simply, I felt the geography needed to come later! There is always a danger in cross-curricular studies that historical perspectives will dominate. However, the pupils surprised me. Their focus became fixed on the stream instead; it helped that we had had a period of intensive rain! Indeed it was my own faltering efforts to explain the (hugely altered) valley's physical geography that really got them enquiring as to *how, what* and *why*!

Enquiry process stage 2: using resources

Back in the classroom pupils' initial sense of time and place were enhanced through looking at photos we'd taken, historical photos and maps. The focus of the stream led us all

What natural features are there?	How does it look on a map?
The brook	*Very blue and green, overgrown.*
What built features are there?	What sort of map would be best?
Houses, roads, street furniture.	*Look for a range of maps both paper and online.*
Can we say how the area has been altered over time?	Can we compare it with an aerial photo?
It has gone from being undeveloped to being heavily populated, then falling back into decline and now repopulated.	*Use Google Maps as well as photos taken for school project.*
What photographic evidence can we find for the area?	Has the area changed regularly, periodically or gradually over time?
Use local archives online to find period postcards when it was a beauty spot. Allow children to search too.	*Create a simplified timeline for the wall. Things did not happen evenly!*
Can we collect new photos ourselves?	
Compare and contrast. Ask parents and grandparents to send in photos.	
What shape does the settlement have? Is there a reason for this?	Are there documents (secondary sources) that describe the place?
It is built on the surrounding hills with the factory owners' large houses in prime spots at the head of the valley.	*Create a fictional diary of the place and use children's fiction based in workhouses.*
Is there a local expert (primary source) or resource we can draw upon to help us?	Are there any creative surprises that we can use to engage pupils?
Use the local history society and the school governor who has lived here all his life.	*Show a video tour, dress up as a Victorian, open a long-lost letter, use a photo of a person, have an announcement from the head teacher, show an artefact, show previous students' work.*

▓ **Figure 9.2** Questions about Barrow Bridge that informed my lesson planning

They wanted somewhere new to live.	People liked the trees.	They went to church there.	They wanted fresh air.
People wanted to grow vegetables.	They liked the stream.	They liked the countryside.	The children wanted somewhere to play.

▓ **Figure 9.3** Children's initial ideas about why people settled in Barrow Bridge to investigate further to realise that this is, in fact, a straightened and diverted brook with a concrete storm drain, culvert and two-metre man-made waterfall. As with many settlements of its era, this water source was essential for the industry's development.

The persistent question remained: *Where did the brook come from?* The children's responses showed a lack of awareness of the large catchments needed to feed even a relatively small body of water. Answers ranged from 'the sky' to the 'big reservoir on the hill'. What excited us all was the discovery that while the brook's source was the hills that surrounded both the valley and our school, it was a tributary of the River Mersey and ended up in the Irish Sea. What a journey for a small brook near our school! Here the interconnected nature of life became clear suggesting that what we see or do locally can very quickly become part of a regional, national or international 'big picture'. Again, I was surprised by the pupils' limited locational knowledge. Many pupils appeared unaware that we are an island nation. Figure 9.4 shows one creative way I developed pupils' knowledge of the brook and river's course from source to sea.

■ **Figure 9.4** Pupils made drawings of different sections of the river, which they joined together
Source: photo by Anthony Barlow

Key resources I used to develop their historical thinking on the second fieldtrip were a band of excellent 'more knowledgeable others' in the guise of school governors and local historians. They led the pupils round the village and mixed historical insight and personal stories of days gone by which fuelled pupils' interests. This allowed me to balance direct, informative and instructional teaching and the enquiry-led, active engagement.

Enquiry process stage 3: collecting further data and making sense

As Roberts states in her suggested four-stage enquiry process, enquiries should collect data to allow pupils to make sense of the world. Balancing subjective, qualitative approaches with more quantifiable approaches was important. This was done in a variety of ways as can be seen below alongside how we used that data.

Place knowledge	Place research	Post-visit thinking
Personal pupil knowledge	Look and listen	What might possible,
Family knowledge	Read and research	probable and preferable
Expert knowledge	Discuss	futures look like?
Oral history	Collect data (e.g. sketch,	What would happen if . . .?
Also through:	count)	What might . . . say if . . .?
Maps, plans	Hypothesise, fantasise,	Would you like to . . .?
Photographs	synthesise	Can you place . . . in
Stories/imagined worlds	Understand	context?
	Surveying (e.g. using an	
	environmental index)	

Re-presenting the place creatively
Demonstrating knowledge and understanding through:
Writing stories and poems
Drawing maps and recording the journey
Using ICT to display, interpret and explain
Fieldwork as a spur for further research
Drama, dressing up and role play (e.g. having a 1900 day)
Examining found and collected artefacts
Making maps and models
Collecting opinions and questionnaires
Interpreting fieldwork data

▦ **Figure 9.5** How pupil responses and creative engagement was part of the enquiry and fieldwork process

COLLECTING DATA: ENVIRONMENTAL INDICES

To balance the subjective, adult perspectives of place I felt pupils needed evidence to draw their own conclusions. First, we used a number scoring system to quantify the environment. I encouraged pupils to scaffold their understanding by picking four contrasting locations and make judgements on what they 'thought about what they could see'. This gave them a chance to stop and reflect on a set of 'environmental indices', scoring them from 1 to 5 using four categories:

▦ street furniture;
▦ wildlife and nature;
▦ litter and graffiti; and
▦ roads and pavements (Barlow 2009).

Pausing in the environment meant pupils began to notice many more ways locations can be defined, referenced and described. These ranged from number, word and symbolic representations (street names/signs, building numbers and date stones/plaques) to the materials they are built from. It also started discussions on architectural styles, especially in relation to types of housing (e.g. terraced, semi-detached, detached), housing styles (e.g. 'mock Tudor'), elements that make up different buildings (e.g. ionic/doric columns) and decisions made over time on land use (e.g. 'greenbelt land').

COLLECTING DATA: DATA LOGGERS

Using hand-held data-logging devices such as *Log-it Explorer* can show the light (lux), heat (°C) and sound (dB) in areas assessed on fieldwork. These devices are easy to use and provide a way to complement the environmental indexes describe earlier. The resulting data is also relatively easy to plot in bar charts and graphs and further allowed an evidence-informed discussion of pupil views and perspectives on an area.

MAKING SENSE: WRITING CREATIVELY USING BLOGS AND PLAY SCRIPTS

This project worked well because it extended beyond the time allotted for geography in the curriculum. This meant that it became integrated into other lessons including literacy and ICT lessons thereby realising a wider variety of pupil learning outcomes. Perhaps the best response came through a task suggested by pupils to use computers to write a blog post in the character of a child labourer in the long-forgotten cotton mills. Through structuring the narrative round a teacher-drawn map of the area, the pupils imagined the day in the life of the character and wrote in the form of a diary in an online blog. Pupils worked best when they talked through their story first after a brainstorming session where they thought of key words and visualised the journey they/the children would make. Figure 9.6 shows some examples of the blog devised by eight-year-old pupils. I have highlighted certain words and phrases to show the range of appropriate subject-specific vocabulary that they used. More structure and a whole-class shared word bank might have been even more helpful here.

Using historical photos in situ and photographing pupils holding views in front of what is there now, provided an excellent context and stimulus for further writing. The following extract from two seven-year-olds' play scripts imagines the demolished mill alongside real and observed features such as the tunnel. The map the children refer to was their altered map where they imagined treasure could be found.

BARROW BRIDGE ADVENTURE PLAY SCRIPT BY TED AND SAM
Child 2: Let's go and look in Mr Bazley's office. [Real historical figure]
Child 1: OK, let's go then!
Child 2: It's still not there!
Child 1: I know.
Child 2: Let's look at this map. [Children's own version of teacher's]
Child 1: Where does it go?
Child 2: It looks like it goes to the cigarette tunnel. [Real place]
Child 1: Let's go then!
Child 2: But how can we get out.
Child 1: We are going to have to sleep here until the morning for this place to be open again.

MAKING SENSE: CREATING MAPS FOR DIFFERENT PURPOSES

In order to develop skills in creating maps, children need to use and make maps in a variety of contexts. Drawing maps showing physical features is difficult for young children even in urban fringe areas such as Barrow Bridge. I needed to model how to draw such a map and explain, for example, the river's course from its source in the hills to the Mersey

11 June, 10:25 a.m.
Post 7 **Barrow Bridge** I learned about lots of different things with Clive, Mr Stockton and Mr Perris told us lots about **Barrow Bridge**. They told us about the **mills** and I found out that they were **six floors high.** I was amazed. I also found out where the **1st, 2nd, 3rd, 4th** and **5th** street are. My group with Mr Perris went up the 35 steps which led to the 1st, 2nd, 3rd, 4th and 5th street. But we did not go up the 63 steps because we did not have time. Finally there was the **river** the **river** was very important to the people in Barrow Bridge because it made all the **machinery working in the mills** and it is right under the **mission** which can also be called **the church**.

11 June, 10:31 a.m.
When we went to **Barrow Barrow Bridge** we learned lots about. The **post box** and that it was made in victorian time when the **mill** was built. It was on the **old shops wall**. we also went up some **steps to Bazley street** I counted **36** of them and turned it around it it made **63**. We looked up **Bazley street** and could just see the **garden center** and **tennis courts**.
Next we went to the 63 steps and after a breath taking climb we arrived at the top and we where told about the **pub** called the **kicking donkey** and that it was the only place that you could go and have a drink.

* * *

Lower achievers showed a poorer response, but still showed a sense of chronology on the journey and a sense of place names.

11 June, 10:30 a.m.
Post 11 **All about Barrow Brige!**
Next we saw lot's of nummber's around and on wall's just like nummber 1096. There was a **river** right at **Barrow Bridge Misson** on one side children where throwing leave's on one side of the river and going to the other side of the river to see the leave's coming under the river. We went up the 63 step's we saw a sine near the tree it said the best mum in the world. and we saw **two big water fall rither's.** Next we saw some dog's and a high **litter** on the floor. After That we saw some house's and athe **letter box** whitch is the **post office** letter box. By MS.

▨ **Figure 9.6** Extracts from the blog about the Barrow Bridge fieldwork by Year 3 pupils, with key vocabulary highlighted

and the Irish Sea. Maps referencing human geographical features were much easier for pupils to draw as their memories of roads, individual buildings and street furniture dominated even towards the end of the teaching sequence. For SEN pupils, placing photos in consecutive order proved an effective additional strategy which helped them to remember their journey. Another approach I used where pupils could keep alive the experience of where they had been was to create their own personal or mental maps. An ICT program such as 2Simple's 2DIY facilitates this activity as it allows pupils to add labels.

A final way I encouraged pupils to recall the fieldtrip we had been on was to create a junk model map. The power of having the whole class of thirty pupils sitting around a map they have all contributed towards cannot be beaten. To create this map (shown in Figure 9.7) I used the work they had already completed alongside aerial photographs, teacher and pupil-drawn and Ordnance Survey maps. The map was made from large sugar

■ **Figure 9.7** Pupils creating a junk model map

paper sheets painted as a base-map in green, grey and blue (signifying the land, roads and water features). Significant buildings were represented by turning cereal boxes of a variety of shapes inside out and then painting and using pens to recreate their features as mentioned above. The scale of individual buildings, of the base-map, of water features and the spacing between objects were all discussed and proved a wonderful way to demonstrate concepts of location, scale and perspective. The children responded to this exercise with great enthusiasm and the quality of their work was extremely high. Some pupils even followed this up to create a Monopoly-style game based on their journey to Barrow Bridge (see Figure 9.8).

Enquiry process stage 4: reflecting on learning

As our enquiry evolved, the idea of *change* in the place and over time emerged as one of the most important concepts. More broadly, this was *what* had (and *was*) happening and *how* (and *why*) things had (and *were*) happening. We also began to develop ideas about *what might happen* in the future. So to finish this sequence of enquiry-led learning with some assessment of what had been learned I decided to ask pupils to plan for ideas of how to improve the area for the future. I used postcard scenes of visitors from decades past packed round the (long since filled-in) artificial lake. Fed by the brook, the lake was clearly a popular attraction which prompted questions over the purpose of the place today. We discussed the reason why anyone would send a postcard from where we lived! The

■ **Figure 9.8** The fieldwork inspired the children to create a game

most significant postcard showed the weekend and public holiday funfair, so we asked the question: *What if the funfair returned? What might local residents think? How would it change the area we had seen? What could the consequences be?* We held a debate on the pros and cons; something I had struggled to do before with children of this age. However, perhaps because of the depth of learning and the creativity mind-set developed by children through this project, ideas came easily to them. The discussions prolonged their memories of the visit and engaged them both cognitively and emotionally. In these sessions, the fourth stage in the Roberts enquiry process, (reflecting on learning) was really brought to life.

CONCLUSION

The old adage declares, 'There's no place like home'. Where is your home? It may not be where you are teaching, and that presents a challenge for teaching history and geography. Do you, then, feel part of the community? In England, schools have been asked to integrate the idea of 'community cohesion' in their planning for some years now and more recently have to focus on the 'respect' and 'prevent' agendas. Current debates about citizenship, multicultural Britain and identity reinforce the idea that schools have ignored parts of our 'island story'. While many a political wind affects those of us charting a course across the curriculum's choppy waters, what all these agendas retain is a sense that fostering an understanding and knowledge about pupils' communities is crucial to pupil safety, fulfilment and attainment. *Knowing* a place is more than just being able to locate and describe it. It is much more about being able to make connections, to see beyond and read the area's human and physical traces. It involves having a view on its past, present and possible futures. In today's increasingly mobile, transitory and (some might argue) fractured society, *who* makes up a place is every bit as important *what* makes it up. You might find that, as a teacher, the story of the place in which you teach is no longer passed on as a collective memory from one generation to another. However, just below the surface, there might lie landmarks and stories which help explain what has gone before and point towards what might come in the future.

These are big issues for children to tackle in primary education. Yet exploring them can help to the lay the foundations for a young person's identity. Creative, enquiry-led approaches which cross curriculum boundaries can start to reveal the nature of places through time. While not easy, and sometimes needing significant personal research, the rewards from such studies, as I hope this chapter shows, can be immense.

REFERENCES AND FURTHER READING

Barlow, A. (2009) Fresh eyes on our natural world. *Primary Geography* 70: 12–13.

Catling, S. (2011) Children's geographies in the primary school. In G. Butt (ed.), *Geography, Education and the Future*, pp. 15–29. London: Continuum.

Davidson, G. (2006) Geographical enquiry. Geographical Association think piece. Available at www.tes.com/teaching-resource/gtip-think-piece-geographical-enquiry-6425603 (accessed 8 January 2016).

DfE (2013a) *Geography Programmes of Study: Key Stages 1 and 2*. London: DfE.

DfE (2013b) *History Programmes of Study: Key Stages 1 and 2*. London: DfE.

Dillon, J., Morris, M., O'Donnell, L., Reid, A., Rickinson, M. and Scott, W. (2005) Engaging and learning with the outdoors. Available at www.bath.ac.uk/cree/resources/OCR.pdf (accessed 8 January 2016).

Hopkins, D. (2008) *Teacher's Guide to Classroom Research*. Oxford: Oxford University Press.

House of Commons Education and Skills Committee (2005) *Education Outside the Classroom: Second Report of Session 2004–05*. London: House of Commons Education and Skills Committee. Available at www.publications.parliament.uk/pa/cm200405/cmselect/cmeduski/120/120.pdf (accessed 14 January 2016).

Kelly, A. (2009) GTIP think piece – every child matters, geography matters. Available at www.geography.org.uk/gtip/thinkpieces/everychildmatters (accessed 14 January 2016).

Lambert, D. (2011) Reframing school geography; a capability approach. In G. Butt (ed.), *Geography, Education and the Future*, pp. 127–40. London: Continuum.

Mackintosh, M. (2005) Children's understanding of rivers. *International Research in Geographical and Environmental Education* 14(4): 313–22.

Malone, K. (2008) Every experience matters. Available at www.face-online.org.uk/face-news/every-experience-matters (accessed 14 January 2016).

Martin, F. (2006) Everyday geography: re-visioning primary geography for the 21st century. *Geographical Education* 9(3): 31–7.

Ofsted (2011) Geography learning to make a world of difference. Available at www.gov.uk/government/publications/geography-learning-to-make-a-world-of-differ-ence (accessed 8 August 2011).

Pickford, T., Jackson, E. and Garner, W. (2013) *Primary Humanities*. London: Sage.

Pollard, A. (2014) *Reflective Teaching in Schools*. London: Bloomsbury.

Rawling, E. (2008) *Planning Your KS3 Curriculum*. Sheffield: Geographical Association.

Rickinson, M., Dillon, J., Teamey, K., Morris, M., Young Choi, M. Sanders, S. and Benefield, P. (2004) *A Review of Research on Outdoor Learning*. London: NFER.

Roberts, M. (2003) *Learning Through Enquiry*. Sheffield: Geographical Association.

Roberts, M. (2013a) *Geography through Enquiry: An Approach to Teaching and Learning in the Secondary School*. Sheffield: Geographical Association.

Roberts, M (2013b) The challenge of enquiry-based learning. *Teaching Geography* (Summer): 50–52.

Steel, B. (2010) GTIP think piece – primary fieldwork. Available at http://geography.org.uk/gtip/thinkpieces/fieldworkprimary (accessed 8 January 2016).

Tuan, Y.-F. (1975) Place: An experiential perspective. *Geographical Review* 65(2): 151–65.

Weeden, P. (1997) Learning through maps. In D. Tilbury and M. Williams (eds), *Teaching and Learning Geography*, pp. 168–79. London: Routledge.

Websites

More examples of work undertaken by the pupils and Anthony can be seen online here:

▨   www.geography.org.uk/projects/makinggeographyhappen/understandingthelocalarea/thegeography

▨   www.geography.org.uk/projects/younggeographers/resources/stpeters

Other useful websites include the following:

▨   *Maps of locations in the UK:* www.ordnancesurvey.org.uk/opendata

▨   *Historic photographs of Barrow Bridge village, Bolton (useful for contrasting locality work):* www.boltonlams.co.uk/collections/collection/5

▨   *Respect agenda:* http://webarchive.nationalarchives.gov.uk/20070306080821/www.respect.gov.uk

▨   *Prevent agenda:* www.gov.uk/government/publications/protecting-children-from-radicalisation-the-prevent-duty

GEOGRAPHY AND MATHEMATICS
A creative approach

Jane Whittle

A creative approach to teaching encourages pupils to apply wonderings and skills in varied contexts. In this chapter I explore the potential for creative connections between geography and mathematics to motivate pupils to participate in active, lively and engaging lessons. I also consider the impact that this may have on the teacher with regards to their practice and planning.

A CASE FOR CROSS-CURRICULAR WORK

The skills and attitudes required by successful mathematicians and geographers have some similarities. Both subjects encourage discussion, sorting and description of ideas – mathematics can be applied through geographical stimuli while mathematics can support the understanding of geographical principles or help to solve an enquiry question. The mathematics curriculum for England, Scotland, Northern Ireland and Wales share the common principle that mathematics can be seen as a vehicle for making sense of the world. It is in this transfer and application of knowledge that creative links between the two subjects come to light. As Barnes (2010: 25) states: 'while creativity varies in degree and impact, it always involves making connections between two previously unconnected items or ideas'.

There are powerful arguments to support the cross-curricular teaching of mathematics, which when integrated with geography provides opportunities for pupils to present their understanding in creative ways. Boaler (2009: 44) highlights this explicitly when she argues that 'when we work as mathematicians in solitude, there is only one opportunity to understand the mathematics'. However, when we combine the two subjects, exciting opportunities for creative links can be found, while maintaining the integrity of both subjects in their own right.

When we observe our pupils working through investigations and listen to their mathematical talk, we witness the ways pupils are beginning to develop what Askew (2003: 85) describes as 'the process of mathematizing'. The more opportunities we give our pupils to experience this in geographical contexts, the more sophisticated their explorations of mathematics and the world may become. On a local level this may involve thinking about the organisation of the classroom furniture or considering the amount of food wasted in the canteen. On a global scale, topics such as patterns of trade or the movement of migrants and refugees could illustrate how mathematics helps us to learn more about world events.

Creativity

There are similarities between creative mathematics and geography. In order to foster creativity, both subjects require pupils to make connections. These may be connections to a local or global issue, to the materials presented or pupils may make connections through applying skills, for example using maths to sort out information about a place. In a cross-curricular approach pupils also begin to see the connections between subjects, especially in seeing the world with 'maths eyes'. In order to do this, children need to have higher-order thinking modelled to them by the teacher and their peers.

HOW CAN MATHS TRAILS ENCOURAGE CREATIVITY?

Maths trails in their simplest form are explorations in an area of the school locality, which focus on selected mathematical themes. They can be indoor, outdoor or digital. The concept of a 'trail' can take two forms:

- ▨ pupils can freely explore a place, such as the playground; or
- ▨ pupils can be given a map, webquest or objects to follow along a route specifically designed by the teacher.

Allowing pupils the freedom to roam a place in search of mathematics gives them opportunities to make personal connections. They may be brave enough to venture to an area that once frightened them or see that the hopscotch game painted on the floor is in fact made of squares. In a more focused, teacher-designed trail, the teacher has the opportunity to make observations of children and their mathematical behaviours in a realistic geographical context. As Milner and Jewson (2010: 190) write: 'trails can be an excellent way of structuring local area work and serve to focus attention on specific themes or issues'. In terms of providing a cross-curricular approach, maths trails focus on discovering mathematics in a place. This requires pupils to form judgements and challenge their perceptions of that place. Maths trails support the following.

SKILL ACQUISITION

Maths trails can involve practising the skill of one-to-one correspondence or looking for geometrical shapes in the corridor. It can involve recording the flow of vehicles or people past a point or hunting for number bonds attached to trees in the playground.

APPLICATION OF KNOWLEDGE

By completing a trail, pupils gain a stronger sense of the environment around them, both physically and spatially. Pound and Lee (2015) state this is important in making mathematics relevant to children and their world. A key part of applying maths is in the language pupils use to describe and explain. In undertaking a trail, the teacher has the opportunity to observe how children use and apply language in a real context.

AWE AND WONDER

Through maths trails, pupils have the opportunity to think positively about the elegance of mathematics (Robinson and Koshy 2004). Geography aims to promote a sense of awe and wonder in children. Mathematics, too, can introduce an aesthetic and existential dimension by focusing on real and purposeful contexts. Boaler (2009: 13) describes the contrast of 'fake' maths versus 'real' maths and argues that the latter must be brought into classrooms 'as a matter of urgency'.

ENQUIRY INTO THE LOCALITY

A fundamental feature of creative geography teaching is to provide pupils with experiences in their familiar environment – the locality of the school.

In using maths trails, pupils extend the scope of their enquiries into a related curriculum area, which reduces the pressure on the school timetable. A tally chart trail of transport along the high street may lead to a discussion of the number of cars on a road. Is this something that could be addressed further through enquiring into issues in the school locality, for example?

SENSE OF PLACE

Writing in the *Primary Geography Handbook*, Paula Richardson declares:

> The buildings, streets and environment around your school are a valuable learning resource. Whatever their age, pupils can undertake a great variety of activities outside the classroom. This work stimulates their curiosity, promotes creative engagement and leads them to value their locality.
>
> (Richardson 2010: 135)

Just as pupils need time to find the elegance in mathematics, they also need time to reflect on and build personal attachments to a place. This appreciation of place is crucial to a child's development both geographically and psychologically as has been repeatedly affirmed (see Ashbridge 2006; Buxton 2006; Scoffham 2017).

CREATIVITY

As the following sections explain, trails can be planned with creativity in mind, or alternatively, the creativity can arise from the pupils' explorations, discoveries and wonderings. In either event, maths trails provide opportunities for a new way of seeing, allowing pupils to take mathematics from the classroom and connect it to the natural and built environment. In being given time to create their own trails, pupils are encouraged to think and search for mathematics. Maths trails are flexible in their approach and thus are suitable for any age of the primary years. Haylock and Thangata (2007) recognise the importance of mathematical play in order to develop concepts in younger children, which can be addressed more formally in later years. It is sometimes tempting for Key Stage 2 teachers to assume play and local area study have been covered in the early years and that pupils should now be proceeding to more 'grown-up' work. However, maths trails always give pupils the possibility to learn or find something new, because the school locality is never static and neither is a child's passion for enquiry.

JANE WHITTLE ▨ ▨ ▨ ▪

USING A MATHS TRAIL WITH A YEAR 3 CLASS

Maths trails can be one-off events, stimuli for a maths week, or they can form a natural part of a teacher's repertoire of techniques for supporting pupils' mathematical understanding. The following case study shows how maths trails were introduced at the beginning of a school year to form the basis of local area enquiry and exploration of mathematics with my Year 3 class.

Being passionate about teaching mathematics creatively and making it accessible for my students aged 7–8, I began the year with a maths trail around the class and school corridors. In taking this approach, I wanted to introduce my class to the feeling of participating in a trail while gauging an understanding of their opinions and knowledge of mathematics.

1 Discussion

I began by asking the class, 'What is maths?', asking them to draw on prior experience of home and school mathematics. Figure 10.1 shows the responses that were recorded. Generally the pupils tended to focus on the procedures in mathematics and made only limited connections to the elegance of mathematics in context.

- All with numbers – you don't need anything else (Child A)
- Calculations, sums, minus, counting
- Adding and subtraction
- In maths, we can do things like sums and counting
- Times tables
- Symbols (+ x ÷ –)
- Maths means to learn
- It's an activity
- Numbers are in the date, the clock and the dice
- It's problems
- It's sorting
- It's putting numbers and things in their place
- Without numbers and years, we wouldn't be alive
- Years are made with days and days are numbers

▨ **Figure 10.1** Pupils' responses to the question 'What is maths?'

2 Preparing the trail

I explained to the pupils that we were going to enquire and explore around school, looking for examples of mathematics. In order to keep the integrity of geography, I explained the concept of searching a place and finding new things. The children then made a simple 'Maths mask' to help with their searching. This mask needs to be no more than a paper plate with eye-holes that children fix to their face with string. My children decorated their masks to make them look 'mathematical', which allowed me to gauge their individual ideas and understanding of the subject.

3 The trail

The trail started in the classroom and moved into the corridors with pupils recording examples of mathematics in their own way. They were encouraged to look high and low, and even under furniture. In doing the trail, most children showed a more developed understanding of the breadth of mathematics. This allowed me to reinforce mathematical language and terms such as 'symmetry' and 'tessellation'. The trail took place in the first week of the school term and children were constantly commenting on changes to displays or the ways in which new teachers had changed the furniture around in the class. A curious teacher asked one boy 'What are you doing?' to which he replied, 'We are discovering the school'. This child had recognised the sense of awe and wonder in this activity.

4 Back in the classroom

With the maths masks off, we reflected on the trail in two ways. I began with the thinking routine, 'I used to think, but now I also think …', in order to help pupils make deeper connections and responses to the question 'What is maths?' The responses showed they were now more curious about everyday mathematics in the school locality (Figure 10.2). Following this discussion, I asked the children about the place we had explored and the things they had noticed. Their responses showed that while they were searching for mathematics they were also able to think and reflect on the locality of the school.

I used to think..., now I also think...
- It's about shapes – everything has a shape (Child A had now been convinced that there was more to maths than just numbers)
- Big and little
- It's about objects
- It's sizes and symbols
- It's about signs – they have a shape

- We can count a lot of things
- We use numbers and letters
- The world has lots of shapes – even the plants, planets, the sun and the galaxy
- It's not just about numbers, it's about shapes, numbers and patterns
- Why did somebody invent maths? Because they wanted to learn

■ **Figure 10.2** Pupils' reflection ideas following the trail

5 Going further

By introducing the children to trails, I set up an expectation that the maths they were going to do in the coming year was not going to be a 'sit-down' subject. Two terms later, the children are now familiar with many types of trail, and, following each one, always have something to add to our original discussion on what mathematics is and what they know about their environment.

DIFFERENT TYPES OF MATHS TRAIL

The following section gives examples of maths trails that can be adapted to cater for the needs of different classes. Trails can be completed individually or collaboratively. In collaborating and interacting, children construct meaning together and begin to recognise that creativity is not always an individual feat – indeed it nearly always involves sharing ideas. The following trails aim to integrate creative mathematics and geography and show how this fusion can foster learning, motivation and a response to the environment.

Counting trails

In the indoor and outdoor environment of a school, there is a wealth of counting opportunities. Materials, letters, door numbers, gateposts, trees – all give potential for counting. Counting trails can take the form of counting objects as a class or pupils could be asked to record how many of something they see. For example, children could have a map of the outdoor area, count how many minibeasts are found at each point marked on their map, and record their results using their own method. As Robinson and Koshy (2004: 74) remind us, 'creative behaviour in mathematics may be seen when a child uses a new way of recording something'. In formal recording, counting trails provide an opportunity to apply the skill of making tally charts.

Shape-hunting trails

Enquiry into shapes in the environment can lead to an interesting discussion about why some shapes are more common in the playground or in buildings. Pupils can look for shapes in the environment or, alternatively, the teacher can hide shapes for pupils to find. Directional vocabulary is an important part of both the geography and mathematics curriculum, and planning a shape hunt/trail allows for questions such as 'What shape was behind the bin?' Alternatively, pupils could hide the shapes and set clues for their peers with the focus being on both shape and the acquisition of directional vocabulary.

Peg trails

Peg trails are fun to organise and extremely effective in promoting learning. Prior to the lesson, the teacher needs to hang cards on trees, fences or benches in the area to be explored. Pupils then have to respond by pegging up a card of their own in the correct place. Peg trails for early years children could involve the numbers one to ten – each child has a number and they must peg their number to the matching hanging card. You could adapt the trail to focus on number bonds to ten, or to reinforce odd and even numbers; the scope is endless. Older children could be given the answer to a mathematical sum that they have to match to the correct calculation (Figure 10.3).

Once children are familiar with this sort of trail, it can easily form a weekly starter/plenary or formative assessment activity. Exploring and venturing into new areas is important in geography and using a peg trail can encourage children to go to places they do not normally visit. Peg trails allow for a competitive element in that the teacher can challenge their pupils – perhaps to finish a trail in less than three minutes. Peg trails also provide instant assessment of pupils' mathematical application of skills in that the teacher can view the pegs and the pupils' responses before taking them down to try the trail again.

■ **Figure 10.3** A Year 2 student from International School of Bologna, racing to complete the peg trail in under two minutes
Source: photo by Jane Whittle

Pattern trails

Children's curiosity for finding patterns in the built and natural environment can form the basis of many maths trails. In the classroom, pupils can replicate the patterns they have found. Alternatively, pupils could photograph the patterns they find on the trail and insert their photographs into a Word document to make a digital map or annotate their photographs using an App. Another option is to print the photographs, which can then be made into maps and combined to make a class 'atlas' of patterns.

Trails with maths maps

In this trail pupils investigate an area such as the playground and, armed with a clipboard, make a map of the mathematics they find. In Figure 10.4 pupils had the option to create their own map or use a teacher-produced one. Pupils were also given a tape measure to aid their enquiries and were encouraged to work collaboratively to measure more challenging objects (Figure 10.5). To develop their mapping skills, children could be asked to make a mathematics route map around part of the school. Teachers of Key Stage 2 pupils could also create maps and routes for pupils to follow and include coordinate questions as an extra challenge (Whittle 2010). Pupils have an innate curiosity for map-making and the freedom of these activities allows them to demonstrate their ability in both mathematical recording and mapwork.

▦ **Figure 10.4** An example of a maths map, completed by a Year 3 student

▦ **Figure 10.5** International School of Bologna Year 3 students measuring the height of a bush
Source: photo by Jane Whittle

Measuring trails

Measuring trails encourage creative ways of applying the skill of measuring in different spaces and places. Delaney (2010) states that children need opportunities to engage with a resource to allow them to make connections. When they measure different objects, pupils begin to do this through problem-solving. For instance, they need to choose the appropriate resource – a ruler, metre stick or tape measure if they are investigating distance. This may also lead to an interesting discussion about standard units of measurement around the world. Pupils can also be encouraged to find examples of right-angles around the school and record their results. A more challenging exercise, which will probably involve a lot of discussion, is to measure the height of a tree (see websites). The teacher could design a trail of trees for pupils to measure to allow for discussion of height and to stimulate questions about trees in the locality.

Leaves and sticks trails

Autumn is the ideal time for collecting leaves and sorting them by colour, size or type (Figure 10.6). Pupils have the right to explore and understand the natural world around them and a creative teacher will find opportunity to do this through a combination of mathematics and geography.

■ **Figure 10.6** International School of Bologna Year 1 students sorting leaves into different types
Source: photo by Jane Whittle

Alternatively, leaves and sticks could be measured. The problem-solving teacher could pose the question, 'How can we find the perimeter/calculate the area of this leaf?' Data collected could be presented in a bar graph and saved to compare to next year's leaf fall. Running around collecting leaves can motivate the disaffected learner and encourage timid children to use maths equipment in a non-threatening situation. Pupils can consider the Countryside Code and reflect on a responsible use of the natural environment during a trail. Respect for the environment is an integral part of geographical thinking.

Trails starting from a story

The world of fiction can be used as a gateway into applying mathematics. In their role play or free play, pupils can create trails for characters in the stories they read or they can create mathematical worlds to roam in. Taking a counting book as the focus for the role play, pupils can apply their counting skills as they free play, using the book as the context for practicing one to one correspondence. Two examples of counting books which lend themselves to both small world play and role play areas are *Over in the Meadow: A Counting Rhyme* (Voce 2011) and *My Granny Went to Market* (Blackstone and Corr 2006). Alternatively, using books with a journey focus allows pupils to recreate this journey with a mathematical focus. An ideal text for this would be *A Friend Like You* (Hubery 2010). Pupils can create the route Panda and Monkey took using toys or puppets to move the characters through the route. A maths trail could also be created by hiding many purple butterflies (like the ones in the story). The pupils use their toys or puppets to help find the butterflies, describing where they found them along the route. Using a story in this way encourages pupils to delve straight into the mathematical and geographical activity. They already have an understanding of the sense of place from reading the book, so personal connections have been made, thus allowing for creativity to develop naturally.

Digital trails

As the scope of technological devices increases, the potential to create digital maths trails develops. Digital trails could be in the form of a webquest whereby the teacher guides the pupils through a range of websites and games with a maths and geography focus. It is also possible to conduct a number of the trails suggested in this chapter using digital cameras or smart phones, creating instant access to data collected back in the classroom. Pupils can demonstrate creativity in their presentation of this data selecting from a host of programmes, movie makers and 'app'-makers to share their learning. Geocaching is a further way to develop digital trails (Figure 10.7). Donadelli (2014) explains that geocaching helps to develop geographical skills such as wayfinding and using compass directions. It is also highly engaging and because of its playful nature motivates even the most reluctant learners.

Most school localities will have geocaches waiting to be explored already and there are a wealth of themes that could be taken. These could include, geocaches with mathematical tasks to complete at each stop, a treasure hunt approach using a theme being studied in the classroom, pupils could decide on what to leave inside a geocache box which would help people to understand more about their school. As the geocache community continues to grow, the scope for sharing this sort of trail goes on increasing. Pupils may also want to develop their own geocache group with feeder secondary schools, or local groups. Geocache trails are an engaging transition activity in order to help KS2

■ **Figure 10.7** Geocaching motivates pupils and develops skills such as wayfinding and using compass directions
Source: photo by Giovanni Donadelli

pupils learn more about their new school environment. With each geocache found, pupils are discovering more about direction, coordinates and orientation while finding new and sometimes creative places.

Land-use surveys from trails

As part of a child's geographical experience in the primary years, opportunities should be given for enquiry into land use in the locality. The trail will involve following a predetermined route and recording different land use using a key. The main land-use categories are housing (include gardens), shops/businesses, transport, parks and farmland. When it comes to analysing the results, mathematics will come into play as pupils make graphs and interpret any numerical data they have collected. The teacher can draw out patterns and connections in an extended plenary. Displaying the work alongside photographs will demonstrate the impact of this combined mathematical and geographical learning journey.

Designing a trail

Pupils can be encouraged to design trails for their peers, younger pupils or even their parents, for a family maths day, for example. Milner and Jewson (2010: 183) suggest that 'pupils learn best when activities revolve around their own interests and concerns'. To ensure pupils understand the cross-curricular nature of the activity, in planning their trail they can complete a writing frame, which asks: 'What is the maths focus of your trail? What might you discover about the place? What geographical and mathematical skills will you need to complete your activity? How will you know if your trail was successful?

Assessment

As a teacher becomes more familiar with using trails they will find creative ways of assessing pupils. One option is to film a particular group of pupils during a trail to collect evidence of their performance. Alternatively, the pupils could watch the film as a means of self-assessment and reflect on the activity. Pupils and teachers could also take photographs while doing the trails for a maths trail scrapbook to share with other classes. This book could stay with the class as they move through the school and develop their maths trail expertise. The above examples are flexible in their design, and teacher and pupils' creativity can become the driving force for a synergy between mathematics and geography. In order to document creativity in pupils, the teacher needs to plan times to step back, observe and allow children time for originality.

OTHER APPROACHES

Geographical and mathematical stimuli can be used to engage the creative learner in more ways than can be described in this chapter; however, the following examples aim to give a sense of more creative partnerships between the two subjects.

Problem-solving

At the heart of creativity is the ability, curiosity and drive to pose questions and solve problems. Problem-solving is a key characteristic of a mathematics curriculum and it is common to find problems with a geographical context. There are plenty of opportunities for teachers to devise problems that are meaningful for children. For example, pupils could be asked to consider the following problem: 'How can we better fit everyone in the hall at lunch?' Another challenge would be to draw a plan to show how to accommodate three new pupils in your class. This would encourage pupils to reflect on the effectiveness of the classroom space, measure table and chair lengths and devise possible solutions to the problem.

Mathematics and weather

Weather is part of a child's everyday experience and can be used as a stimulus for collecting data and finding patterns, providing opportunities for cross-curricular discussions. Pupils could measure rainfall and record their data or observe patterns in cloud formations. They could design and make their own snow measuring devices or compare and contrast where mini-beasts live in different weather conditions. The creativity in these activities lies not only in the richness and variety of the stimulus but in the analysis of the data. In classrooms where year-long data is kept, pupils will begin to acquire a stronger sense and understanding of the geography of weather.

Education for sustainability

Sustainability is an important geographical concept and it involves mathematics both explicitly and implicitly. In discussing energy and water use in school, pupils are encouraged to become active members of their community and enquire into the use of lights or taps being left to run. This allows for real data to be collected and classified using mathematical strategies. In terms of encouraging sustainability, pupils could create a mathematical, sustainable garden, perhaps involving the planting of vegetables and measuring their growth, providing more scope for mathematics in the environment. Older pupils could measure the area of the garden and make plans or maps of how the area could be used effectively. Alternatively, pupils could be challenged to make recycled sculptures or use Unifix cubes to create homes for creatures living in the garden. This could be extended further by setting criteria for the area used for the homes.

World maths map

Children have an innate curiosity for patterns and places around the world and this allows the creative teacher to plan opportunities to enquire into global mathematics. Haylock and Thangata (2007: 5) write about a teacher's responsibility to open up a 'world of delight and beauty to our pupils'. Mathematics can be taught from a multicultural perspective, and thinking about the internationalism of the subject, could lead to a whole-school world mathematics display. This may include:

- examples of tessellation, polygons and non-polygons in flags;
- how numbers are written in other languages (particularly those of non-English pupils in the school);
- the world in numbers (number of countries, city populations, longest rivers, heights and distances, and so forth, displayed around a world map);
- children's own holiday photos showing maths (their own maths trails);
- maths textbooks and resources used around the world;
- famous mathematicians from across the globe;
- patterns in materials, buildings and artwork, both modern and historical; and
- significant data about the globe.

THE ROLE OF THE TEACHER – WAYS OF SEEING

This chapter has focused on (a) developing creative links between geography and mathematics and (b) finding ways to promote children's natural creativity. However, in order for the ideas presented to be brought to life, teachers need to reflect on their current practice. In what ways do they consider the curiosity they themselves have for the world, as this will impact the sense of awe and wonder they transmit in lessons? In addition, teachers need to consider the responsibility they give to their pupils to guide their own learning to allow for creativity to emerge.

CONCLUSION

Traditionally, mathematics has been seen as a 'right or wrong', passive subject, based on recall. While skill acquisition continues to be crucial, teachers are now encouraged to explore real world mathematical contexts and support pupils to apply their skills in more creative ways. The teacher plays an important role within this in terms of selecting geographical activities which allow pupils to make use of mathematics, experience the world through 'maths eyes' and supporting pupils to appreciate mathematics as a cross-curricular tool. Through using maths trails, exploring the natural environment and taking an international perspective, teachers have the chance to support their pupils to become life-long creative enquirers into mathematical spaces and places. Both geography and mathematics are driven by a desire to make sense of the world and they have a surprising amount in common.

ACKNOWLEDGEMENTS

With thanks to Patricia Mallon and Leon Hutchison, and pupils and parents at the International School of Bologna.

REFERENCES

Ashbridge, J. (2006) Is geography suitable for the foundation stage? In H. Cooper *et al.* (eds), *Geography 3–11*, pp. 115–27. London: David Fulton.

Askew, M. (2003) Word problems: Cinderellas or wicked witches? In I. Thompson (ed.), *Enhancing Primary Mathematics Teaching*, pp. 78–85. Maidenhead: Open University Press.

Barnes, J. (2010) Geography, creativity and place. In S. Scoffham (ed.), *Primary Geography Handbook*, pp. 24–33. Sheffield: Geographical Association.

Blackstone, S. and Corr, C. (2006) *My Granny Went to Market*. Oxford: Barefoot Books.

Boaler, J. (2009) *The Elephant in the Classroom*. London: Souvenir Press.

Buxton, C. (2006) Sustainable education: what's that all about and what has geography field-work got to do with it? In H. Cooper *et al.* (eds), *Geography 3–11*, pp. 49–65. London: David Fulton.

Delaney, K. (2010) Making connections: teachers and children using resources effectively. In I. Thompson (ed.), *Issues in Teaching Numeracy in Primary Schools*, pp. 72–83. Maidenhead: Open University Press.

Donadelli, G. (2014) Outdoor learning and geocaching. *Primary Geography* 85: 22.

Haylock, D. and Thangata, F. (2007) *Key Concepts in Teaching Primary Mathematics*. London: Sage.

Hubery, J. (2010) *A Friend Like You*. Battleboro, Vermont: Good Books.

Milner, A. and Jewson, T. (2010) Using the school locality. In S. Scoffham (ed.), *Primary Geography Handbook*, pp. 180–93. Sheffield: Geographical Association.

Pound, L. and Lee, T. (2015) *Teaching Mathematics Creatively*, 2nd edn. Abingdon: Routledge.

Richardson, P. (2010) Fieldwork and outdoor learning. In S. Scoffham (ed.), *Primary Geography Handbook*, pp. 134–47. Sheffield: Geographical Association.

Robinson, D. and Koshy, V. (2004) Creative mathematics: allowing caged birds to fly. In R. Fisher and M. Williams (eds), *Unlocking Creativity: Teaching across the Curriculum*, pp. 68–81. London: David Fulton.

Scoffham, S. (2017) Streetwork: investigating streets and buildings in the local area. In S. Pickering (ed.), *Teaching Out of Doors Creatively*. Abingdon: Routledge.

Voce, L. (2011) *Over in the Meadow: A Counting Rhyme*. Somerville, MA: Candlewick.

Whittle, J. (2010) Maths and geography – making connections. *Primary Mathematics* 14(2): 4–8.

Further reading

Alexander, R. (2008) *Towards Dialogic Teaching: Rethinking Classroom Talk*. Thirsk: Dialogos.

Barmby, P., Harries, T. and Higgins, S. (2010) Teaching for understanding/understanding for teaching. In I. Thompson (ed.), *Issues in Teaching Numeracy in Primary Schools*, pp. 45–57. Maidenhead: Open University Press.

Beeley, K. (2013) *50 Fantastic Ideas for Maths Outdoors*. London: Featherstone Education.

Briggs, M. and Davis, S. (2008) *Mathematics in the Early Years and Primary Classroom*. London: Routledge.

Briggs, M. (2009) Creative mathematics. In A. Wilson (ed.), *Creativity in Primary Education*, pp. 94–104. Exeter: Learning Matters.

Craft, A. (2009) Changes in the landscape for creativity in education. In A. Wilson (ed.), *Creativity in Primary Education*, pp. 5–21. Exeter: Learning Matters.

Fisher, R. (2004) Creativity across the curriculum. In R. Fisher and M. Williams (eds), *Unlocking Creativity Teaching across the Curriculum*, pp. 160–71. London: David Fulton.

Hankin, R. (2015) It all adds up! *Primary Geography* 88: 22–3.

Higgins, S. (2003) *Parlez-vous* mathematics? In I. Thompson (ed.), *Enhancing Primary Mathematics Teaching*, pp. 54–64. Maidenhead: Open University Press.

Loveless, A. (2009) Thinking about creativity: developing ideas, making things happen. In A. Wilson (ed.), *Creativity in Primary Education*, pp. 22–35. Exeter: Learning Matters.

MacNaughton, A (2015) Tut, tut, it looks like rain. *Primary Geography* 88: 19–21.

Martin, F. (2004) Creativity through geography. In R. Fisher and M. Williams (eds), *Unlocking Creativity: Teaching across the Curriculum*, pp. 117–32. London: David Fulton.

McClure, L. (2007) *Primary Project Box: KS1 Units 1 and 2*. Sheffield: Curriculum Partnership/Geographical Association.

Pike, S. (2014) Adding up the issue. *Primary Geography* 84: 10–11.

Robertson, J. (2014) *Dirty Teaching. A Beginner's Guide to Learning Outdoors*. Carmarthen: Independent Thinking Press.

Skinner, C. (2005) *Maths Outdoors*. London: BEAM.

Swan, M. (2003) Making sense of mathematics. In I. Thompson (ed.), *Enhancing Primary Mathematics Teaching*, pp. 112–24. Maidenhead: Open University Press.

Tanner, J. and Whittle, J. (2015) *The Everyday Guide to Primary Geography: Local Fieldwork*. Sheffield: Geographical Association.

Useful websites

- *How Big is Your Tree?* www.plt.org/family-activities-how-big-is-your-tree
- *Ian Thompson:* www.ianthompson.pi.dsl.pipex.com/index.htm
- *Worldometers:* www.worldometers.info
- *32 Maps That Will Teach You Something New About the World:* twistedsifter.com/2015/06/maps-that-will-teach-you-something-new-about-the-world
- *Coolmath geography games:* www.coolmath-games.com/1-geography-games
- *Kids Know It Network geography games:* www.kidsgeo.com/geography-games
- *Ordnance Survey Mapzone:* www.ordnancesurvey.co.uk/mapzone
- *The Little Big Book Club:* www.thelittlebigbookclub.com.au/sites/ thelittlebigbookclub.com.au/files/files/title_resource/granny_goes_to_market_learningtime_45_august _2013.pdf
- *Visible Thinking:* www.visiblethinkingpz.org/VisibleThinking_html_files/03_ ThinkingRoutines/03c_Core_routines/UsedToThink/UsedToThink_Routine.htm
- *The Countryside Code:* www.youtube.com/watch?v=a2x1eVLi154

JANE WHITTLE ▨ ▨ ▨ ■

- ▨   *Scale of the Universe:* www.scaleofuniverse.com
- ▨   *Geocaching:* www.geocaching.com
- ▨   *MapTools:* www.maptools.com

GEOGRAPHY AND THE CREATIVE ARTS

Julia Tanner

This chapter focuses on the role of the creative arts in geographical education in the primary school. In the first section I explore creativity in geography and the role of the creative arts in education, including their contribution to children's well-being. This leads to a discussion about how the creative arts can motivate and engage children, thereby raising achievement. In the second section I consider the implications for classroom practice and suggest a variety of practical ideas for teachers who wish to develop imaginative cross-curricular approaches. These include creative practices drawn from movement and dance, drama and role play, and visual art. The final section focuses on the exciting possibilities for using creative arts approaches to communicate the results of geographical enquiries in rich and meaningful ways.

CREATIVITY

There are many definitions of creativity, which variously emphasise that it can be seen as 'a property of people (who we are), a process (what we do), or products (what we make)' (Fisher 2004: 8). The definition that I adopt here comes from the National Advisory Committee on Creative and Cultural Education (NACCCE) who defined it as 'imaginative activity fashioned so as to yield an outcome that is of value as well as original' (NACCCE 1999: 29).

Creativity and geography

Creativity, when it is broadly conceived, has natural synergies with geography. Geography is a subject that is driven by curiosity about the world as it is now and how it might become. Good geographical learning involves an enquiry process in which children:

- ask questions,
- use a wide variety of sources to find the answers; and
- record and report their findings.

Each of these stages offers possibilities for creative rather than routine approaches, such as asking quirky and unexpected questions, seeking unusual sources to provide answers, or communicating findings through innovative, arts-based approaches.

The creative arts

There is a rich literature attesting to the value of creative and expressive arts for psychological wellbeing (Maslow 1971; Csikszentmihalyi 1992; Devlin 2010). There is also a long tradition of using art, drama, music, dance and movement in therapeutic contexts to address psychological illness and distress (Jones 2005; Warren 2008). Reviewing the evidence, Neilson, King and Baker (2015) conclude that the creative arts promote recovery from mental ill health by encouraging activity, enabling painful feelings to be addressed indirectly, fostering a sense of capability and greater self-esteem, and facilitating social interaction. Recently, with the rise of the positive psychology movement, more attention has been paid to the role of creative arts in actively promoting the positive wellbeing of individuals and communities. For example, Arts Council England (2012) contends that the value of the arts is threefold:

1   to enhance people's capacity for life by helping them to understand, interpret and adapt to the world around them;
2   to enrich people's experience, bringing colour, beauty, passion and intensity to lives; and
3   to provide a safe context for the development of skills, confidence and self-esteem.

Human societies have always used the arts for a variety of purposes. The arts can capture the beauty of nature, places or noble ideas; help us reflect on and question cultural values; unite people in public and private celebrations; express and interpret strong emotions; and bring profound pleasure and joy.

The value of the arts is manifold. While I was writing the first version of this chapter I went to an exhibition of David Hockney's innovative and magnificent new paintings. Many of them, such as 'Winter Tunnel in Snow' (see Plate A) portray ordinary country scenes. Like other people in the gallery that afternoon, my partner and I discussed the pictures at length, noticing different elements, studying the details and viewing them from various perspectives. Later I found myself noticing the beauty of the ordinary winter trees in the ordinary suburban roads in a new, more appreciative way. Hockney's pictures had enabled me see things differently and also tempted me to pick up some oil pastels to try some sketching.

The arts have the capacity to enrich and enhance our lives. They can focus our attention, provoke us to see things differently, allow for alternative interpretations, elicit unexpected responses, expose new insights, pose new questions and inspire creative thought and activity. There is a dynamic reciprocal relationship between the practical process of making art (the generative aspect of creativity) and experiencing art created by others (the evaluative aspect of creativity). In this way, existing works of art or performances can be revelatory and act as a powerful inspiration for the children's own creative work. One excellent example of this is the National Gallery's project 'Take One Picture' (see below). It is also possible for teachers and schools to create vivid and memorable learning experiences that provoke imaginative and creative responses (Figures 11.1 and 11.2).

Kinaesthetic Adventure Learning Park

Lower Fields Primary School in Bradford is a school that takes kinaesthetic leaning seriously. In September 2010 it opened its Kinaesthetic Adventure Learning Park. This is described by the school as an 'outdoor arena which can become an environment from any time or place in the universe'. It comprises a large open space enclosed by walls. At one end is an enclosed area that can be turned into different imaginary places, such as a tomb, a cottage, a coalmine or a cave. The purpose of the Learning Park is to provide direct, first-hand experiences to ensure learning is memorable, meaningful and fun. The area is used by every year group in school for one week each term.

The creative approach to learning adopted by the school is illustrated by the events that led up to the formal opening event. During the construction of the Learning Park, the contractors apparently unearthed a strange map (see Figure 11.2). This event was witnessed by a Year 4 class who, needless to say, were eager to study the map and discover its secrets. As it was a map unlike any other, this proved an exciting challenge. Later, all classes in the school speculated on the meaning of the map and on other mysterious objects – including an old manuscript recounting a fantastic legend – which have subsequently been found. At the opening event, a time traveller unexpectedly burst into the event, and children and visitors had the opportunity to discuss the map and manuscript with him. At the time of writing, 18 months later, the meaning of the map remains unknown. It is on display in the school reception area, together with some examples of children's responses to it.

As a confirmed cartophile, I can confirm that I have never seen a map like it. The more I studied it, the more details I saw, and the more mysterious it seemed. It provokes the fundamental questions we often forget to ask about maps: Where does it show? Who made it? Was it commissioned by somebody? For what purpose? Who or what was the intended audience? What is its significance? What is its value?

The location in which the map was found provokes further questions. How did it end up in a school field in Bradford? Did it somehow get lost, or thrown away, like many archaeological artefacts? Was it hidden there deliberately, and if so, why? Did whoever hid it expect to retrieve it themselves, or was someone else intended to find it, and when? Is it significant that it was discovered in 2010? Is someone seeking it? If so, why? Are their motives good or bad?

I have little doubt that this map, and the manner of its finding, will continue to excite children's interest and stimulate their critical and imaginative thinking for many years to come.

Figure 11.1 The Kinaesthetic Adventure Learning Park creates engrossing and memorable learning experiences

Young children are innately creative, with a natural tendency to fantasise, to explore their physical and social environment and to experiment with things, processes and ideas. They express these creative impulses through their desire to play, move, draw and paint, their urge to make and do and their propensity for speculating and asking questions. In the creative arts curriculum we build upon these innate tendencies by introducing children to major cultural traditions. In promoting the role of the creative arts in education, Deirdre Russell-Brown argues that:

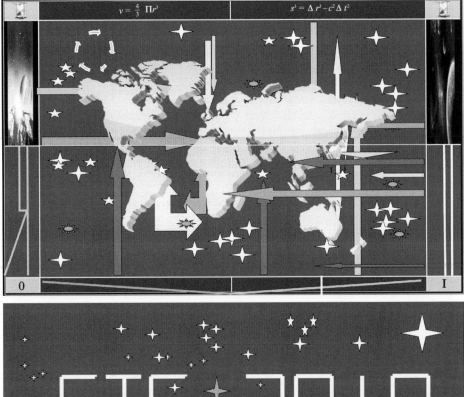

Figure 11.2 The mystery map and old manuscript that the contractors claimed to unearth when they built the park
Source: © John Edwards

Children need to experience and understand the complexity and beauty of the world of music, drama, dance and the visual arts for themselves. Being involved in the arts gives children the tools for lifelong learning within the arts so that they have the opportunity for pleasure and for self-development, creativity, self-expression, opening up a range of new experiences and opportunities they may never have known existed.
(Russell-Brown 2009: 299)

The value of creative activities for young children's development has long been championed by early childhood and progressive educators, such as Frobel, Dewey and Vygotsky. More recently, significant international reports have investigated the role of the arts in education. UNESCO (2006) contends that good-quality arts education is a key component of education. In USA, the President's Committee on the Arts and Humanities (2011) presented strong research evidence that arts teaching increases academic achievement and that integrating the arts into other subjects can dramatically improve results, particularly for 'disengaged' learners. In Britain, too, the government-commissioned Henley Review affirmed that cultural education is a 'strong influence on wider academic attainment in schools' (Henley 2012: 17). Significantly, the Cambridge Review of Primary Education (Alexander 2010) argues that creative arts are an essential element in a genuinely broad and balanced primary curriculum.

Geography and the creative arts

Geography is concerned with the study of places and environments and the interaction between people and places. The relationship between geography and the creative arts is strong and enduring. Many public sculptures are created for specific sites, often reflecting their unique qualities or what is valued in the place. Throughout history, many artists, musicians, dramatists, choreographers, novelists and poets have been inspired by places, or moved to represent them in their work. The works of art they have produced are testimony to the power of places to excite emotions and provoke responses. Furthermore, many artists and writers have imagined and fashioned powerfully evocative fictitious places with their images and words. While some of these, such as Dickens's London, are based on recognisable places, others are conceived as fantastical worlds, such as C. S. Lewis's Narnia or Escher's drawings of impossible landscapes and buildings.

In previous work, I have explored the ways in which geographical teaching and learning can contribute to children's well-being by providing opportunities for children to explore, acknowledge and express their feelings about places and geographical issues (Tanner 2010). In particular, I have drawn attention to the significance of children's attachment to places that have personal significance for them, and how this can be nurtured and fostered through meaningful first-hand learning experiences and expressed through creative activities (Tanner 2009). The wider application of the creative arts in primary geography is a fertile interface, which suggests ways to enrich, enliven and enhance geographical learning and teaching.

USING THE ARTS TO ENHANCE GEOGRAPHY

Most primary teachers appreciate the value of the creative arts in motivating and engaging children; in deepening and enriching their learning; in enabling them to express their feelings; in fostering their personal, social, emotional, cognitive and physical development; and in providing non-written modes of communication. They build on children's natural desires to move, do and make; foster holistic learning, engaging head, heart and hand; and offer thrilling possibilities for innovative cross-curricular projects. In this section, I explore some of the approaches teachers can use to exploit creatively the potential of movement and dance, drama and role play, and all forms of art in primary geography.

Movement and dance

It is said that human communication is more about body language than the words we use. The way we move, the postures we adopt and our gestures and facial expressions convey much about our feelings and thoughts. Very young children can communicate their desires and emotions effectively through non-verbal sounds and their bodies, and as they grow, they delight in their ability to move in new ways, such as running, jumping and skipping.

In primary education, we build upon children's innate desire to move and experiment with their bodies through movement, mime and dance. These provide opportunities for children to explore the potential of their bodies for expressing feelings and communicating with others. They can experiment with using movement to express emotions, capture a mood, represent an idea or tell a story.

There is much potential for using movement, mime and dance to deepen and enhance children's understanding of physical geography. The processes that shape the land often work over very long time-frames (such as river valley formation), which cannot be directly observed (for example, the build-up of pressure before a volcanic eruption). Children can use dance/movement to explore, represent and communicate physical geography processes such as:

▦ the journey of a pebble from a stream spring along a river course (via waterfalls, rapids, meanders and lakes in times of low and high flow) to the estuary;
▦ the movement of the waves on a beach, in calm and stormy weather;
▦ the violence of volcanic eruptions and earthquakes; and
▦ a hurricane or tsunami crossing the ocean and hitting land.

In human geography, movement or dance can be used to explore the idea that our environment may affect how we feel, to try to imagine ourselves in other places or in 'other people's shoes'. Some ideas include:

DEVISING PLACE 'FREEZE-FRAMES'

Invite the children to imagine a familiar place, such as the playground, in different sorts of weather (e.g. a hot sunny day, a very blustery day, a snowy day) and to experiment with moving as appropriate. Use 'freeze-frame' to capture the stance, and ask children to say how they feel in this pose. Discuss the impact of the different types of weather on how they move and feel.

IMAGINING UNFAMILIAR PLACES

A similar approach can be used to help children imagine themselves in an unfamiliar place, provided you have an evocative stimulus (e.g. a picture-book, a painting of a landscape, a piece of music) with a strong sense of place as a starting point. Ask the children to imagine themselves transported to that place. What can they see, hear, smell? Invite them to start moving, exploring the place. How do they feel, finding themselves in this place?

MAKING DANCES FROM PAINTINGS

The previous activity could be developed into a more collective piece, focusing on the social interaction between people in the place. Artworks that depict highly peopled landscapes, such as Breugel's winter landscapes or Lowry's industrial townscapes, can be an excellent stimulus for this. Careful study of the picture will reveal people engaged in all sorts of activities, and the children can experiment with holding their stances and then creating a movement or dance piece that conveys the mood of the picture, or develops a story that takes place there.

MIMING JOURNEYS FROM PICTURE-BOOKS

Many story- and picture-books for young children involve journeys, which can be mimed to imagine the experience of moving in or travelling through different sorts of environments. Well-loved examples include *We're Going on a Bear Hunt* (Rosen and Oxenbury 1993), *Rosie's Walk* (Hutchins 2009) and many traditional stories.

TRADITIONAL DANCES FROM OVERSEAS

It may be possible for children to work with a creative practitioner to learn and recreate the traditional dances or music of places they are studying as overseas localities. Such activities are excellent motivators and can lead to valuable new learning as long as stereotypes and post-colonial images are avoided.

Drama and role play

Drama presents extensive possibilities for exploring the nature of places and people's responses to them, including the conflicts and tensions associated with environmental challenges. Some of the best dramas involve discovering the unknown rather than acting out what has already been decided. Cremin (2015: 26) argues that drama gives children the opportunity to engage with fictional situations and investigate the issues within them before returning to the real world with more understanding and insight. In delineating what she calls the 'primary drama continuum', Cremin points out that drama encompasses a very wide range of activities from the informal (e.g. playground games, small-world play and puppetry) to more formal events (e.g. school performances and theatre outings). As she points out, most of these activities trigger children's imaginative involvement, offering rich opportunities to explore different possibilities and perspectives. Many common drama activities identified on the primary drama continuum could be harnessed to enhance and extend geographical learning.

SMALL WORLD MODELS

Younger children may enjoy creating their own version of real places such as towns, parks, farms or zoos, or fantasy worlds with small-world equipment, and playing out different scenarios with people and animal figures.

ROLE PLAY

Role-play areas can be created to represent significant aspects of common geographical topics, such as an estate agent's office (houses and homes), a local TV studio (change in the local area), a school/home/shop (overseas locality) or an environmental campaign office (rainforests).

ANIMAL PUPPETS

Animal puppets or masks can be used to support exploration of issues of animal habitats, perhaps based on a storybook such as *We All Went on a Safari* (Crebs 2003), *Backyard Bear* (Rockwell 2006) or *The Crocodile Who Didn't Like Water* (Merino 2013). Puppets and masks can serve as helpful 'props', enabling children to embody alternative personas and explore scenarios from different perspectives.

IMPROVISED OR 'PROCESS' DRAMAS

Improvised classroom drama, individually, in groups, or with the whole class and teacher in role, provides many opportunities for children to use their imaginations, consider situations, exchange ideas, try alternative perspectives and envision and rehearse possibilities. Improvised drama is commonly used in conjunction with fiction, which, typically, contains many moments of tension (e.g. conflict, misunderstandings and dilemmas), which can be explored through common drama conventions such as tableaux, thought-tracking, hot-seating, freeze-frame or improvised flashback/flash-forward. These techniques can be deployed to help children explore how they think and feel about the issue when they are in character, and the consequences of their thoughts and feelings.

DEBATES OR SIMULATIONS

With careful use of resources and detailed preparation to build belief in the scenario, role play or simulation can be used to debate a controversial issue. Examples include plans to redevelop derelict sites, building a supermarket on open land or creating a new wildlife area. You could collect information giving different perspectives from newspaper cuttings, campaign group leaflets or your local government planning department. Pupils could then adopt different roles, design campaign materials and prepare for a simulated TV studio discussion with the teacher in role as the presenter of the programme, inviting contributions from interested parties and the audience.

FIELD VISITS

Field visits to locations with a strong sense of place can offer powerful stimuli for drama activities. Many National Trust and English Heritage properties have education programmes that include place-specific role-play activities, but your local open spaces or woodland or derelict sites could also prove fruitful locations for exploring geographical issues through drama.

The visual arts

The visual arts offer numerous opportunities for exciting geographical and cross-curricular work. We live in an environment saturated with visual images such as photographs, diagrams, pictures and maps, and as Sara Lipati points out, children often possess very high levels of unconscious and unacknowledged visual literacy (Lipati 2004: 133). Visual literacy is the ability to interpret, negotiate and make meaning from information presented in the form of an image. The concept is based on the idea that images can be 'read' and that meaning can be communicated through visual media. The practical implication of this is that children are highly skilled in decoding visual clues, and, as Lipati illustrates, well able to discuss the meaning of images they encounter.

The emphasis on images in geography offers rich opportunities for children to develop skills in critical visual literacy. These include adopting a critical approach in interpreting, negotiating and making meaning from images, and understanding that all images are created/constructed and selected, often with a particular purpose and/or audience in mind (Tanner 2012). Questions about the creation of an image include: Who created this image? What was their purpose in creating it? What audience did they have in mind? Were they trying to provoke a particular response, such as awe and wonder, sympathy, or anger? Questions about the interpretation of an image include issues of response and meaning: What do I see when I look at this image? What do others see? How do I feel when I look at this image? How do others feel? What does it mean?

Artists working in all media have been inspired by the world around them to try to represent particular places, or to capture their sense of place. They have produced drawings, paintings, prints, photographs, collages, embroideries, banners, ceramics, models, sculptures and, more recently, digital images. Primary school children can experiment with all these materials and processes in exploring the relationship between landscape and people, and its representation. Mackintosh and Kent (2014) offer numerous ideas for using a wide variety of art forms to develop pupils' geographical thinking, knowledge, understanding, and to extend their geographical skills.

Special places

Ask the children to think about a place that is special to them, and to create a sketch or painting of the place. Invite individuals to talk about their place, saying why it is special. Discuss the sorts of things that make places special, and explore the range of emotions that special places can invoke.

CAPTURING A SENSE OF PLACE

Visit somewhere with a strong or dramatic sense of place (for example, an old or religious building, clifftops, a local forest, a wild space, a historic townscape) and focus on experiencing it with all the senses, and on talking about how the children feel in this place. Discuss the emotions they experience. Use this as a stimulus for individual or collective art work that captures the spirit of the place, such as a mural, wall hanging or clay frieze (Figure 11.3). Tanner and Whittle (2015) provide many suggestions for developing creative activities in exploring and investigating a range of places in the school grounds and local area.

■ **Figure 11.3** Making a model of Tower Bridge
Source: photo by Paul Owens

PHOTOMONTAGE

Ask children to take surprising/unexpected/quirky photographs of places around the school and grounds, or the local area, and create a photomontage.

LOCAL ARTISTS

Use the internet or local contacts to identify artists or photographers who create images of the local area, and invite the children to consider their work. Discuss why they may have chosen the particular sites to illustrate or represent. If possible, invite the artists into school to discuss their work. If you have the opportunity to work with a creative artist in school, consider the possibility of working with a place/geographical theme, perhaps celebrating the unique features of the local area.

ENVIRONMENTAL ART

Look at images of environmental art (e.g. Andy Goldsworthy) and use found materials such as stones, sticks, leaves or litter to create environmental art in the school grounds or a local open space. Invite the children to consider how it feels to create art that is temporary, and may be altered by the weather or the actions of others.

MODELLING

Older primary children may appreciate the opportunity to the use small-world equipment usually found in Foundation Stage or Key Stage 1 classrooms to create a model of a proposed development, or to envision how the world might be if, for example, their community committed itself to halving its carbon footprint.

IMPROVEMENT PROJECTS

Plan and undertake an environmental improvement project that involves the creative arts, such as creating an embroidered wall-hanging for the school hall, a mural for the playground, a storytelling chair or an open-air theatre in the school grounds, or get involved in local community arts environmental projects.

RESPONDING TO PAINTINGS

Study a picture depicting a landscape. Ask the children how they feel when they look at the picture. Can they guess how the artist felt about the place? Do they know any places that make them feel like this? Create pictures in the style of the artist/picture.

COMPARING LANDSCAPES

Compare landscape pictures of the same sort of environment (rural, urban, coastal) by different artists and notice the geographical features they show. Discuss the differing ways the artists represent the similar features, e.g. cliffs, stormy seas, clouds, trees and buildings. Which do the children find most appealing, most accurate or most effective at conveying what it might be like to be there? Provide opportunities for the children to experiment with creating their own pictures incorporating landscape features.

TAKE ONE PICTURE

This excellent National Gallery project offers many stimulating ideas for using individual pictures, including several landscapes, as the stimulus for cross-curricular work. Many of the ideas could be used to investigate and compare the different regions and countries of United Kingdom (England, Wales, Scotland and Northern Ireland) as well as the wider world. Internet searches will reveal details of relevant works to complement local and distant locality studies (e.g. famous Welsh landscape artists, images of rainforest). Figure 11.4 lists some artists whose work has a strong sense of place, which could be used to explore a variety of different aesthetic and geographical issues.

THE POTENTIAL OF STORY

High quality picture, story and fiction books have enormous potential as a stimulus for cross-curricular work in the primary classroom and to support intercultural understanding (Dolan 2014). Many children's books convey a strong sense of place, transporting children to unfamiliar or unimagined environments, or explore geographical themes such weather, journeys, or sustainable development. Many of the ideas for learning activities in this chapter can be used in conjunction with picture or story books. For an extensive list of suitable books, organised by age range and geographical theme, see Tanner and Whittle (2013).

COMMUNICATING THROUGH THE ARTS

This final section explores the communicative power of the creative arts. In developing my thinking on this topic I have drawn on the long tradition in arts practice of working

Visual artists who convey a strong sense of place

Pieter Breugel the Elder – highly peopled sixteenth-century Flemish rural scenes
John Constable – early nineteenth-century East Anglian rural landscapes
Canaletto – highly detailed architectural paintings of eighteenth-century Venice and London
MC Escher – fantastical geometrically 'impossible' buildings
David Hockney – bold and colourful contemporary images of California and east Yorkshire
Edward Hopper – early/mid-twentieth-century (mostly urban) USA townscapes
Thomas Gainsborough – eighteenth-century English rural landscapes
LS Lowry – early twentieth-century northern English cityscapes
Claude Monet – nineteenth-/twentieth-century French impressionist paintings of outdoor scenes
Marianne North – nineteenth-century rural botanical landscapes of the Americas and Far East
Henri Rousseau – French post-Impressionist, exotic jungle scenes
WilliamTurner – early nineteenth-century impressionistic British landscapes
Vincent van Gogh – Post-Impressionist, later nineteenth-century Dutch and French landscapes

▨ **Figure 11.4** Artists whose paintings have influenced our perceptions of places

across different art forms, and the concept of 'remodelling' developed by the Exeter Extending Literacy Project (EXIT). Among many stimulating ideas for supporting children in reading and writing non-fiction, Wray and Lewis (1997) suggest a wide range of activities to promote interactive reading, which, in a geographical context, can be applied to the full range of resources commonly used, such as books, maps, diagrams, websites, photographs and artefacts. Remodelling activities require children to restructure information from one format or genre to another, such as using prose text in an information book to produce a grid, diagram or board game. The extensive text-restructuring list of possible formats offered by Wray and Lewis involves mostly verbal and/or graphic forms, but I believe there is enormous potential in working with the freer, more creative approaches that the arts offer.

In a seminal work on the nature of creativity, Koestler (1964) argued that originality, discovery or creativity occurs through the dynamic interaction of discrete frames of reference. In Figure 11.5, I have experimented with this idea in the application of the creative arts to authentic geographical enquiries. I have listed possible learning activities drawn from creative arts practice, and some ways in which these can be presented and used to communicate with real audiences.

Re-modelling offers many possibilities. Could children transform the information in standard geographical resources such as maps, photographs, information books, websites, field data, and photographs, into a puppet show, a mime or an art exhibition? Could their response to new experiences on a residential field trip be expressed in a handmade memory book, an installation in a corner of the school hall or a rap performance? Could the outcome of a study of some threatened local woodland be an environmental art trail, a piece of street theatre, a textile collage, an art exhibition or a multimedia presentation? The arts are a powerful vehicle for presenting complex emotions and ideas, and, given

Possible approaches	Possible outcomes	Possible audiences
Movement	Dance performances	Peers in the class
Mime	Drama performances	Peers in the year group
Dance	Poetry performances	Older children
Sculpts	Simulated events	Younger children
Role play	Puppet shows	School Council
Improvisation	Playmats	Class teacher
Puppetry	Art exhibitions	Other teachers
Masks	Handmade picture-books	Head teacher
Drama performance	Photography exhibitions	Pupils in other local
Mark-making	Sculpture exhibitions	schools
Paper craft/bookmaking	Exhibition of models	Pupils in twinned school
Drawing	Installations	Parents and carers
Painting	Sculpture trails	Governors
Printing	Poetry trails	Members of local
Photographs	Environmental	community
Collage	improvements	Local community groups
Textile art/embroidery	Environmental art trails	Local councillors
Sculpture	Published storybooks	Local planning officers
Modelling	Published poetry books	National politicians
Clay work	Campaigns	
Installations	Websites	
Environmental art	Multimedia presentations	
Poetry and raps		
Stories		
Posters and leaflets		
Maps and diagrams		
Animation		
Video		

■ **Figure 11.5** Some opportunities for applying creative arts approaches in authentic geographical learning experiences

encouragement and appropriate resources, primary aged children are likely to generate plenty of imaginative ideas for themselves.

CONCLUSION

As noted earlier, many reports attest to the value of comprehensive creative arts provision in the development of children and young people. The benefits for wider society and for economic growth have also been well documented in national and international reports (Winner *et al*. 2013; UNESCO 2013; Arts Council England 2014; Warwick Commission 2015). A recent British Government policy statement argued that:

> Arts and culture strengthen communities, bringing people together and removing social barriers. Involving young people in the arts increases their academic performance, encourages creativity, and supports talent early on.
>
> (DCMS/DfE 2013: 1)

For this potential to be realised, children need opportunities for experiencing and working with the arts across the whole primary curriculum. In this chapter, I have explored the specific opportunities offered by primary geography, focusing on how movement and dance, drama and role play, and visual and 3D art can be used:

▨ to enhance children's learning about places, physical and human geography and environmental issues by providing approaches that deepen understanding;
▨ to enrich and enliven geographical topics by extending their scope through creative cross-curricular approaches; and
▨ to convey the outcomes of geographical learning in novel and engaging ways.

I believe that the creative arts have much to offer primary geography and hope that the ideas in this chapter will inspire you to adopt creative approaches in devising exciting and meaningful learning experiences for the children you teach.

ACKNOWLEDGEMENT

Many thanks go to John Edwards, Head Teacher of Lower Fields Primary School, who had the vision and drive to create the Kinaesthetic Adventure Learning Park.

REFERENCES AND FURTHER READING

Alexander, R. (2009) What is primary education for? *Times Education Supplement* (20 February). Available at www.tes.com/article.aspx?storycode=6008992 (accessed 17 April 2016).

Alexander, R. (ed.) (2010) *Children, Their World, Their Education*. London: Routledge.

Arts Council England (2005) *Children, Young People and the Arts*. London: Arts Council England.

Arts Council England (2012) *Be Creative, Be Well*. London: Arts Council England.

Arts Council England (2014) *The Value of Arts and Culture to People and Society: An Evidence Review*. Manchester: Arts Council England.

Boniwell, I. (2008) *Positive Psychology in a Nutshell*. London: Personal Well-being Centre.

Carr, A. (2005) *Positive Psychology*. London: Brunner-Routledge.

Catling, S. (2009) Creativity in primary geography. In A. Wilson (2009), *Creativity in Primary Education*, pp. 189–98. Exeter: Learning Matters.

Craft, A., Jeffrey, B. and Leibling, M. (eds) (2001) *Creativity in Education*. London: Continuum.

Crebs, L. (2003) *We All Went on a Safari*. Oxford: Barefoot Books.

Cremin, T. (2015) (2nd edn) *Teaching English Creatively*. London: Routledge.

Csikszentmihalyi, M. (1992) *Flow: The Psychology of Happiness*. London: Rider.

DCMS/DfE (2013) *2010 to 2015 Government Policy: Arts and Culture*. Available at www.gov.uk/government/publications/2010-to-2015-government-policy-arts-and-culture (accessed 13 January 2016).

Devlin, P. (2010) *Restoring the Balance: The Effect of Arts Participation on Wellbeing and Health*. Newcastle-Upon-Tyne: Voluntary Arts Network.

Dolan, A. (2014) *You, Me and Diversity: Picture Books for Teaching Development and Intercultural Education*. Stoke on Trent: Trentham Books.

Fisher, R. (2004) What is creativity? In R. Fisher and M. Williams (eds), *Unlocking Creativity: Teaching Across the Curriculum*, pp. 6–20. London: David Fulton.

Henley, D. (2012) *Cultural Education in England*. London: DCMS.

Hutchins, P. (2009) *Rosie's Walk*. New York: Aladdin.

Jones, P. (2005) *The Arts Therapies: A Revolution in Health Care.* London: Brunner-Routledge.

Koestler, A. (1964) *The Act of Creation.* London: Hutchinson.

Levine, S. K. and Levine, E. G. (eds) (1999) *Foundations of Expressive Arts Therapy: Theoretical and Clinical Perspectives.* London: Jessica Kingsley.

Lipati, S. (2004) Creativity in music and art. In R. Fisher and M. Williams (eds), *Unlocking Creativity: Teaching Across the Curriculum*, pp. 133–49. London: David Fulton.

Mackintosh, M. (2003) The art of geography. *Primary Geographer* 49: 36–37.

Mackintosh, M. and Kent, G. (2014) *The Everyday Guide to Primary Geography: Art.* Sheffield: Geographical Association.

Martin, F. (2004) Creativity through geography. In R. Fisher and M. Williams (eds), *Unlocking Creativity: Teaching Across the Curriculum*, pp. 117–32. London: David Fulton.

Maslow, A. H. (1971) *The Farther Reaches of Human Nature.* Harmondsworth: Penguin.

Merino, M. (2013) *The Crocodile Who Didn't Like Water.* Zurich: NorthSouth

NACCCE (1999) *All Our Futures: Creativity, Culture and Education.* London: DfEE.

Neilson, P., King, R. and Baker, F. (eds) (2015) *Creative Arts in Counselling and Mental Health.* London: Sage.

Ofsted (2010) *Creative Approaches that Raise Standards.* London: Ofsted.

President's Committee on the Arts and Humanities (2011) *Reinvesting in Arts Education*: *Winning America's Future through Creative Schools.* Washington, DC: President's Committee on the Arts and Humanities.

QCA (2005) *Creativity: Find It! Promote It! Promoting Pupils' Creative Thinking and Behaviour Across the Curriculum at Key Stages 1, 2, and 3.* London: QCA.

Robinson, K. (2011) *Out of Our Minds: Learning to be creative.* Chichester: Capstone.

Rockwell, A. (2006) *Backyard Bear.* New York: Walker & Company

Rosen, M. and Oxenbury, H. (1993) *We're Going on a Bear Hunt.* London: Walker Books.

Russell-Brown, D. (2009) Learning to teach the creative arts in primary schools through community engagement. *International Journal of Teaching and Learning in Higher Education* 20(2): 298–306.

Snyder, C. R. and Lopez, S. J. (2002) *Handbook of Positive Psychology.* New York: Oxford University Press.

Tanner, J. (2009) Special places: place attachment and children's happiness. *Primary Geographer* 68: 5–9.

Tanner, J. (2010) Geography and emotional intelligence. In S. Scoffham (ed.), *Primary Geography Handbook*, pp. 34–47. Sheffield: Geographical Association.

Tanner, J. (2012) How do you see it? Using geographical images to promote meaningful talk. *Primary Geography* 78: 22–3.

Tanner, J. and Whittle, J. (2013) *The Everyday Guide to Primary Geography: Story.* Sheffield: Geographical Association.

Tanner, J. and Whittle, J. (2015) *The Everyday Guide to Primary Geography: Local Fieldwork.* Sheffield: Geographical Association.

UNESCO (2006) World Conference on Arts Education. Available at http://portal.unesco.org/culture/en/ev.php-URL_ID=9485&URL_DO=DO_PRINT-PAGE&URL_SECTION=201.html (accessed 17 April 2016).

UNESCO (2013) *United Nations Creative Economy Report 2013: Special Edition Widening Local Development Pathways.* Paris: UNESCO. Available at www.unesco.org/culture/pdf/creative- economy-report-2013.pdf (accessed 13 January 2016).

Warren, B. (ed.) (2008) *Using the Creative Arts in Therapy and Health Care: A Practical Introduction.* London: Sage.

Warwick Commission (2015) *Enriching Britain: Culture, Creativity and Growth: The 2015 Report by the Warwick Commission on the Future of Cultural Value.* Warwick: University of Warwick.

Wilson, A. (ed.) (2005) *Creativity in Primary Education*. Exeter: Learning Matters.
Winner, E., T. Goldstein and Vincent-Lancrin, S. (2013) *Art for Art's Sake?* Paris: OECD Publishing.
Wray, D. and Lewis, M. (1997) *Extending Literacy: Children Reading and Writing Nonfiction*. London: Routledge.

Websites

▨ *Cultural Learning Alliance:* www.culturallearningalliance.org.uk/manifesto
▨ *Government policy for arts and culture 2010–15:* www.gov.uk/government/publications/2010-to-2015-government-policy-arts-and-culture
▨ *Take One Picture:* www.takeonepicture.org

CHAPTER 12

GEOGRAPHY AND MUSIC
A creative harmony

Arthur J. Kelly

This chapter starts by discussing the relationship between music and geography. It draws, in particular, on literature relating to cultural geography, which, over recent decades, has shifted attention towards social relations (Johansson and Bell 2007). It moves on to discuss the relationship between music, memory and geographical learning, focusing on the role of the affective domain, imagination and emotion. An ethnographic approach (Martin 2008), where music is employed to engage with pupils' geographical imaginations (Massey 2005) through dialogic teaching (Alexander 2008), is advocated. It is argued that such a strategy could empower teachers to become architects of a more relevant, inclusive and creative curriculum, ensuring that a diverse range of needs are challenged and catered for. The chapter concludes by outlining a range of practical ideas that teachers can use with their pupils to develop geographical knowledge, understanding and skills. There are also suggestions for further activities, such as creating music in response to place.

OVERTURE

> Music is by nature geographical.
>
> (Connell and Gibson 2003: 280)

The word 'music' derives from the ancient Greek *mousike*, art of the muse, the muses being the goddesses who inspired creative practices. This chapter outlines the creative synergy between geography and music. This synergy has the potential to create high-quality, meaningful, enjoyable and memorable learning experiences across the primary age phase at the same time as providing teachers with insights into contemporary geographical understandings. It is argued that the use of music as a cultural artefact can be a springboard for two different aspects of creativity: (a) teaching creatively; and (b) teaching for creativity and provide an exciting stimulus for enquiry based teaching and learning.

GEOGRAPHY AND MUSIC

> One might wonder what geography can say about music and vice versa.
>
> (Crang 1998: 89)

There is a well-developed academic interest in how music is geographical and Johansson and Bell (2007) provides a range of examples. Studies include the way music is linked to space and place, how music has geographical roots and the routes music takes around the world. While definitions of culture are diverse and complex, the importance of place and identity, the relationships between the local and the global and the links between culture and economy have all been explored from a geographical standpoint (Mitchell 2000). The following paragraphs provide a brief overview of some relevant literature, situated within the field of cultural geography.

Music is an aspect of culture that has been studied by geographers. A range of themes have been explored including:

- music and the production of space and place (e.g. Connell and Gibson 2003);
- the role of music in the structuring of community and identity (e.g. Whiteley *et al.* 2005); and
- the links between music and geographies of emotion (e.g. Wood and Smith 2004).

Much of this work is concerned within an exploration of 'popular' music as a cultural artefact, but, as will be seen below, this does not preclude the use of other musical genres in teaching and learning geography. Three interrelated areas are of particular relevance to the primary context and are now explored in more detail: (a) music and place; (b) music and identity; and (c) music, emotion and the geographical imagination.

Music and place

Place is a fundamental geographical concept and has been described by Matthews and Herbert (2004) as a 'unifying bond' that links disparate studies, particularly in human geography. Understanding the relationship between place and music can deepen our understanding of the concept. As Matthews and Herbert explain:

> The unique quality of place is that it goes beyond the objective and has affective meanings … Place catches the very basis of the geography around which we build our lives.
>
> (Matthews and Herbert 2004: 165)

Identity and belonging are central to our concept of place, as are meaning and experience. Furthermore, Connell and Gibson (2003) suggest that auditory media, such as music, are involved in the generation and articulation of *narratives* about place. They contend that many everyday understandings about place are mediated through popular music.

Music is rooted in culture, which is traditionally linked to place. This relationship is often expressed through musical styles and genres that include Mersey beat, 'Jamaican' reggae, 'Irish' music, New Orleans jazz, Chicago blues, and so forth. The symbolic representation of place is also evident in western classical traditions; for example, Rodrigo's *Concierto de Aranjuez* is a musical articulation of the town and landscape of Aranjuez in Spain. Additionally, the relationship between music and place may be apparent in the lyrics. At a simplistic level, this takes the form of 'name-checking' particular locations, as in songs such as 'New York, New York', 'The Leaving of Liverpool' and 'Carrickfergus'. The use of place names in song may also contribute to the construction of images of the place. Frank Sinatra created his idea of New York from a fusion of words and music. Paul

Simon has given us the image of the Mississippi delta 'shining like a national guitar'. Meanwhile, Bruce Springsteen has constructed a particular notion of blue-collar America (Figure 12.1).

Geographers have long recognised that the nature of place is both multifaceted and contested. Some of these complexities can be highlighted by examining the relationship between music and geography. Cohen (1995) reminds us that the production of place through music has always been a political and contested process and that music is implicated in the struggle for identity and belonging. Music may also link us to past places as well as where we are now in an almost Flaubertian manner. As she puts it, 'many people maintain a link with their past through attachment to specific places and music is often used to remember such places' (*ibid.*: 437). Many of us share the experience of hearing particular pieces of music or songs and being transported to particular places (and people) in our past. In addition, music may also transport us to places we have never been to or places in our geographical imaginings.

Music and identity

There is no doubt that music – in both its production and consumption – can be an important influence in shaping the typically hybrid identities of people and places, of engendering a sense of place and deep attachment to place.

(Hudson 2006: 633)

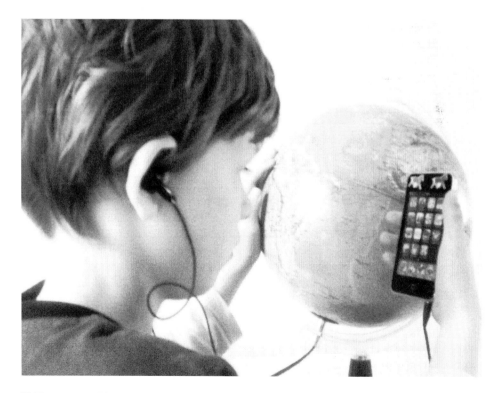

■ **Figure 12.1** Music is linked to place at a profound level

There have been a number of studies that explore the relationship between music and identity. This relationship operates on a range of scales – individual, community, regional and national. Taking a biographical approach, Cohen (1995) provides a case study of the relationship between music, place and identity, which illustrates its multifaceted nature. Stokes (1997) suggests that identity can be influenced through listening to, performing, dancing to and even thinking about music. Music, he suggests, can be the prison bars or the key to freedom. Many teenagers have gained freedom from their parents' world through discovering 'their' music, which then plays a part in establishing their identity. As a parent of two teenage children I see this unfolding at first hand as lines are drawn between *their* music and *mine*. Music plays a role in production of distinct cultural identities within which individual identities may be framed. Leonard (2005) examines how music and dance are used to construct an Irish 'cultural identity' by second- and third-generation Irish immigrants living in Coventry and Liverpool. Her research suggests that the role of music as a connective tissue among diaspora populations is important in establishing a collective identity and shared sense of community. Other displaced groups such as Jamaicans and Africans use music in similar ways to maintain their links with their country of origin. It is also recognised that the cultural heritage of the homeland can become fossilised as it travels through time and space, thus losing its dynamism and fluidity and that these constructions of community and the past form a series of overlapping and competing narratives (Bennett 2005).

There are many examples of the role music plays in confirming ethnicity and regional and national identities (see Baily 1994 and Mach 1994). Bennett (2005) also points out that music can be particularly important in times of war and national crisis: Vera Lynn's 'White Cliffs of Dover' and Elvis Costello's 'Shipbuilding' provide different temporal and political examples. Interestingly, the hymn 'Nkosi Sikelel'i Afrika' changed from being an act of political defiance against apartheid to being part of the South African national anthem. The way it mixes languages and forms is designed to attempt to reflect the plurality of the 'rainbow nation'.

Music, emotion and the geographical imagination

> It is probably now well accepted, though it is still important to argue, that a lot of our geography is in the mind.
>
> (Massey 2005: 48)

Emotion and imagination are recognised as having a role in geography (see Davidson and Milligan 2004). There is a growing appreciation that our emotions influence how we engage with the world, and that emotional ways of knowing enable us to form unique personal geographies. This interest in emotional geographies is relevant across a range of themes and scales, from the emotional aspects of social life in the city to the role of emotion in building our sense of identity and nationalism. Wood and Smith (2004) explore the relationship between music and geographies of emotion, making interesting links between music, emotion, well-being and quality of life that echo the links between creativity and well-being. They point out that part of the power of music is that it expresses a range of emotions that we cannot rationalise. In this way it 'communicates something which tells us who people are, what has happened to them, where they are going, why and how' (*ibid.*: 544).

The complexity of how and why music evokes emotion has been the subject of extensive research by music scientists. While there seems to be a broad consensus that most people are moved by music, we need to be careful of attributing a simple cause-and effect relationship. Ball (2010) reminds us that rather than being passive recipients of music, we construct our own interpretations. It has the ability to evoke memories that may be either personal or communal, and that lie outside the music itself.

THE POWER OF MUSIC

> Understanding why we like music and what draws us to it is a window on the essence of human nature.
>
> (Levitin 2008: 7)

Music is a powerful form of communication, which is universal across human cultures and seems to be related to basic human needs and expression. It can provide a deep response at an individual level but also acts as a glue that binds us together. Levitin (2008: 11) describes it as 'the most beautiful human obsession'.

There is a significant body of research rooted in neuropsychology and music cognition, which explores the relationship between music and the human brain. Levitin (*ibid.*) points out that listening to music involves the oldest and newest parts of the brain as well as prediction and emotional reward systems. There is a logical structure to music but the affective element is also important and the links to memory are clear. As Levitin puts it, 'when we love a piece of music, it reminds us of other music we have heard, and it activates memory traces of emotional times in our lives' (*ibid.*: 192).

Ball (2010) provides an overview of how our minds respond to and come to understand music, and provides evidence to support the claim that music is 'part of what we are and how we perceive the world' (*ibid.*: 31). MRI scans suggest that listening to music is an integrative activity that links left and right brain areas, utilises cognitive and emotional systems, and engages both the heart and the mind. This may be contrasted with the brain areas to do with language, which seem to be more strongly lateralised. Ball contends that, as a stimulus, music is like a 'gymnasium of the mind' and plays a key role in development, cognition, education and socialisation. This means it appeals to pupils whatever their level of ability.

Film directors and advertising executives utilise the power of music to influence our emotional responses and buying preferences. Both are aware of the power music has to influence us, from the creation of catchy jingles to the use of a wide range of music to create mood. Educators, too, should be taking the power of music more seriously and using it to promote interest and engagement. Studies suggest that in listening to music the brain is far from passive. It is involved in seeking patterns, looking for clues, unpacking sensory data, accessing old stories and constructing new ones. Even if the music appears to be 'aural wallpaper', brain activity is still stimulated.

DIALOGIC ETHNOGRAPHY

> Dialogue is the antithesis of a state theory of learning, and its antidote.
>
> (Alexander 2010: 307)

The past twenty five years has taught us that curriculum is mutable, with a premium being placed on core knowledge in the current curriculum (DfE 2013), which in geography is reflected in locational knowledge. However, the curriculum forms the landscape of teaching and learning while pedagogy is its geology and it is argued here that a curriculum built upon the enquiry process and embracing what is termed 'dialogic ethnography' would have a robust pedagogical base and be exciting, stimulating and relevant.

Martin (2008) argues that teachers often fail to realise that geography is part of everyday life. One of the results is that they are reluctant to engage in creative practices. However, contemporary constructions of both music and geography emphasise the relevance of real-world experience. Also, as previously discussed, music is a cultural form, which interests, stimulates and engages most people. This fits in with the new paradigm that Martin (2008) proposes for primary geography. As Martin argued in an earlier piece:

> There is … a real need to re-connect people with the subject in ways that recognise what their starting points might be … Everyday geography means … connecting the knowledge that teachers and pupils bring with them from their daily experiences to the knowledge and ways of understanding that geographers have developed over the years.
>
> (Martin 2006: 5)

This argument places an emphasis on children's everyday worlds and experiences and embodies and ethnographic approach. This can potentially mitigate against a curriculum that distances pupils from their interests and opts instead for comfortable topics based around safe questions and safe answers (Catling 2005). This dislocation could be ameliorated by creative approaches, such as the integration of music and geography, which are child-centred and involve an appreciation and celebration of personal geographies (Kelly 2009). These approaches also empower teachers as decision makers to become curriculum makers and design learning experiences that are relevant to their pupils' needs.

This approach can easily be linked to the enquiry process. The basis of the enquiry process is that pupils should be supported in asking geographical questions, which develop geographical knowledge, understanding and skills. The nature of these questions may vary from the generic to the specific. The power of a questioning approach is that it recognises that geographical knowledge is dynamic rather than static. As, Roberts (2013: 17–18) reminds us, 'geographical knowledge is a construction rather than something "out there" to be found … It is formed by the questions and imagination that geographers bring to the task.'

Within the ethnographic model, the relationship between teacher and learner is characterised by dialogue and co-construction rather than monologue and delivery. Alexander (2008) has championed dialogic teaching. He declares, 'dialogic teaching harnesses the power of talk to engage children, stimulate and extend their thinking, and advance their learning and understanding' (*ibid.*: 37). Martin (2008) takes the notion of dialogue to a higher level by suggesting that the curriculum should be designed to harness the dialectical relationship between children's everyday geographies and the academic discipline. It is suggested here that the use of music as a stimulus for dialogic enquiries into children's lived geographies is an exemplification of this process.

INCLUSIVE GEOGRAPHIES

This creative approach may also lead to more inclusive teaching practices which potentially can engage all pupils including those identified as having Special Educational

Needs and Disabilities (SEND), English as an Additional Language (EAL) and those from minority ethnic backgrounds. It is now accepted that to make lessons inclusive, teachers need to consider potential barriers to learning for particular groups. In terms of SEND there is a wealth of literature outlining the potential of music to stimulate, engage and support learning for pupils with a range of needs (see Corke 2002; Ott 2011; Hammel and Hourigan 2011). While these texts offer advice regarding teaching music as a distinct subject to SEND pupils much of this is of relevance to teaching geography and music creatively. It should also be noted that aspects of proposed strategies would benefit all pupils – in relation to improved self-esteem (Ott 2011), for example, and the importance of a 'playful' approach to teaching (Corke 2011) which can be linked to creative teaching (Chapters 2 and 4). It is important to recognise that the label SEND is a broad category that covers a diversity of individual needs and that these should be met. Adaptive expertise, the skill of being able to adjust learning to meet the needs of classes, groups and individuals is required (Cochran-Smith, Feiman-Nemser and McIntyre 2008). For example, pupils with particular needs such as Autistic Spectrum Disorder who need structure may experience overstimulation and the opportunity to go a quiet place.

This ethnographic approach also provides opportunities for us to recognise, celebrate and utilise the diversity within our classrooms, a diversity which is sometimes ignored. Even within what appears to be a homogeneous classroom such approaches can highlight the hidden, sometimes ignored, diversities. English schools are characterised by increasing 'obvious' diversity, with around 20 per cent of pupils maintained state primary school having a first language other than English (DfE 2015). Furthermore, the trend is increasing – 16 per cent in 2010 and 18 per cent in 2013. This diversity is part of our national identity and to ignore it, whether we are teaching in schools with an 'ethnic' minority or a majority, would not represent good practice. There is currently an interest in the teaching of 'fundamental' values in British schools as part of the requirements to promote spiritual, moral, social and cultural development (DfE 2014) and the fusion of geography and music can provide opportunities for primary aged pupils to:

- develop their self-knowledge, self-esteem and self-confidence;
- acquire an appreciation of and respect for their own and other cultures promoting tolerance and harmony between different cultural traditions;
- show respect for other people;
- demonstrate understanding that other people having different faiths or beliefs to oneself (or having none) should be accepted and tolerated, and should not be the cause of prejudicial or discriminatory behaviour.

As with SEND, pupils learning English as an Additional Language and from minority ethnic groups are not homogeneous and include a spectrum ranging from those who are relatively new English learners to those who are fluent. Such pupils will obviously be drawn from a wide range of places around the world and contexts may also vary, from schools where there are less than five percent are from ethnic 'minorities' to school where the majority are themselves minorities. The approach advocated here would:

- allow discussion of culture and language from an early age;
- enable open dialogue on racial and social attitudes;
- offer more than tokenism; and
- encourage peer support and language development through socialisation.

Research into the sociocultural aspects of being a bilingual learner, highlight all of these features as elements of successful classroom teaching (Wardman 2012). They also contribute to a positive geographical education for *all* pupils.

CLASSROOM APPLICATIONS

The following teaching and learning ideas are not presented in any particular order and are based upon the geographical and pedagogical points outlined previously. They are designed to make learning enjoyable and memorable while promoting empathy and understanding. They can be adapted to suit different abilities according to the professional judgement of the teacher. All are intended to harness the energy generated by the emotional link with the music to provide a springboard for geographical enquiry. Key geographical questions should be emphasised throughout (see page 178).

Favourite music

If we are to pursue an ethnographic pedagogy (Martin 2008), we need to start with the pupils themselves. Ask the children to discuss the music they like listening to. Encourage them to consider what appeals to them about particular songs or compositions. Are they influenced by their family, friends or faith community (i.e. their cultural background)? Appreciation of and respect for different viewpoints should be encouraged (DfE 2014). This can lead to an exploration of the places *where* they listen to music and links to particular people and memories. Pupils could bring examples of music to share with the class. Similarly, they could survey their parents' or family's preferences. The key point here is to celebrate the diversity of preferences and the shared enjoyment of music. Children's use of technology could also be explored. How do they listen to music? Do they have personal stereos/MP3 players? Are there issues in listening to music in public places (noise pollution) or the outdoors (safety)?

Describing music

Music can also be used to develop pupils' 'emotional palette'. Some pupils may have difficulty expressing emotional responses beyond 'happy' or 'sad'; many others will find themselves at a loss for suitable words. One way to address this problem is to provide a vocabulary bank to describe the emotions, feelings and moods evoked by music. This can be developed by playing pieces from around the world and getting pupils to choose words that describe how they feel about them. You could also use 'classical' music to introduce children to other cultural traditions and to develop their historical perspective.

Music and place

The strong link between music and place is relatively easy to explore as there are many examples. Most countries and regions have particular musical styles and many have particular types of music or instruments associated with them. Taking Latin America as an example, (which encompasses the Spanish, Portuguese and Francophone regions of South and Central America) it is possible to explore musical styles rooted in place from Argentina to Uruguay For example, the tango is rooted in Argentina, flamenco in Spain and samba in Brazil. Children can to develop their knowledge of places around the world though listening and responding to music from these different places. Some examples of different styles include:

- Argentina – tango
- Brazil – bossa nova and samba
- Chile – cumbia
- Guatemala – marimba
- Puerto Rico – bomba

A display could be made locating the musical styles or instruments on a map of the continent. Once pupils have addressed the fundamental enquiry question 'Where is this place?', they could use secondary sources (e.g. maps, photographs) to explore further geographical questions. In addition to recognising different types of music from around the world, pupils could also explore the breadth of music from within individual countries in order to avoid stereotyping.

Musical stereotypes

An issue that may arise is that children may develop musical (and place) stereotypes if they listen to just one type of music from a particular place; for example, within the Latin American countries mentioned above there is actually a diversity of different styles and global influences. These styles will be linked to the colonising powers, slaves transported from Africa and indigenous musical traditions. Initially, these simple 'musical images' can be useful reference points and raise their awareness of other people and cultures. However, to avoid stereotyping, children need to hear a range of music from a particular country. This will help them to appreciate that there is diversity within other places, just as there is in their own. For example, Brazil is a large and diverse country with a range of different musical traditions which go beyond the simple styles listed above, and the different styles can be attributed to different parts of Chile. As well as listening to different styles and tempi, you could explore the emotions that music conveys – joy, sadness, loss and hope – and the way that this is part of our common humanity. I have used this strategy successfully in teaching about diversity within particular African countries. The life, vibrancy and emotional palette of music from different parts of Africa can provide a stark counterpoint to the negative media images of that continent. Exploring different musical traditions can help to convey how diverse the continent of Africa is. This strategy can help develop emotional literacy at the same time as exposing pupils to diverse cultures. The life, vibrancy and emotional palette of music from different parts of Africa can provide a stark counterpoint to the negative media images of that continent. Exploring different musical traditions can help to convey how diverse Africa, or any other continent is. This strategy can help develop emotional literacy at the same time as exposing pupils to diverse cultures. Music from different cultures can also be played ambiently in lessons or assemblies, perhaps linking to an overseas locality. This can be useful in encouraging pupils to accept and respect cultural differences – the 'other' becomes part of their world. Always ensure that children are given an opportunity to discuss how the music makes them feel and ensure that they know where it comes from, using maps and globes to help. The internet is a rich source of different musical styles from around the world which can be used to support teaching.

National anthems

National anthems are often not the most inspiring or emotionally stirring pieces of music (to the outsiders at least). However, listening to national anthems and their lyrics can be linked to work on overseas localities and introduces aspects of culture. For example, if the class is studying Mexico, then this is a natural opportunity to listen to the Mexican national anthem. The key point is to try to understand the music and its significance for the people who live in or originate from the country concerned.

National identity and music

From the previous sections it is evident that music is linked to place, identity and nationhood. To take examples from the British Isles, the harp is seen as a symbol of Welsh culture, the bagpipes Scottish, just as the bodhrán represents Ireland. It was interesting to see how British identity/ culture was expressed through music and performance at the opening ceremony of the 2012 Olympics (and how Brazilian identity and culture were represented in the closing ceremony). Watching video clips pupils could be prompted to consider what images of identity are being constructed. Although we have a National Anthem for the United Kingdom it is pertinent to observe that there are 'unofficial' anthems which are used to express identity of individual countries at major sporting and other cultural events (e.g. 'Flower of Scotland', 'Land of my Fathers', 'Jerusalem'). It would be useful for older pupils to be provided with the lyrics to these songs while listening to them and to consider what constructions of place are being articulated.

Another way to develop understanding of the cultural diversity of the United Kingdom would be to listen and respond to traditional folk music and instruments. How are they similar, how are they different? Traditional elements are often subsumed in contemporary popular music and re-interpreted in different ways. It would be useful for pupils to explore the musical roots of their locality, either through engaging with traditional or contemporary 'folk' music, where there are different regional traditions. By exploring music and identity at these varying levels pupils can develop an appreciation of the multifaceted nature of identity and how it is linked to place. For further ideas of how pupils can explore UK identity see *The UK: Investigating Who We Are* (Scoffham and Whyte 2011).

Musical journeys

Some pieces of music depict journeys through sound and lyrics; 'Route 66' (Chuck Berry) is an obvious example from popular music. The 'Little Train of the Caipara' from *Bachianas Brasileiras No. 2* (Villa-Lobos) is another. The latter piece describes a journey through rural Brazil. Given pictures of the landscape, pupils could imagine themselves on the journey and create a map showing what they might see. You could extend this idea to musical representations of landscape and weather/seasons. *Fingal's Cave* (Mendelssohn) was inspired by the basalt columns in the uninhabited island of Staffa in western Scotland, Beethoven's Pastoral Symphony depicts a passing storm, Vivaldi's *Four Seasons* chronicles changes over a 12-month cycle. There are many other examples.

Places in songs

A fun way of developing map and atlas skills, as well as locational knowledge, is through a focus on lyrics in songs. Places are often mentioned in song lyrics but tend to go unnoticed. Play the pupils extracts from these selected songs and challenge them to find the places on a map:

- 'New York, New York' – Frank Sinatra
- 'Philadelphia' – Bruce Springsteen
- 'California Gurls' – Katy Perry
- 'San Francisco (Be Sure to Wear Flowers in Your Hair)' – Scott McKenzie
- 'Do You Know the Way to San Jose?' – Dionne Warwick
- 'Is This the Way to Amarillo?' – Peter Kay
- 'Viva Las Vegas' – Elvis Presley
- 'Wichita Lineman' – Glen Campbell
- 'Walking in Memphis' – Cher
- 'Georgia on My Mind' – Ray Charles.

When the children have found all the places mentioned and worked out if they are cities, states and so forth they could plot them on a map of the USA and plan a journey linking them together. How would they travel? What would they see? Vocabulary relating to compass points, distances and obstacles such as mountains and deserts can also be developed through this exercise. Obviously this example just focuses on the USA in song titles but could be adapted to other parts of the world. Include lyrics and extend the work with home learning by asking pupils to find as many songs as they can that mention places. Can they find a way of going around the world in 80 songs? Can they visit each continent? As always with these ideas, get pupils to discuss how the music makes them feel and locate them before moving on to other geographical questions.

Creating music

The preceding ideas have involved pupils in listening to and responding to recorded music. In other words, they have been consumers. However, there is also huge potential for pupils to create their own music in response to place and to make up their own songs. An obvious stimulus for composition would be the school itself. One way to do this would be to compose different pieces based on places within the school. For example, how would pupils evoke the character of the dining-hall at lunchtime or the classroom during lesson time through music? Maybe they could devise a *Playtime Concerto*, which could either tell the story of the playground activities or capture the mood of relaxation and leisure. Children could also compose musical responses to other places using photographs as a stimulus. The contrast between a bustling urban scene, a stormy seashore or a sunny day in the country can be expressed in many different ways and make a really creative contribution to work in related geography topics.

CODA

This chapter has explored the relationship between music and geography and suggested that music is a fundamental human disposition with deep emotional resonance, which has the potential to create meaningful, enjoyable and memorable geographical learning experiences. Music, with its dynamism, hybridity and multiplicity, could almost be a metaphor for more nuanced understandings of place and geography. The academic case is grounded in a pedagogy that embraces dialogic teaching, and an ethnographic approach that supports teachers in both teaching creatively and harnessing children's creativity. The chapter has also exemplified some teaching strategies, all of which have been applied in the classroom. The harmonies and resonances between music and geography have the potential to bring excitement and relevance to teaching and learning. These harmonies operate at a number of different levels ranging from individual emotional impact to intercultural understanding. Music can connect us with each other and the wider world. Ultimately, music is part of what it means to be human, just as the desire to explore, know and understand is, too. I would argue this is what geography is all about.

REFERENCES

Alexander, R. (2008) *Towards Dialogic Teaching: Rethinking Classroom Talk*. York: Dialogos.

Alexander, R. (ed.) (2010) *Children, their World, their Education*. Abingdon: Routledge.

Anderson, B., Morton, F. and Revill, G. (2005) Practices of music and sound. *Social and Cultural Geography* 6(5): 640–3.

Baily, J. (1994) The role of music in the creation of an Afghan national identity, 1923–1972. In M. Stokes (ed.), *Ethnicity, Identity and Music*, pp. 45–60. Oxford: Berg.

Ball, P. (2010) *The Music Instinct*. London: The Bodley Head.

Bennett, A. (2000) *Popular Music and Youth Culture: Music Identity and Place*. London: Macmillan.

Bennett, A. (2005) Music, space and place. In S. Whiteley *et al.* (eds), *Music, Space and Place: Popular Music and Cultural Identity*, pp. 2–8. Farnham: Ashgate.

Bonnett, A. (2003) Geography as the world discipline: connecting popular and academic geographical imaginations. *Area* 35(1): 55–63.

Catling, S. (2005) Children's personal geographies and the English primary school curriculum. *Children's Geographies* 3(3): 325–44.

Cochran-Smith, M, Feiman-Nemser, S. and McIntyre, J. (eds) (2008) *Handbook of Research on Teacher Education* (3rd edition). London: Routledge.

Cohen, S. (1995) Sounding out the city: music and the sensuous production of place. *Transactions of the Institute of British Geographers* 20: 434–46.

Cohen, S. (2007) *Decline, Renewal and the City in Popular Musical Culture*. Farnham: Ashgate.

Connell, J. and Gibson, C. (2003) *Sound Tracks: Popular Music, Identity and Place*. London: Routledge.

Corke, M. (2002) *Approaches to Communication through Music*. London: David Fulton.

Corke, M. (2011*) Using Playful Practice to Communicate with Special Children*. London: David Fulton.

Crang, M. (1998) *Cultural Geography*. London: Routledge.

Davidson, J. and Milligan, C. (2004) Embodying emotion sensing space: introducing emotional geographies. *Social and Cultural Geography* 5(4): 523–32.

DfE (2013) *Geography Programmes of Study: Key Stages 1 and 2*. London: Department for Education.

DfE (2014) *Promoting Fundamental British Values as Part of SMSC in Schools*. London:

Department for Education.

DfE (2015) *Schools, Pupils and Their Characteristics: January 2015*. London: Department for Education. Available at www.gov.uk/government/statistics (accessed 13 January 2016).

Duncan, J. and Ley, D. (1993) *Place/Culture/Representation*. London: Routledge.

Hammel, A. and Hourigan, R. M. (2011) *Teaching Music to Students with Special Needs: A Label-Free Approach*. Oxford: Oxford University Press.

Hudson, R. (2006) Regions and place: music identity and place. *Human Geography* 30(5): 626–34.

Johansson, O. and Bell, T. (Eds) (2007) *Sound, Society and the Geography of Popular Music*. Farnham: Ashgate.

Kelly, A. (2009) Sounds geographical. *Primary Geographer* 68: 34–6.

Leonard, M. (2005) Performing identities: music and dance in the Irish communities of Coventry and Liverpool. *Social and Cultural Geography* 6(4): 515–29.

Levitin, D. (2008) *This Is Your Brain on Music*. London: Atlantic Books.

Mach, Z. (1994) National anthems: the case of Chopin as a national composer. In M. Stokes (ed.), *Ethnicity, Identity and Music*, pp. 61–70. Oxford: Berg.

Martin, F. (2006) Everyday geography. *Primary Geographer* 61: 4–7.

Martin, F. (2008) Ethnogeography: towards liberatory geography education. *Children's Geographies* 6(4): 437–50.

Massey, D. (2005) *For Space*. London: Sage.

Matthews, J. and Herbert, D. (2004) *Unifying Geography: Common Heritage, Shared Future*. London: Routledge.

Mitchell, D. (2000) *Cultural Geography: A Critical Introduction*. Oxford: Blackwell.

Ott, P. (2011) *Music for Special Kids: Musical Activities, Songs, Instruments and Resources* London: Jessica Kingsley.

Roberts, M. (2013) *Geography through Enquiry: Approaches to Teaching and Learning in the Secondary School*. Sheffield: Geographical Association.

Scoffham, S. and Whyte, T. (2011) *The UK: Investigating Who We Are*. Sheffield: Geographical Association.

Stokes, M. (ed.) (1997) *Ethnicity, Identity and Music*. Oxford: Berg.

Wardman, C. (2012) *Pulling the Threads Together: Current Theories and Current Practice Affecting UK Primary School Children who Have English as an Additional Language*. London: British Council.

Whiteley, S., Bennett, A. and Hawkins, S. (eds) (2005) *Music, Space and Place: Popular Music and Cultural Identity*. Farnham: Ashgate.

Wood, N. and Smith, S. (2004) Instrumental routes to emotional geographies. *Social and Cultural Geography* 5(4): 533–47.

Websites

■ *Sing Up* is an organisation that provides tools, songs and music linked to geography (and other curriculum areas): www.singup.org

■ *Songlines* is a journal that focuses on the genre of world music, and the sampler CDs can provide a way in to this area: www.songlines.co.uk

■ *Putumayo* is a source of a range of resources relating to music and multicultural under-standing: www.putumayo.com/en/putumayo_kids.php

■ *Oxfam Education* provides ideas for using music as a stimulus to develop global citizen-ship: www.oxfam.org.uk/education/resources

■ *Oxfam Education* have produced a series of lessons designed to celebrate music from around the globe: http://www.oxfam.org.uk/education/resources/global-music-lessons-for-ages-7--11

▦ *Audacity* is an excellent piece of freeware that allows you to edit and shape sounds for the classroom: www.audacityteam.org

▦ *Global Dimension* is a useful site providing more general advice on using sound more generally to explore the world near and far: www.globaldimension.org.uk

▦ *The Woodland Trust* website includes examples of music and songs inspired by trees and woodland: www.woodlandtrust.org.uk/naturedetectives/blogs/nature-detectives-blog/2015/06/creative-outdoor-activities/

GEOGRAPHY AND SUSTAINABILITY EDUCATION

Paula Owens

This chapter discusses how creative geography teaching can help children understand and engage with sustainability issues and be genuinely involved in designing outcomes with future well-being in mind. Young children have a good deal of curiosity about the world that they live in but they also worry about the future of the planet. When they are given opportunities to participate in relevant creative and critical problem-solving enquiries, their learning can become powerful. Such teaching helps children to be better informed and thus more able to tackle issues such as climate change, unequal development and loss of biodiversity, which may otherwise seem daunting. It also provides an agenda of hope.

GEOGRAPHY AND EDUCATION FOR SUSTAINABILITY

'Education for sustainability' (ESD) is a term used to describe an approach to education that considers how we might better look after the planet we have inherited for the benefit of present and future generations. It has a wide remit and takes into account ideas such as stewardship, justice, equity and human rights. Although there are many definitions of ESD, they all involve focus on the future and how we might change it through our actions to offer a preferable quality of life for everyone. Thinking about how we might be best equipped to make decisions that will impact on our own and others' everyday lives, and the environments that sustain us, are powerful and relevant ideas for education, requiring both creative and critical thought. Owens (2011: 8) raises the following questions:

- What is education for if it is not to empower us with the knowledge, skills and values to live well on this Earth and with each other?
- What good is education if it does not build the capacity to question and change lifestyles and habits that threaten the one planet that sustains us?
- How effective is education if it does not carry a message of hope – that we can make a difference?

Hicks (2014) discusses what education is for and reminds us that it is never value free; thus we need to be able to better understand the role of ideology in debates about its purpose. Education undoubtedly has a vital importance in the arena of sustainability. It was a core part of the Millennium Development Goals which operated from 2000 to 2015, and it is now embedded in the 17 'Sustainable Development Goals' (also known as the 'Global Goals for Sustainable Development') adopted by world leaders at the UN's annual General Assembly in 2015. Two of these are particularly relevant to ESD:

▨ Goal 4 is about 'quality education' and aims to 'ensure inclusive and equitable quality education and promote lifelong learning opportunities for all' (UN 2015).
▨ Goal 16 aims to 'Promote peaceful and inclusive societies for sustainable development, provide access to justice for all and build effective, accountable and inclusive institutions at all levels' (*ibid.*).

While time will tell the effectiveness of the Sustainable Development Goals, the proactive language sets out a clear agenda for the role of education and institutions in actively promoting sustainable development.

Sustainable development is commonly thought of as having three mutually supporting dimensions – economic, social and environmental. These work together and link to the idea of quality of life for all, recognising that we live in an interconnected world. They also relate to some of the 'big' questions that geography seeks to answer, namely:

▨ Where is this place? What is it like and why?
▨ Why and how is it changing? What will it be like in the future? What kinds of futures do we want?
▨ What do people do here? How are their actions influenced by, and how do they impact on, environments at different scales?
▨ How is this place connected to other places? How am I connected to other people and places?
▨ Who gets what, where, when and how? Who decides?
▨ What's it got to do with me? Why should I care?

Sustainability education is relevant across the entire curriculum and is best approached through holistic teaching and learning. It has a particular association with geography and requires careful underpinning with geographical thinking and knowledge. Issues concerning sustainability and the environment have a values-led and affective base, often articulated as a need to 'care for the world', which can sometimes eclipse other necessary components of knowledge and critical thinking. While values and emotions are intrinsic and inescapable facets of sustainability, being properly equipped to respond to these issues also demands some degree of cognitive understanding about how and why human, biological and physical worlds interact with and affect each other. This is part of the remit of geography education. Melding these ingredients together successfully to produce new ways of thinking about the world and some of the daunting issues we face, requires creativity of approach, thought and deed.

TEACHERS' KNOWLEDGE OF EDUCATION FOR SUSTAINABILITY

Research by Symonds (2008) found that the majority of teachers had limited knowledge of ESD and that it was often piecemeal and impacted only on small groups of pupils. Surveys by Ofsted (2008, 2009) reveal that sustainability education is more noticeable in primary than secondary schools. However, this finding is tempered by the observation that 'while a small number of schools were doing this well, many schools were only doing this as a peripheral activity and not through the mainstream curriculum' (Ofsted 2008: 5).

With respect to geography, Ofsted (2011) raised concerns about the quality of teaching and the amount of time allocated to it. Unfortunately, a climate of poor geography teaching does not bode well for successful work on sustainability. As Martin and Owens (2010: 9) note, 'if you are doing ESD then you're probably doing geography!' Imagine, for example, trying to teach about sustainability without understanding how local and global events are connected or how human, physical and environmental processes interact. If we need to improve ESD, we also need to improve the teaching and learning of geography.

A survey by WWF (2010) into pedagogical approaches to sustainability found that success was dependent on teachers' subject knowledge; the support structures in schools; and teachers' capacity to root learning within the knowledge and skills of the curriculum. The WWF report recommended that both initial training and ongoing CPD should develop teachers' ability to engage with successful pedagogical approaches and build the subject knowledge necessary to support pupil enquiry, independent thinking and debate. Subsequent reports (e.g. UNECE 2013) have continued to stress the importance of developing teacher competence and the value of a whole school approach.

Many of the teaching and learning strategies that underpin quality geography are consistent with those that encourage effective ESD. These include (a) developing autonomy and critical thinking; (b) developing skills of enquiry, creativity and imagination; and (c) collective decision-making and using a range of media and text resources (Smith 2012). The 2011 subject report from Ofsted specifically mentions sustainability as a component of good practice. This adds weight to the argument that sustainability is an indicator of high-quality geography which offers a real context for learning and enables pupils to make links between their own and others' lives in meaningful ways.

Many schools are enthusiastic about the idea of a 'creative curriculum' although Ofsted (2010) warns that successful creative curriculum practice is dependent on teachers' subject knowledge. When teachers are confident in their understanding of geography as a subject they are better equipped to make and apply relevant and powerful links to other curricular areas. Successful geography teaching requires that pupils know some 'core knowledge' about the world, but it also draws on other kinds of knowledge, such as that provided by personal and everyday geographies, which help to develop deeper *understanding* about the complex nature of the world we live in. Core knowledge on its own is useful, yet it can be static if not viewed in contexts of diversity, conflicting opinions and change. Personal and everyday geographies recognise the interpretations and experiences gathered through our everyday transactions. These latter kinds of knowing are, by definition, varied and subjective, yet they are hugely pertinent to the way that learners perceive, interpret and imagine the world around them.

In addition, it is important to note that the 'creative' aspects of exploration and imagination need to be complemented by critical thinking to avoid learning becoming 'woolly'. When creativity and critical thinking work together they generate purposeful learning that can be applied to real-world contexts. This can be thought of, diagrammatically, as a diamond-shaped process in which divergent and creative ideas are honed and focused towards a purposeful outcome (see Figure 13.1).

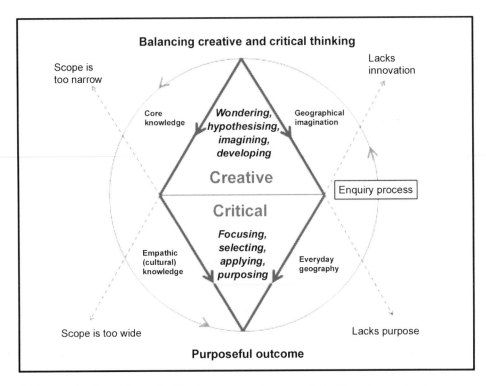

Figure 13.1 Creativity and criticality are complementary but different aspects of purposeful learning

TEACHING GEOGRAPHY AND EDUCATION FOR SUSTAINABILITY CREATIVELY

When taught well, geography enables creative enquiry opportunities because it offers investigations into real places, situations, and issues and invites active agency, giving children a meaningful voice (Catling 2009). It has also been suggested that geography is particularly well suited to developing creative thought because it synthesises material and ideas from different subject areas (Scoffham 2013a), thus helping pupils to 'think outside the box' when, for example, imagining how issues are connected and how problems might be tackled. Making connections, envisaging futures, problem-solving and collaboration in purposeful contexts are all indicators of creative activity (Hicks 2012). Indeed, where schools have developed their approaches towards sustainability, an increasing emphasis on creative thinking has been seen as a result (Ofsted 2009). The following headings indicate some of the key areas through which creativity can be developed.

Making geography enjoyable and relevant

The Geographical Association manifesto puts forward ideas about the nature and relevance of modern geography as a 'living' subject (Geographical Association 2010; Figure 13.2). Geography uses an enquiry approach to support and encourage curiosity about the

Living geography:
- is directly relevant to people's lives and the world of work;
- is about change – recognises that the past helps explain the present, but is current and futures-orientated;
- has a scale 'zoom lens', so that the local is always set in a global context;
- is 'deeply observant' – it looks beneath the surface to identify the mechanisms that change environments and societies; and
- encourages a critical understanding of big ideas like 'sustainable development', interdependence' and 'globalisation'.

Figure 13.2 Some principles of 'living geography'
Source: Geographical Association (2010: 13)

wider world and aims to develop pupils' ability to give creative and critical responses to everyday issues. Starting from what pupils know, and want to know, provides intrinsic motivation. It makes learning enjoyable as pupils can investigate aspects of life that are relevant to them. You might start by asking pupils to tell stories about who they are and where they come from. Sharing stories about who we are can build social bonds in the classroom and contribute to ESD: it helps us to understand more about the characteristics of places from our own and others' perspectives; deepens feelings of value, and strengthens notions of national identity. Mapping and explaining where we live, play and shop is also an important part of geography, developing our geographical imagination, or ways in which we view the world.

Fieldwork

Children today have less first-hand contact with outdoor environments than previous generations. This can be partly explained by the pull of indoor virtual lifestyles, reduced access to outdoor play spaces and increased parental concerns about safety (Gill 2012; Pickering 2016). Yet children enjoy being out-of-doors where there is often far more scope for exploration and discovery than in the home or classroom. Fieldwork immerses pupils in experiences that allow them to engage with their local environment and better imagine distant ones. We also learn more about our environment when we experience it at first hand and have the opportunity to use all our senses. The process of immersing ourselves in such experiences helps to develop positive values and feelings towards the world around us and provides us with incentives for stewardship. Fieldwork, Lambert and Owens (2013) argue, is an essential aspect of engaging with sustainability and promoting creativity.

Being outside can open up new experiences: sights, smells, touch, sounds and feelings that stimulate the imagination and heighten awareness. Research has shown that fieldwork promotes vocabulary acquisition so necessary for engaging with environmental dialogues (Ward 1998). It can also provide an affective component, through positive emotional experiences that promote the development of deep and lasting memories. Such memories can positively influence adult values and attitudes (Catling *et al.* 2010). If we want children to genuinely care about their surroundings and the wider world we need to help them connect to it first and foremost.

Investigating the locality through first-hand exploration is one of the best ways of developing knowledge about local issues. You might have already identified an issue that requires focused enquiry, such as the closure of a local shop or a proposal to build new houses or roads; or you might discover an issue while exploring the local area: for example, a walk around the school to record good and negative aspects of the local environment will produce many ideas about how the area might be improved. You could also undertake simple explorations of the school grounds in which pupils are free to collect and record sights, sounds and other phenomena that interest them (Figure 13.3). This is a simple awareness technique that develops pupils' capacity to see their surroundings in new ways and to begin to think critically about the quality of an environment. Such explorations encourage children to make careful and deep observations, raise questions and make connections of which they were not previously aware. One of the other benefits is the sense of awe and wonder that can be found from being outside, which might stem from noticing everyday natural phenomena such as the patterns of clouds, spiders' webs or the colour of autumn leaves. Or it might be discovered in the complexity and beauty found in some parts of the built environment. Awe and wonder are, in themselves, powerful motivators for imaginative thought and response. They remind us that the world is an amazing place.

▨ **Figure 13.3** Year 3 student, International School of Bologna, collecting information about the school grounds
Source: photo by Jane Whittle

Investigating current issues

Flexibility is a key feature of effective planning for creativity as everyday events and issues can crop up that trigger sparks of curiosity and motivation in children, offering fruitful and creative sources of enquiry. Flexibility is especially relevant for geography as it deals with the 'here and now', and so is particularly susceptible to the need to be 'current'. Very often, unplanned learning opportunities emerge from news stories, often, sadly, because of a disaster such as a volcanic eruption or a tsunami, where lives have been lost and livelihoods threatened. Even very young children can be aware of these events, which they can find worrying as they fear for their own safety. Using such stories to start a geographical enquiry can help children make sense of them and feel less threatened. It also helps to empower them as they become actively engaged in tackling a problem perceived as a threat.

In one Year 2 class, children discussed the effects of a volcanic eruption and, particularly, how it had disrupted air travel. One of the consequences was that tourists had become stranded, including some teachers following a holiday period. In addition, some fruit and vegetables started to run low in supermarkets. This led pupils to develop all kinds of interesting ideas about how the stranded teachers might be able to get home and led them to think about why we rely on certain fresh foods to be transported by aeroplane. The new thinking by pupils enabled them to appreciate the importance of interdependence and how we are globally connected to each other.

Many classes use the 'What's in the news?' approach in geography, but few develop this further to actively investigate a particular news topic. Using sources of information such as newspapers and television media can provide a starting point for pupils to voice their concerns and pose their own questions. Sometimes a simple image can be used to ask pupils, 'What's going on here?' and 'How do you feel about …?', which is enough of a hook for pupils to begin to imagine and respond to what might be happening. Using a mix of knowledge and emotional response in connection with issues-based thinking is also a very powerful way to create new understanding. As Hicks (2014) advocates, the affective world is every bit as important to life and learning as the cognitive dimension. When we access feelings and emotions we are better equipped to drive positive change – one of the crucially important outcomes of learning in ESD.

Sometimes children can become fired up by exposure to a particular issue. For example, when a Year 4 class learnt, through a speaker from the Hawk and Owl Trust, how barn owls were losing their natural habit and were in decline, they wanted to know more. Such was their enthusiasm that the teacher adapted her lesson plans to make the most of their curiosity and drive. Instead of designing money boxes, children designed owl boxes, and the study of habitats in science was given a new slant through a real-life problem. The pupils also investigated the human and physical and pressures which had led to the problem and undertook active geography fieldwork to investigate the kinds of habitats favoured by owls and to decide where to site new boxes. This example is typical of how geography can provide a real focus point for cross-curricular work (Figure 13.4).

Some issues are current but also long-term, which gives ample scope for curriculum planning, although they can be daunting to tackle. Perhaps the most challenging of these is rapid climate change, as it poses immediate and real threats to the status quo of life on Earth and is now generally agreed to be attributable to human activity through the use of fossil fuels. The Intergovernmental Panel on Climate Change (IPCC) was established in 1988 to synthesise and report on the science and research of climate change and this extract from their 2014 report, starkly summarises the situation:

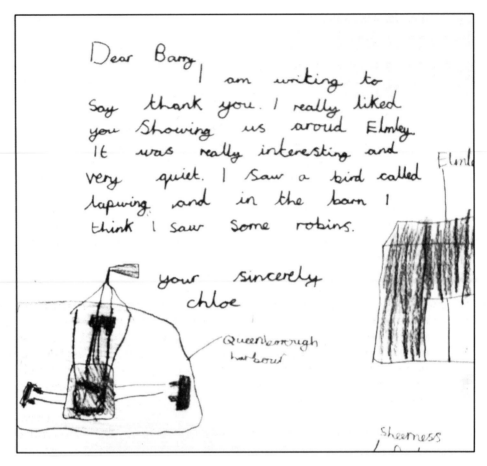

▧ **Figure 13.4** A letter from a Year 3 pupil, Eastchurch School, Isle of Sheppey, Kent, following a visit to a local nature reserve

Warming of the climate system is unequivocal, and since the 1950s, many of the observed changes are unprecedented over decades to millennia. The atmosphere and ocean have warmed, the amounts of snow and ice have diminished, and sea level has risen.

(IPCC 2014: §1.1)

Understanding the language of this debate requires sound underpinning with subject knowledge and facts before the more value-laden aspects of how we might respond are explored.

'Climate change' refers to the fluctuation of climate conditions on Earth over varying periods and is a variation that we know we can expect to happen again. However, 'rapid climate change' differentiates the unexpectedly fast pace of change, which is leading to environmental conditions to which humans and other living creatures may find it hard to adapt. 'Global warming' is a natural phenomenon thanks to the presence of carbon dioxide, which means that our planet has just the right conditions for life to flourish, whereas 'enhanced global warming' refers to the human-induced build-up of carbon dioxide, methane and other gases in the Earth's atmosphere that is causing global temperature rise on a rapid scale. Understanding the terminology of complex processes such as this can seem anything but creative, yet creativity flourishes where there is secure subject knowledge, so helping pupils to differentiate between, and use, appropriate vocabulary is vital.

As well as understanding and using correct vocabulary and terminology, children need to develop better awareness of climate change processes. Drama can be a useful approach here, especially where younger children are concerned. Pupils could act out, through dance, for example, how carbon dioxide in the Earth's atmosphere captures some of the sun's energy reflected back from the Earth. This would allow pupils to see in a concrete way how much more energy can be captured if the amount of (e.g. number of dancers) carbon dioxide increases. Encourage pupils to think of good questions to ask that allow them to probe and challenge assumptions about issues such as climate change: a dialogical space for exploring known or given boundaries between accepted truth and fiction is an essential part of creative and critical thinking.

Imagining the implications of rapid climate change around the world and possible solutions requires a good deal of creativity. Having a developing understanding of this complex problem and a secure vocabulary allows children to begin to engage in meaningful dialogues and action. As part of the government-funded Global Learning Programme (GLP) of 2015, several schools on the Isle of Wight held a cross phase 'Transition project' in the style of a United Nations conference. The schools joined together and listened to invited speakers put forth different views about solutions to climate change before creating their own policies. Meanwhile the Ashden Trust has been developing a project of mentoring and coaching for UK schools called LESSCO2 so that they can both actively reduce their carbon footprint and energy bills and also build this into curriculum experiences. This model is particularly effective when trying to bring about change as participating schools can join together in a network of support.

Empathy and role play

Trying to imagine other people's views and perspectives can be difficult, especially when there are conflicts of opinion. Empathising through role play can be one way in which this kind of imaginative thinking can be developed, and was the approach used by class teacher, Sarah Lewis, in collaboration with Dr Emma Mawdsley, a lecturer in geography at Cambridge University. This teacher wanted her Year 4 pupils to develop more complex thinking, and accept that, often, there were no simple answers to environmental problems; rather, there were complex trade-offs between conflicting areas of need. To this end, a group of characters representing different aspects of life on the island of St Lucia were portrayed on a website. Pupils were able to learn about their life, ask Dr Emma questions about their needs and were challenged to take on the 'Role of the Mantle' by becoming experts about environmental policy. The culmination of this work was a presentation to visiting 'ministers' where the pupils would outline identified policies.

Through this activity, innovative solutions to conflicts on St Lucia, such as the tensions between the fishing industry, the health of the reef and tourist yachts, were identified. The pupils used a variety of maps, graphs, 3D models and written and oral reports to present their work. They demonstrated their ability by not only achieving complexity of thought but also by identifying solutions such as beach zoning, which are actually in use on the island but of which they were hitherto unaware (Lewis and Mawdsley 2007). 'Empathic geography' of this kind has been identified by Lambert and Owens (2013) as a powerful approach to creative geography.

Using storybooks

Stories about place can be powerful and stimulating influences on the geographical imagination (Rawling 2011; Tanner and Whittle 2013) and invite personal responses. They take us out of our place in the world and help us to imagine other situations, landscapes, cultures and contexts. In this way they can help to scaffold enquiry, interpretation and learning. Cremin (2009) notes how the choice of text is important for enabling creative engagement and how picture-books can be especially powerful in facilitating a range of responses and meaning-making. Picture-based and other relevant storybooks can provide examples of features and environmental vocabulary that can set children off on an enquiry bolstered by relevant knowledge and their own questions.

Books by authors such as Jeanne Baker are particularly evocative through their use of illustrations, which invite children to enter into a futures-oriented world. For example, *Where the Forest Meets the Sea* (1987) and *Window* (2002) are both enduring and relevant tales of our time in which the story is set in the context of an encroaching built environment.

Some books have the power to enchant and inspire us to think about the diversity and beauty of the wider world, for example *Ben's Magic Telescope* (2003) by Brian Patten. Others help us learn where everyday resources come from such as in *The World Came to My Place Today* by Jo Readman (2004). A number of books have captured concerns about global issues such as climate change include *Who Will Save Us?* by Rebecca Morch (2007) and *The Trouble with Dragons* by Debi Gliori (2009), while *Dolphin Boy* by Michael Morpurgo (2004) invites us to discuss the impacts of change at a local scale. Books that deal with changing environments and other issues offer a safe space for children to explore and respond to scenarios that they might hitherto have been unable to imagine. They can also allow children to apply some of these ideas to help them better imagine other scenarios.

Even traditional tales can be used in creative hands as a starting point for sustainability enquiries. Jonathan Kersey subverted the story of Little Red Riding Hood to develop an idea with his Year 2 pupils in which the big bad wolf became the good wolf who helped Little Red Riding Hood to successfully recognise and negotiate dangers in the neighbourhood (Figure 13.5). This was developed through active fieldwork and made into a film through a cross-curricular project with a geography focus. The creativity of this project was inherent in how pupils had collaborated to create new meanings from their locality through a mix of fieldwork and film, while the sustainability dimension arose from pupils' new perspectives and identified actions with regard to the quality of their environment (Lambert and Owens 2013).

Pupil participation

Genuine participation is an essential part of both the process and outcome in sustainable learning and typifies high-quality geography. It is really important that pupils feel that they have a genuine voice, share responsibility and have the freedom to suggest outcomes

Geographical skills and fieldwork
- ■ Identify locations within Southborough that present dangers or difficulties for pedestrians.
- ■ Use maps and plans to mark a route to visit these locations and use them as film locations to retell a narrative story.
- ■ Visit locations and record film footage.
- ■ Record environmental hazards and dangers with photography and sketches.
- ■ Identify the causes of some of the environmental hazards in Southborough.
- ■ Recognise how aspects of the environment can be sustained, developed and improved.

■ **Figure 13.5** Extract from initial planning sheet, Southborough Primary School: the true story of Little Red Riding Hood

that are taken seriously. Building this aspect into teaching and learning can seem risky initially, but jointly constructed curricula can help to develop children's sense of autonomy and improve motivation.

When children feel connected to their learning and have what Hicks (2014) calls an 'agenda for hope' there is a real sense of empowerment and motivation. It is precisely this kind of learning environment that nurtures creativity and critical thinking. You can use children's own questions to frame enquiries and work together with them to develop their skills. Make space for their suggestions about how an enquiry will happen and what the purpose of it might be: together you can decide if there are realistic actions that might be taken. For example, some Year 4 pupils gathered data about litter in the environment; canvassed local residents, and worked with the local council in deciding where new bins ought to be sited. In another example, a whole school produced an 'Eco-exhibition' which was opened to the general public. Pupils became the 'experts': each year group studied an aspect of sustainability and their work was set out in a display with a selected group of pupils available to talk about what they had done and why, as well as answering queries. Year 1 children showed off their Eco super-heroes: who they would be and what one thing they would change to improve the world, while Year 6 explained climate change. Enquiries like these, where children lead learning, are powerful drivers for creative work.

Collaborative learning

Working together is a vital part of sustainable thinking and learning, and of creativity too. Collaboration happens easily in classroom situations, less often through links with the local community, and is even rarer with distant communities. Yet, in our globalised world, where our actions impact on local and global environments, learning from people who live in other parts of the world is valuable as it helps us to imagine a wider range of acceptable responses to local problems.

Many schools now have links with schools overseas or, at the very least, study contrasting localities overseas, and this provides a huge potential to promote learning from and about other cultures and promoting international goodwill. While we cannot actually go to overseas localities and experience them at first hand, we can employ empathic geographies to help us learn about them. We can also employ creative techniques such as 'hot-seating' and 'putting ourselves in the picture' to imagine what life is like there, having securely underpinned imaginative thought with background information from as many sources as possible (e.g. sights, sounds, tastes, artefacts and stories).

It is essential to challenge stereotypical thinking about others' lifestyles, especially when there is a stark contrast in material wealth (Scoffham 2013b). Try to focus on questions such as 'What can we learn from this community?' rather than the shallow and often inaccurate stance, 'How can we help this community?' The best school partnerships are equal in terms of learning and giving and provide enormous motivation for pupils to respond to and learn from other cultures. True, collaborative geographies can help to mutually develop and enhance geographical imagination and widen perspectives.

Campus, community and curriculum

Ideally, sustainability needs to be embedded within the curriculum; apparent across the school campus in both deed and ethos, and is mindful of and collaborative with, local and global communities. Learning about sustainability does not only happen in the classroom and designated curriculum activities; it also emerges in hidden agendas, such as the way the buildings and grounds are managed and the quality of the links with the community, both local and distant. Many schools have found that they can clarify what they do using the following three headings: care: caring for oneself, caring for others, and caring for environments. This approach can be neatly combined with the idea of working across the campus, community and curriculum.

One area that rightly warrants a lot of attention is our use of resources especially that of energy. Our energy use has many geographical implications, such as, for example: How do we source our energy? How does energy use impact on local and global environments (e.g. global warming)? Why do some people in other parts of the world not have ready access to electricity? How do other people and communities solve their energy problems? How do we travel to school? Several schools now have 'energy monitors' who help ensure that their school takes every precaution against wasting energy and endeavours to reduce its carbon footprint. Ofsted (2009) has highlighted how, in some examples of best practice, schools are influencing the local community to act more sustainably.

Some Key Stage 2 pupils were investigating wind energy as their school was going to have a wind turbine installed. They were asked to consider the pros and cons of this type of energy use from different perspectives. In particular, they were asked to think about their own opinions, those of neighbours and to also imagine how wildlife in the school grounds, such as little owls, might feel about this change. These pupils were engaging with sustainability through creative and critical thinking rather than being 'greenwashed' into merely making positive comments about a technology that the school had chosen to adopt (see Figure 13.6).

CONCLUSION

Sustainability and the environment are key ideas for geography and require a creative approach in which children are enabled to:

▩   envisage previously unimagined places and futures;
▩   empathise and understand other viewpoints and perspectives;
▩   think about possible solutions that might help solve local and global issues; and
▩   imagine themselves as capable agents of change.

Energy from the Wind – what do we think about it?

The Little Owl thinks that the wind turbine

A bit scary, quite dangerous, noisy, distracting, taking room up on the field, ugly.

Some people think that the wind turbine is a good thing because

it is cheap to run, less likely to have a global warming, important and renewable that mean it will never run out.

Other people think that the wind turbine is not a good thing because

They might think it is going to be noisy and it will destruct there

I think that the wind turbine is

important, beautiful, saves the environment and saves us money.

Draw your wind turbine here

▨ **Figure 13.6** Thinking about wind turbines from different viewpoints: from a Year 4 pupil from Eastchurch School, Isle of Sheppey, Kent

It also requires a critical approach to received wisdom and an ethos in which children feel free to question and enquire about alternative explanations and actions. It is a most important and relevant aspect of our children's education.

Sustainability is about considering a range of opinions and recognising that sometimes we do not have all the answers or that our knowledge may be uncertain. It is also about recognising that people have conflicting views and that these may be value-led: solutions to conflicting opinions may involve trade-offs and compromise and it is often difficult to select an outcome that will suit everyone. This is why sustainability is so complex, yet it is all the more important to provide children with the necessary skills and knowledge to think about it creatively.

ACKNOWLEDGEMENTS

Thanks to:

▧ The Geographical Association and their Quality Mark Schools.
▧ St Joseph's Catholic Primary School, Surrey, Dr Emma Mawdsley and teacher Sarah Lewis.
▧ Teacher Jonathan Kersey and pupils at Southborough Primary School, Kent.
▧ Jan Austin and pupils at Eastchurch Primary School, Isle of Sheppey, Kent.

REFERENCES AND FURTHER READING

Catling, S. (2008) *Young Geographers: A Living Geography Project for Primary Schools, 2008 – An Evaluation Report*. Sheffield: Geographical Association.

Catling, S. (2009) Creativity in primary geography. In A. Wilson (ed.), *Creativity in Primary Education*, pp. 189–98. Exeter: Learning Matters.

Catling, S., Greenwood, R., Martin, F. and Owens, P. (2010) Formative experiences of primary geography educators. *International Research in Geographical and Environmental Education* 19(4): 341–50.

Cremin, T. (2009) *Teaching English Creatively*. Learning to Teach in the Primary School Series. Abingdon: Routledge.

Geographical Association (2010) *A Different View: A Manifesto for Geography*. Sheffield: Geographical Association.

Gill, T. (2012) *No Fear: Growing Up in a Risk Averse Society*. London: Calouste Gulbenkian.

Hicks, D. (2012) The future only arrives when things look dangerous: reflections on futures education in the UK. *Futures* 44(1): 4–13. Available at http://teaching4abetterworld.co.uk/docs/download17.pdf (accessed 9 January 2016).

Hicks, D. (2014) *Educating for Hope in Troubled Times: Climate Change and the Transition to a Post-Carbon Future*. London: Institute of Education Press.

IPCC (2014) *Climate Change 2014: Synthesis Report. Contribution of Working Groups I, II and III to the Fifth Assessment Report of the Intergovernmental Panel on Climate Change*. Geneva: IPCC.

Lambert, D. and Owens, P. (2013) Geography. In R. Jones and D. Wyse (eds), *Creativity in the Primary Curriculum*, pp. 98–115. Abingdon: David Fulton.

Lewis, S. and Mawdsley, E. (2007) Geojoes St Lucia challenge. *Primary Geography* 64: 19–21.

Martin, F. and Owens, P. (2010) *Caring for Our World: A Practical Guide to ESD for 4–7 Year Olds*. Sheffield: Geographical Association.

Ofsted (2003) *Taking the First Step Forward: Towards an Education for Sustainable Development*. HMI 1658. London: Crown.

Ofsted (2008) *Schools and Sustainability: A Climate for Change*. London: Ofsted. Available at www.eauc.org.uk/schools_and_sustainability_a_climate_for_change (accessed 13 January 2016).

Ofsted (2009) *Education for Sustainable Development: Improving Schools – Improving Lives*. London: Ofsted. Available at www.schools.norfolk.gov.uk/view/NCC103946 (accessed 13 January 2016).

Ofsted (2010) *Learning: Creative Approaches that Raise Standards*. London: Ofsted. Available at www.creativitycultureeducation.org/wp-content/uploads/learning-creative-approaches-that-raise-standards-250.pdf (accessed 13 January 2016).

Ofsted (2011) *Geography: Learning to Make a World of Difference*. Available at www.gov.uk/government/publications/geography-learning-to-make-a-world-of-difference (accessed 13 January 2016).

Owens, P. (2011) Why sustainability has a future. *Primary Geography* 74: 7–9.

Pickering, S. (ed.) (2016) *Teaching Out of Doors Creatively*. Abingdon: Routledge.

Pretty, J., Angus, C., Bain, M., Barton, J., Gladwell, V., Hine, R., Pilgrim, S., Sandercock, S. and Sellens, M. (2009) *Nature, Childhood, Health and Life Pathways*. Interdisciplinary Centre for Environment and Society Occasional Paper 2009–02. Colchester: University of Essex.

Rawling, E. (2011) Reading and writing place. In G. Butt (ed.), *Geography Education and the Future*, pp. 65–83. London: Continuum.

Scoffham, S. (2013a) Geography and creativity: developing joyful and imaginative learners. *Education 3–13* 41(4): 368–61.

Scoffham, S. (2013b) What makes stereotypes pernicious. In M. Sangster (ed.), *Developing Teacher Expertise*, pp. 97–9. London: Continuum.

Smith, M. (2012) *GTIP Think Piece – Education for Sustainable Development*. Available at www.geography.org.uk/gtip/thinkpieces/esd/#4 (accessed 9 January 2016).

Symonds, G. (2008) *Barriers and Enablers in ESD and EE: A Review of the Research – A Report for Sustainability and Environmental Education*. Shrewsbury: SEEd. Available at http://se-ed.co.uk/edu/practice-barriers-and-enablers-in-esd-and-ee-a-review-of-the-research (accessed 17 April 2016).

Tanner, J. and Whittle, J. (2013) *The Everyday Guide to Primary Geography: Story*. Sheffield: Geographical Association.

Tilbury, D. (2011) *Education for Sustainable Development: An Expert Review of Processes and Learning*. Paris: UNESCO.

UN (2015) Sustainable Development Goals. Available at www.un.org/sustainabledevelopment/sustainable-development-goals (accessed 9 January 2016).

UNECE (2013) *Empowering Educators for a Sustainable Future*. Geneva: UNECE. Available at www.unece.org/fileadmin/DAM/env/esd/Images/Empowering_Educators_for_a_Sustainable_Future.pdf (accessed 9 January 2016).

UNESCO (2005) *Guidelines and Recommendations for Reorienting Teacher Education to Address Sustainability: Education for Sustainable Development in Action*. Technical paper no. 2. Paris: UNESCO Education Sector.

Ward, H. (1998) Geographical vocabulary. In S. Scoffham (ed.), *Primary Sources: Research Findings in Primary Geography*. Sheffield: Geographical Association.

WWF (2010) *Learning for Sustainability in Schools: Effective Pedagogies*. Godalming: WWF.

Websites

▓ *Ashden:* www.ashden.org
▓ *Sustainable Development Goals:* www.globalgoals.org
▓ *Model UN Conference on Climate Change:* www.geography.org.uk/projects/global-learningprogramme/cpd/climateconference

Storybooks

Baker, J. (1987) *Where the Forest Meets the Sea*. London: Walker Books.

Baker, J. (2002) *Window*. London: Walker Books.

Foreman, M. (2013) *Superfrog and the Big Stink*. London: Andersen Books.

Gliori, D. (2009) *The Trouble with Dragons*. London: Bloomsbury.

Morch, R. (2007) *Who Will Save Us?* Rebecca Morch Publishing.

Morpugo, M. (2004) *Dolphin Boy*. London: Andersen Press.

Patten, B. (2003) *Ben's Magic Telescope*. London: Penguin.

Readman, J. (2004) *The World Came to My Place Today*. St Blazey: Eden Project Books.

Serres, A. (2012) *I Have the Right to Be a Child*. London: Phoenix Yard Books.

Smith, D. J. and Armstrong, S. (2004) *If the World Were a Village*. Toronto: Kids Can Press.

Smith Milway, K. (2009) *One Hen: How One Small Loan Made a Big Difference*. Toronto: Kids Can Press.

CHAPTER 14

KEEPING GEOGRAPHY MESSY

Stephen Pickering

One of the main ideas in this chapter is that geographical themes and issues involve complex problems that rarely have precise or clear-cut answers. This chapter also highlights how learning is itself an untidy process that does not fall into the neat and orderly sequences that many would have us believe. Finding out about the real world is, inevitably, a much messier process than studying sanitised textbook examples. If the curriculum is to be meaningful it involves, as Catling and Pickering (2010) argue, investigating real issues rather than separating children from them. Getting your hands dirty is part of the process of engaging with this fascinating subject.

CREATIVITY: A MESSY BUSINESS

When Phineas Gage set out to work on the railway early one morning in 1848 he had no idea that he was about to lead the way in brain research. His job was to clear rocks so that the railway tracks could be laid, but on 13 September (an unlucky day for Phineas) a spark from the rock set off the gunpowder too early and the metal bar he used for tamping down the explosives was blown straight through his head and out of the top of the skull with such force that it landed 30 metres away. Undeterred, he hitched a ride into the nearest town where a doctor tried his best to cover the hole. Amazingly, Phineas lived for a further 12 years with a hole in his head. But his personality changed from a happy, generous soul to one who was quick to anger and who lacked all inhibitions. Constant swearing was the least worrying of his new personality traits. But this messy accident also heralded the realisation that different areas of the brain are responsible for different emotions and learning, and the start of modern neuroscience.

The findings emerging from current research confirm that the brain, as well as being little understood, is indeed a messy organ (Goswami 2015). There are multiple links and connections; neural pathways vary from one individual to another and brain areas that appear to have one function are sometimes recruited for other purposes. The evolutionary processes that have resulted in overlaps and multiplicity help to give the brain its resilience. In this chapter we investigate how the messiness of geography and the messiness of learning can combine in creative approaches to teaching. Children think in a variety of ways: intuitively, cognitively and emotionally. One of the advantages of creative approaches to teaching is that they draw on a range of different capacities and challenge children to arrange their thoughts in new configurations. If children are made aware of the way in which they learn and which type of thinking they have been engaged in, then they will be better placed to apply these thinking skills to new situations.

TEACHING MAP SKILLS CREATIVELY

Messy maps

Villages, towns and cities often develop haphazardly over long historical periods. Indeed, pupils may discover that their own school is a bit of a mess, consisting of higgledy-piggledy buildings that have been put up for different purposes at different times in the past including mobile classrooms. You might begin by asking the children to define what they understand by the term 'mess'. They will probably start with untidiness and images of their bedroom and move (perhaps with a bit of teacher input!) towards a more general idea that things that are messy lack a sense of order. Now look at local maps and plans, perhaps focusing on the school and its surroundings, a local attraction like a theme park or the area in which children live. This is a great way for children to discover the apparent chaos in the roads, highways and infrastructure that actually give order to their lives. Can they identify any loose or abandoned spaces? Why do they think these areas have become neglected and how might they be used in the future?

Physical maps, particularly when you consider landscape and relief, or even a meandering river, provide further examples of 'messy geography'. Try zooming in and out of an area using Google Earth to view images at a range of scales and perspectives. Make comparisons with traditional maps and discuss the things that seem odd. Can the children explain how the odd and illogical things might have come about? Can they see any order within the apparent mess?

It is important for children to understand that places are complex, particularly as they develop haphazardly over time. You can help them to move beyond simple 'yes/no' answers to more nuanced and evaluative modes of thinking. Embracing complexity and accepting that there are not necessarily clear-cut or definitive solutions to problems is part of creative thinking.

Additionally, learning is almost always enhanced if pupils can understand *why* they are learning. According to Barnes (2015) children often remark that learning seems easier when it makes sense to them. Basically they need to see the relevance of the subject. Neurologist Howard Gardner (1999) asserts that, as an organism, the brain learns best when it is exploring situations and asking questions to which it actively craves the answers. Meanwhile, Antonio Damasio (2003, 2012) has established the importance of the emotional component of learning. The following exercises show how mapwork can be both relevant, providing a local focus, and challenging – the challenge of creative interpretations.

Map detectives

This is a super activity that helps children to make links between maps and the places they portray. It can be easily adapted to suit a range of ages. Arm each small group of children with a digital camera and ask them to take six photographs of small, interesting details around the school grounds (examples might include a special bench, places where the playground markings have been rubbed off or the area under a bench). Older children can mark where they have taken their photos on an outline map of the school. Put each photograph onto a PowerPoint slide and print them off as a slideshow (six slides to a page). Now get the children to swap sheets, give them an outline map of the school, ask them to discover where the photos were taken and mark them on the map. You could also ask pupils to take photographs that illustrate a theme such as sustainable practice, messy places or favourite places. The aim is to connect real places to maps. Children might work with maps of different scales (e.g. classroom or school grounds), depending on which is most appropriate.

Making messy maps

Pupils love to do things differently. Challenge them to create a messy or unusual map of their local area (Figures 14.1 and 14.2). They could use chalk and the playground, or arrange tables and chairs – anything they can utilise – to create a map of the local area in their classroom or hall. To do this they will need to collaborate, discuss features, describe the local area to each other, use artistic licence and consider what makes their local area distinctive. They can follow this up by taking groups on a guided tour of the area, highlighting distinctive features, or even create a documentary film.

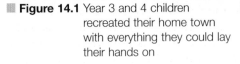

▨ **Figure 14.1** Year 3 and 4 children recreated their home town with everything they could lay their hands on

▨ **Figure 14.2** The children raided the PE store to create their maps

Living maps

One way to help children become familiar with Ordnance Survey maps is to personalise them. Use the set of cards shown in Figure 14.3 with pupils at Key Stage 2. Children will need to read and interpret the map in order to choose appropriate places to apply the statements. You can challenge the children further by getting them to write their own statements to test each other. These questions might be structured around skills. For example, pupils could write two cards that focus on each of the following: scale, signs, symbols and map-reading.

The cards in Figure 14.3 encourage children to evaluate the places shown on the map. (The train station is 3.5km SW as the crow flies.) They imagine what they are like (this is my favourite spot because …). This calls for both cognitive and emotional responses and draws on different neural networks. The exercise works best if you use a map local to your school and create your own appropriate 'living map' cards. You can develop this further by using maps of different scales and compare how the statements vary. The exercise can also be linked with Modern Languages, using, for example, a French map and creating simple French phrases.

What a great place for a picnic!	The church is only 2 km away, but it is much further if you travel by road.	I can't see the town because of the hills.	The slope is really steep here: great for sledging in winter.
This is the centre of the wood.	If you travel due east for 5 km you will reach the centre of town.	Isn't this spot beautiful?	This is probably the busiest road.
I wouldn't like to stay here in the middle of the night!	The train station is 3.5 km south-west as the crow flies.	I think the views from here are best.	If you want a good job you should come to this place.
I wouldn't be able to see this on a larger-scale map.	The bypass is best placed here.	If we are to develop this area, we need a shopping centre here.	This is my favourite spot because…

■ **Figure 14.3** Statements that might be used in a set of 'living map' cards

Messy scale

Scale can be quite a difficult concept for children, particularly those who may not have travelled far in their young lives or who fall asleep as soon as they set off on a long car journey! It is rare for children to engage with maps when travelling in order to gain a sense of distance or scale, yet these fundamental skills are necessary for both understanding maps and developing knowledge of places. They also feature as part of a balanced geography curriculum. Traditionally, scale is often taught as a classroom activity that dovetails mathematics and mapwork. However, children's understanding of scale can be greatly enhanced by fieldwork in the local area. This can, quite literally, be a messy business in which pupils get stuck into their surroundings. However, practical activities help them gain a sense of place and space, which they can then apply when the look at maps when they return the classroom.

Google Earth

Google Earth is a fantastic tool to develop the notion of scale in a local, national or global context. Images from Google Earth can be easily transferred onto an interactive whiteboard using the camera tool and then annotated by the children. Pupils might add a set of research questions or add speech bubbles and thoughts to the map. Using the Street View tool, the children can act as if they are taxi drivers taking the class on a guided tour of virtually any major road network in the world. All it takes is that creative spark from the children, but it develops deep (and quick) thinking as children base their commentaries on previous knowledge, connect learning from different subjects and start thinking about places in a more holistic sense. The idea outlined in 'map detectives' (see above) can also be explored on computer by cropping, cutting and pasting parts of Google Maps at different scales for children to identify. Additionally, you might use a free download called Scribble Maps, where you can draw over Google Maps, highlight various areas and complete a wide range of map exercises.

Mapping our world

There are some excellent games for the interactive whiteboard that explore scale at a continental and global context. The Oxfam website has activities appropriate for children in Year 1 to Year 6. In a section called 'Mapping Our World', children can flatten out a globe, view the world as an alien might see it at a range of scales and challenge each other to dig through the centre of the Earth and guess where they will emerge! This award-winning site encourages children to engage with and learn about the world in a thoroughly creative and imaginative manner.

Travel agent

Put children into groups of five. Each group needs to have two travel agents and three customers. See that the travel agents are armed with an atlas (or Google Earth), a ruler, a calculator (unless you want to encourage mental maths skills) and perhaps some old travel brochures. Each customer takes one of the traveller cards (Figure 14.4) and becomes that person when they enter the travel agents.

The travel agent has to find the best place for each customer to take a holiday and also answer all the questions they may have. As an additional challenge, pupils could be encouraged to make up some cards of their own. This will help them to appreciate that different people have different requirements and also to view alternative perspectives. The children will quickly learn to pore over the atlas, refer to climate graphs and find out interesting facts and statistics. They will learn to how to conduct research and present their data clearly and effectively.

Explorer	Family	Student	Vulcanologist
Personality: Adventurous	*Personality:* Varied (mum, dad + 4 children)	*Personality*: Intelligent	*Personality:* Fiery
Special requirements: Somewhere exciting with extreme climate	*Special requirements:* Fun for all, not too far to travel, something for everyone	*Special requirements:* Wants to travel across at least two climatic regions, meet interesting people and visit places of culture	*Special requirements:* Likes barbeques and chilli
Type of holiday: Wild	*Type of holiday:* Something different	*Type of holiday:* Touring	*Type of holiday:* Wants to explore an active volcano
Needs to know: Climate, distance, equipment needed to survive	*Needs to know:* Where, distance to travel, what they can do for fun (for the whole family)	*Needs to know:* Cheap way to travel and live, places to visit, people to see, climate and environment	*Needs to know:* What to wear, climate, typical food of chosen region
Old person	**Alien**	**Chef**	**Head teacher**
Personality: Inquisitive	*Personality:* Different	*Personality:* Happy and fun	*Personality:* Grumpy
Special requirements: Frightened of flying	*Special requirements:* Brings own human disguise	*Special requirements:* Exotic food	*Special requirements:* Away from children and families
Type of holiday: Cultural, city and rural Not too hot Likes views	*Type of holiday:* Wants to find out about the human race	*Type of holiday:* Touring	*Type of holiday:* Open to suggestions
Needs to know: Total itinerary and distance to travel Weather and the best time to travel.	*Needs to know:* At present, the alien knows nothing – looks to you to plan the perfect holiday to investigate human beings	*Needs to know:* The typical food of the chosen area and the best things to eat Distance to travel and weather	*Needs to know:* Everything (the head teacher is likely to ask lots of questions)

■ **Figure 14.4** Person specifications for the travel agent simulation

TEACHING CREATIVELY ABOUT THE EARTH

The messy Earth

It can sometimes be helpful to use objects as metaphors to illustrate complex or abstract ideas. You can use an apple, for example, as a way of getting children to think about the Earth. An open-ended question such as 'How is the Earth like an apple?' will get them speculating. At first, children generally give straightforward answers based on the core and the skin, and these can be used to develop their knowledge. But when given encouragement, children's ideas will extend far beyond the obvious. The apple is a living thing. Is the Earth? This leads into an interesting discussion on what it means to be alive and whether the Gaia hypothesis rings true or not (Figure 14.5). There are many other instances where open-ended questions and prompts can help stimulate creative responses. You can find out more about strategies and techniques from the Philosophy for Children website.

▨ **Figure 14.5** How is the Earth like an apple?
Source: adapted from Deborah Haines

How is the Earth like an apple?

Draw the outline of the continents on an apple (board marker pens work well) or get the children to draw outlines on apples of their own. Now ask them to consider how the apple resembles the Earth. In my experience, if you ask the question with the correct emphasis, the class is usually divided over the answer. This means you can then challenge the children to suggest similarities and enhance their geographical knowledge as they investigate further. Here are some interesting facts that may surprise children:

1   The peel of an apple is, proportionately, the same thickness as the Earth's crust.

2   Both the apple and the Earth contain water. Apples are about 75 per cent water: the oceans cover about 71 per cent of the Earth's surface.

3   They both contain life. All sorts of creatures live and breathe on and within the Earth and, of course, on and in apples! Indeed, as Capra and Luisi (2014) argue so convincingly, recognising the interdependence of different organisms is fundamental to understanding our planet.

4   Both are alive in some sense. The Gaia hypothesis by James Lovelock and Lynn Margulis describes the Earth as a living system, just like an apple (Lovelock 1979).

5   They are both spheres. Additionally, neither is a perfect shape. The Earth is an oblate sphere, being very slightly flattened at the poles by millions of years of spinning and bulging at the equator. Apples, of course, are distorted by all sorts of events over their growing life. It is even possible to grow a cubed apple!

TEACHING CREATIVELY ABOUT THE ENVIRONMENT

Climate change

No one knows for sure what the future may bring and this uncertainty can be quite hard for children, particularly when they hear stories of doom and gloom through the media. Climate change is a particular area of concern where children often view adults as spoiling the world they are due to inherit. The threat of flooding, drought and other catastrophes can be really frightening and the media seems to delight in bleak and emotive imagery (Figure 14.6). Such media coverage can be disempowering for children and their worries tend to be exacerbated by their lack of knowledge.

▓ **Figure 14.6** Climate change could have disastrous implications for wildlife
Source: adapted from Deborah Haines

Research shows that children learn through 'connectionism' within and across areas of the brain (Goswami 2015). Blocks can occur where learning is stressful; either through content or pedagogy, and this inhibits learning. When schools place too much emphasis on troubling problems, young people tend to become increasingly worried and disinterested (Scott 2010). An alternative is to engage children creatively and to empower them with knowledge. When children can see through the mess of a 'problem' and are given the chance to develop possible solutions, they become troubleshooters rather than victims. The following activities provide examples of a constructive and positive introduction to developing a creative response to environmental issues and sustainability issues.

Messing with climate change

Start with a selection of photographs that all relate to climate change. It helps if these are not immediately clearly linked. For example, you could choose from images of a coal-fired power station, a dried-up reservoir, a flooded town, a traffic jam, a city at night, alive with lights, or a solar-powered cooker. Cut each of the chosen images into a jigsaw of four or five pieces, one for each child in the class. The first task is for the children to complete the jigsaw and form a group with those who have other parts of the same picture. This is a great way to split children up and get them talking. Now give each group a large sheet of paper and coloured pens and ask the pupils to answer the following questions using their photograph:

▨ Describe the photograph. What can you see? What questions would you like to ask about it?
▨ Can you identify any issues – good or bad – connected to this photograph?
▨ What has this issue got to do with our lives?
▨ What can I do to make things better?

Give the children a few minutes to think about each question before you go on to the next. You can choose whether to have a class feedback session after each question or save this till all the questions have been tackled. The last question is vital. It provides the link between the children's own lives and abstract concepts. Climate change, for example, isn't only something that happens to other people thousands of miles away; it affects us too.

The final challenge is to ask pupils to design a creative solution to climate change. It could be anything at all, inspired by the photographs or not. It may be helpful to describe some of the creative solutions already in place around the world like children's roundabouts in playgrounds in arid areas of South Africa, which pump water up into a tank as the children play, or lamp-posts in England that have a solar panel on top and a wind turbine in the crook so that they become net contributors to the electricity grid.

Sustainability

Sustainability starts at home. It is a messy and complex issue, often simplified in schools to turning off lights and not wasting paper. But it is far more than the way in which we create and manage mess. We produce vast amounts of rubbish and waste that we subsequently have to manage. Each item, however, has a long tale behind it that relates to sustainable production, distribution and discard. The issue of using local food over international supplies to reduce food miles becomes more complex if local production involves a greater carbon footprint, with heating costs and large-scale greenhousing, than importing produce from southern Europe. It is important for children to learn to ask questions and challenge ideas, both to enable them to become more effective learners, but also to gain a broader and deeper understanding of complex processes. Sustainability can be portrayed in a very simple way for the children, which, curiously, opens the door to deeper thinking. The diagram below shows how sustainability can be defined in terms of care (Figure 14.7).

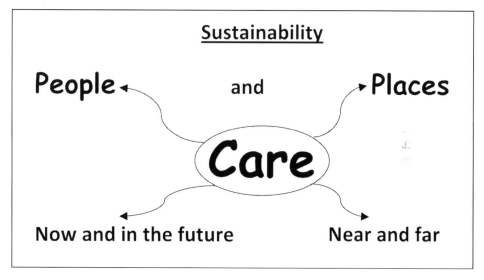

Figure 14.7 There are strong links between notions of care and sustainability

'Care' is a term of which all children are fully aware. Indeed it is used in many contexts throughout early life and this makes it a far more comfortable and easily understood word than 'sustainability'. It is still very important for children to learn and use the term 'sustainable', but the word 'care' can be used to remove some of the myth and confusion. Care also refers to people as much as places and, hopefully, children will be better-placed to move beyond the ideas around recycling and saving energy to working to providing a better life for people around us. The notion of care can be an excellent vehicle for pupils to investigate sustainability with their own sustainable audit following an enquiry cycle designed to allow children to develop creative solutions (Figure 14.8).

Does our school care?

Challenge the children to present their head teacher with a plan to make their school more sustainable under the mission title 'Does our school care for people and places, near and far, now and in the future?' Children should investigate as much as they can about how the school cares for people and places by asking questions, researching, observing and

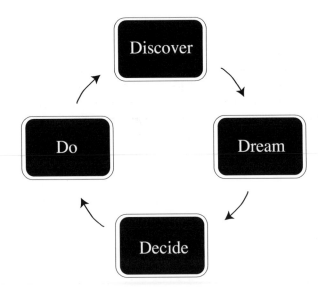

Figure 14.8 The four Ds of the enquiry cycle
Source: adapted from Cooperrider and Whitney (1999)

analysing. It helps if they structure their investigation under the following headings: People, Places, Near, Far, Now, Future. Once they have discovered all they need to know, pupils should work together to *dream up* ways to improve things. This is where the children should be allowed to let their creativity run wild; let them think of the most amazing ways to improve their school. The third stage is the testing one. This is when they have to rein in their creativity alongside actualities. Deep thinking is called for when children have to decide which of their ideas are truly viable and how they could adapt their dreams to make them a reality. The final stage is the 'do'. In this example, the *do* is to present their action plan to the head teacher to make the school more sustainable, thereby helping it truly care for people and places, near and far, now and in the future.

Messy world news

Every day we learn through the media about geographical events that are unfolding around the world. Children naturally want to find out why volcanoes erupt (earth movements), why some places are very wet (climate patterns), why some people dress so strangely (global cultures) and why tigers are becoming extinct (habitat loss). You can build on their enthusiasm by setting up a 'News from around the World' noticeboard in your classroom. Encourage children to bring newspaper cuttings about geographical events and processes from the local to the global. Everything from sporting occasions like the Olympic Games to floods in Europe and Asia can generate great interest in the world and its people. This ongoing activity provides rich opportunities for children to ask the questions that lurk at the back of the mind. It also helps to open their eyes to the wonderful world we inhabit for inspection and debate.

CONCLUSION

Children love mess, be it a messy bedroom, a messy river to scramble around or a muddy field, and this notion of mess really should be embraced within learning too. If children are given the opportunities to accept that there are some patterns and processes, issues and concerns around the world that are 'messy' and for which there is not necessarily a single solution, then they will also find it easier to understand this messy world of ours. But there is a fundamental learning element to this idea of mess as well: mess encourages investigation. It encourages critical thinking and, crucially, it encourages learners to start to think for themselves, to sort in their minds which elements of the mess could be important information and how the mess might mean different things to different people. In other words, accepting that the world is a messy place and getting involved and trying to find creative solutions, or at least reason within the mess, helps children to develop as critical thinkers and effective learners.

ACKNOWLEDGEMENT

The idea for 'Messing with climate change' is adapted from the World Wide Fund for Nature (WWF) Reaching Out programme, with thanks to R. Brakspear and the Worcestershire County Council sustainability team. I am grateful to Anthony Barlow, Jane Whittle and Ruth Potts for their ideas on messy maps, which appear in *Primary Geographer* 73 (Autumn 2010). Finally, I would like to thank children and staff at Upton Primary School, Upton-upon-Severn, Worcestershire, and the Wyche C of E Primary School, Malvern, Worcestershire.

REFERENCES AND FURTHER READING

Barnes, J. (2015) *Cross Curricular Learning 3–14* (3rd edn). London: Routledge.

Capra, F. and Luisi, P. L. (2014) *The Systems View of Life*. Cambridge: Cambridge University Press.

Catling, S. and Pickering, S. (2010) Mess, mess, glorious mess. *Primary Geographer* 73: 16–17.

Cooperrider, D. and Whitney, D. (1999) *Collaborating for Change: Appreciative Inquiry*. San Francisco, CA: Berrett-Koehler.

Damasio, A. (2003) *Looking for Spinoza*. Orlando, FL: Harcourt.

Damasio, A. (2012) *Self Comes to Mind*. London: Vantage.

Gardner, H. (1999) *The Disciplined Mind*. Upper Saddle River, NJ: Prentice Hall.

Goswami, U. (2008) Principles of learning, implications for teaching: a cognitive neuroscience perspective. *Journal of Philosophy of Education* 42(3–4): 381–99.

Goswami, U. (2015) *Children's Cognitive Development and Learning: A Report for the Cambridge Primary Review Trust*. CPRT Research Survey 3. Cambridge: Cambridge Primary Review Trust.

Lovelock, J. (1979) *Gaia: A New Look at Life on Earth*. Oxford: Oxford University Press.

Pickering, S. (2008) *Pupils Advise on Sustainability: Primary Subjects 2, DfCSF/CfSA*. Northwold: Buxton Press.

Scott, W. (2010) *Sustainable Schools: Seven Propositions around Young People's Motivations, Interests and Knowledge*. London: SEED.

Websites

- ▓ *Google Earth:* http://earth.google.com
- ▓ *Oxfam:* www.oxfam.org.uk
- ▓ *Philosophy for Children:* www.philosophy4children.co.uk
- ▓ *Scribble Maps:* www.scribblemaps.com
- ▓ *World Wide Fund for Nature:* www.wwf.org.uk

CHAPTER

15

INSIDE, OUTSIDE AND BEYOND THE CLASSROOM

Stephen Scoffham with Jonathan Barnes, Peter Vujakovic and Paula Owens

Schools, colleges and universities are the key institutions charged with transmitting and promoting learning in a modern society. They are dedicated to education and staffed by people who have a professional interest in learning and an expertise in their subjects. Most tutors and teachers are also trained in communicating ideas and working with groups of students. Yet, as we all know, learning also happens in everyday contexts and in haphazard and unstructured ways. This is especially true of young children who are finding out about the world around them and trying to make sense of it for the first time in their lives. By the time they come to school just about every one of them will have learnt their native language and come to understand many of the nuances of its grammar and syntax. They will have accomplished this extraordinary achievement without any formal instruction and without any externally imposed learning targets or achievement indicators.

Learning happens in many different ways. It doesn't only happen in classroom settings with a group of around 30 children and a teacher working in isolation from the world around them. Learning also happens in the playground as children play together. It happens on the journey from home to school. It happens in leisure pursuits and pastimes and in the home as children interact with their parents, carers and siblings. Schools undoubtedly contribute enormously to children's learning but formal education doesn't suit all pupils equally. Nor are schools children's only source of knowledge and experience.

There is a growing interest in informal learning and the value of outdoor experiences (Waite 2011; Pickering 2016). There is also an on-going debate about what modern schools can and should look like (Robinson and Aronica 2015). These are huge questions which go right to the heart of what we think matters and how we can best equip children to live fulfilling and worthwhile lives. Rather than addressing these questions head on, this chapter provides a sample of non-standard approaches to learning. Different authors offer portraits of how practical activities inside, outside and beyond the classroom can draw on diverse, inter-active teaching methods to stimulate geographical learning.

ARTEFACTS THAT TELL THE STORY OF THE WORLD

Stephen Scoffham

Since the earliest times in human history people have devised artefacts to help them in their daily lives. Four million years ago our ancient ancestors started to gain an advantage over other animals using stone axes and spears. However, the processes involved in designing and making simple tools are also believed to have had a profound evolutionary significance. Tool making required a wide range of skills including manual dexterity, forward planning and social communication. In turn this stimulated a period of rapid brain growth and eventually resulted, according to Capra and Luisi (2014), in the development of language and reflective consciousness. People are thus linked to technology at the very deepest levels.

Today, wherever you live and whatever you do, you are likely to be surrounded by artefacts. All the things that you use will have been devised by people at one time or another in the past and collectively they represent the creativity, values and culture of the societies which generated them. This suggests that even apparently simple everyday items are invested with social meanings. In addition, artefacts are manifest expressions of innovative thinking. Moran and John-Steiner (2003) argue that future cycles of creativity draw on notions which have been internalised from current and past products. One of the implications of this argument is that creativity, while it may appear to emanate from individuals, should also be seen as being vested in groups.

The objects described below have been selected because they each relate to a different aspect of human life and illustrate key geography concepts. They are also likely to be familiar to children and link directly to their everyday lives. Why not set up a geography display table of your own that tells the story of your area or which links to different locations? This might perhaps take a thematic or conceptual approach (Figure 15.1). Alternatively, you could look back to the past or forward to the future.

1 A BOTTLE OF WATER

CONCEPTS: WATER, WEATHER AND THE ENVIRONMENT

We depend on water in lots of different ways. We drink, cook and wash in it. Water irrigates crops, helps to run factories and provides the power to make electricity. Although seas and oceans cover nearly three quarters of the Earth's surface, fresh water represents less than three per cent of the total. Most fresh water lies deep underground or is frozen in the polar ice caps. Nevertheless, there is enough to meet our needs. The problem is that supplies are unevenly distributed and drought and erratic weather conditions are affecting people in many parts of the world. Obtaining supplies of clean drinking water is essential for health. Bottled water is one guarantee of quality. The label will also indicate the source, opening up a discussion about the water cycle, rivers and weather patterns.

2 A FOSSIL

CONCEPTS: ROCKS AND MOUNTAINS

Fossils have been a key source of evidence for piecing together the story of life on Earth. They also show that the rocks that are now at the top of high mountain ranges were once

■ **Figure 15.1** A collection of fridge magnets is one way to develop children's locational knowledge

under the sea. Children love collecting rocks and fossils and they make an excellent addition to any geography display. Ammonites, belemnites and other small sea creatures from the Jurassic period are quite common in many parts of the UK. Fossilised dinosaur bones feature in museum collections and new finds are reported in the media from time to time as they are discovered. Extend the collection to include minerals and brightly coloured stones. You may not be able to identify them all but a simple collector's guide will certainly help.

3 A PAIR OF WOOLLEN GLOVES

CONCEPTS: SEASONS, WEATHER AND CLIMATE

The weather in the UK is notoriously variable. The interaction between warm air from the equator and cold air from the poles means that there are continual changes in temperature and humidity. Children are particularly responsive to the weather and enjoy learning more about it. There are plenty of opportunities for practical work. Recording the weather on a day-to-day basis links strongly with science while seasonal changes are revealed in longer-term patterns. A pair of gloves represents the winter just as a sun hat or sunglasses can symbolise the summer. Finding out what causes the seasons and how the seasons affect plants and creatures takes the work to greater depths.

4 A MAP OF THE LONDON UNDERGROUND

CONCEPTS: MAPS, ROUTES AND JOURNEYS

Geographers are particularly interested in where places and are and how they relate to each other. Maps are a powerful way of representing such spatial information. There are many types of map ranging from the personal maps we carry in our heads to the formal maps found in atlases and gazetteers. The London Underground map has become a classic because it is brilliantly effective at showing the sequence of stations and links between lines. If children are exposed to different types of map, it gives them models they can copy and adapt. There are a surprising number of occasions when you need to find out where places are. Finding out the answer and speculating over routes and connections can be a highly creative process.

5 A CUDDLY TOY

CONCEPTS: HABITATS AND BIODIVERSITY

Children have a deep-seated empathy for the natural environment and tend to be fascinated by living creatures. Finding out about animal habitats is one way of exploiting their interest. Celebrating the variety and wonders of the animal kingdom is also an excellent starting point for wider investigations. Four thousand million years of Earth history have given rise to great diversity. Sadly, many creatures are under threat, particularly due to human pressure and climate change. The cuddly toys that many children have treasured since they were toddlers symbolise not only their interest in animals but also suggest issues to do with biodiversity. There are plenty of links to geography. Bears, for example, are found around the world – koalas in Australia, brown bears in the Rockies, polar bears in the Arctic. Identifying these places and finding out about their climate is an integral part of any study.

6 AN ENERGY-EFFICIENT LIGHT BULB

CONCEPTS: ENERGY AND CLIMATE CHANGE

One of the great challenges at the present time is to find ways of reducing carbon emissions. Scientists warn that without radical measures we face the prospect of damaging global warming and climate change. The humble energy-efficient light bulb could be part of the solution. These bulbs use a fraction of the power of incandescent bulbs, last much longer and give out roughly equivalent amounts of light. Other measures to save energy at home, school and work could make a really significant difference to our carbon emissions and be part of a battery of strategies to combat climate change. However, time is not on our side as levels of atmospheric carbon dioxide need to be drastically reduced to have any meaningful impact.

7 A BANANA

CONCEPTS: FOOD, TRADE AND GLOBAL INEQUALITIES

Much of the food that we eat in the UK comes from other countries. We import grain from the USA and Canada and fresh fruit and vegetables from the Mediterranean. Some other products such as tea, coffee and pineapples come from the tropics. Bananas make a particularly interesting case study. Supplies are shipped to the UK from the Caribbean, central Africa and parts of southern Asia and distributed to shops and supermarkets from warehouses. Some bananas are grown under fair trade agreements that ensure that producers receive reasonable remuneration for their work. Others are sold on the open market where prices fluctuate. Finding out about the terms of trade raises questions about global inequalities. It also reminds us how we are linked to other people around the world through the food chain and how we depend on them for our survival.

8 A MOBILE PHONE

CONCEPTS: COMMUNICATION AND THE FUTURE

Mobile phones have not only become cheaper and more versatile in recent years, they have also become more powerful. As well as sending messages, mobiles are important for navigation and a significant number of internet searches are to do with location. The traffic is not all one-way. Any mobile that contains a battery is tracked by satellite, effectively monitoring the whereabouts of the vast majority of people in economically developed countries. Thus the children in your class are not only going to benefit from the information about the world that is now, literally, at their finger-tips, they are also going to have to come to terms with the privacy implications and learn how to cope with information overload. As a communication tool the mobile phone has eliminated distance and opened up enormous possibilities for intercultural dialogue. In this sense it is profoundly interesting to geographers.

FOCUS EXERCISES FOR OUTDOOR WORK

Jonathan Barnes

If geography teachers are to encourage thinking in, about and through places, then they will need a range of strategies to support children's learning. My own experience and research indicates that there are advantages in starting with activities that involve physical, sensory and emotional engagement with place. The focus exercises described below are designed to give children practical experiences in their immediate environment. Although the activities are tightly framed, the geographical follow-up is left to teacher, child or group. Using touch, smell, sight, hearing, social and emotional entry points, the activities encourage pupils to collect data about different places at an age-appropriate level. They can be applied in any environment, inside or out, in familiar or unfamiliar places. They are also open-ended and can be followed up in a wide variety of ways.

Experience over ten years of using these focus exercises has shown that they frequently generate conditions of 'flow' or timeless involvement (Csikszentmihalyi 1997). Psychologists argue that these occasions are optimum times for deep learning, connection-making and creative thought (Fredrickson 2009). Participation in the exercises also provides opportunities to draw on what is known as 'distributed intelligence' (Lucas and Claxton 2011). This is the type of thinking that arises when we use tools and devices invented by others to augment our ideas. In other words, it occurs when we are sharing and communicating thoughts rather than working in isolation.

HEALTH AND SAFETY

Children's physical and emotional safety needs to be every teacher's primary concern. Fieldwork will not constitute any extra risks to the child if the following simple checks are carried out:

1   Know and follow the health and safety policies of the school/local authority.
2   Always make a preliminary visit to the site to be visited with another person to assess any potential hazards.
3   Note the potential hazards and enter them on the school health and safety documentation.
4   Communicate potential hazards to all adults supervising and all children participating.
5   Speak to children about their responsibility to keep themselves safe and be aware of dangers for others.

DESCRIBING PLACES USING MAPS AND DIAGRAMS

▓   *Emotional map:* Ask pupils to record their feelings about their school or local area with words or colours on an outline map (sad, happy, lonely, frightened, excited and so on). Get pupils to report back on their findings and present information in posters.
▓   *Sound map:* Make a map using symbols or words to record the dominant sound in each area. Make large composite maps to the show the character of the area you have surveyed.
▓   *Smell map:* Get pupils to mark the location of the smells that they identify in each place they visit. Show the boundaries between them. Discuss any changes that could

be made to the area to address any negative features, e.g. unpleasant sounds and smells.

■ *Touch map:* Make a map to show different textures and surfaces along a journey. Create a local map for someone in a wheelchair or with a visual impediment as an extension activity.

■ *Panorama:* Select a place where you can see in different compass directions. Ask pupils to draw an outline of what they can see on the skyline to the north, east, south and west. Use thick marker pens and large sheets of kitchen paper. Assemble and present a collection of different 360-degree drawings of the area as a classroom follow-up activity. Add a large movable arrow to show wind direction. Paint a continuous skyline to create a freeze to decorate the school.

■ *Sound diagram:* Ask pupils to draw a small circle to represent a plan view of their head, adding ears at the side and a nose at the front. Now get them to listen carefully to the sounds around them. They should mark the location of each sound on their diagram, using arrows to show moving sounds such as cars and aeroplanes. Devise a walk across the school site to make a sound transect or cross-section of quiet and noisy places. Compare how the sound environment of the school changes during the day. You could also discuss noise pollution or the contribution sounds make to the character of the environment. Try making a musical map of the area to reflect local sounds and noises (Figure 15.2).

■ **Figure 15.2** Pupils at Woolmore Primary School, Tower Hamlets, listen to sounds and assess the quality of the environment while on a trail
Source: photo by Jonathan Barnes

▓   *Colour match:* Ask children to use paint swatches (available in different colours from DIY shops) to find matching examples in natural and built environments. They should attach around half a dozen examples to a length of double-sided tape attached to a cardboard strip (no living animals please!). Discuss the colours that were easiest and hardest to find. Consider how colour contributes to the quality of the environment. Devise a short trail focusing on a specific colour such as red or yellow as a follow-up exercise.

CASE STUDY 1 DESCRIBING AN URBAN AREA

Three-hundred-and-twenty children walked excitedly and carefully along Robin Hood Lane to visit Canary Wharf in the London Docklands less than 500 metres from the school gates. Nursery children were paired with Year 6 pupils, Reception with Year 5 and the Year 1s held hands with Year 4s. The children worked in mixed-age groups of six with the support and care of teachers, teaching assistants and adult helpers. The aim of the visit was to collect as much information as possible about the area. Children conducted traffic surveys, made rubbings, noted the routes taken by people, hunted for geometric shapes, took photographs and absorbed sights and smells. None of this information could have been gathered from a website or written sources. For some pupils it was the first time they had really looked at the shiny glass-and-steel office blocks or seen the River Thames. Back at school their work blossomed as they recalled and recounted their experiences in the following days.

RESPONDING IMAGINATIVELY TO PLACES

▓   *Journey sticks:* Individual children use a strip of card with double-sided tape on the front to collect five small items from a short walk. (Do not collect any living creature.) Get them to theme their collection (e.g. life, decay, same colour etc.) or simply collect items at random. Discuss the choices and compare results. Using the journey sticks as a prompt, pupils describe and/or map the route they followed. See if they can make up a story that links the different items collected in an imaginative way. Talk about the landmarks that help us find our way between places, e.g. journey from home to school.

▓   *Haiku:* Write your own haiku (a three-line classical Japanese poem that uses only 17 syllables; five in line one, seven in line two and five in line three). Start by choosing a tiny detail of the environment. Describe it in the first two lines and then lift it to a higher philosophical plain by asking a deep question arising from it. Traditionally, Japanese haikus make some mention of the seasons too. Working in groups, ask the children to share their haikus with each other and the rest of the class. Take photographs or make drawings to illustrate or complement the haikus. Make a display of haikus that give poetic impressions of the local area.

▓   *Fridge-magnet poems:* Fold an A4 sheet into 16 rectangles, then unfold it to reveal the spaces. Ask pupils to explore their surroundings and write down 16 random words that relate to their chosen spot and environment. Get the children to arrange their words into a meaningful poem or sentence. They could add extra words and they don't have to use all the words they have collected. Repeat the exercise, restricting children to geographical words and ideas.

CASE STUDY 2 USING A LOCAL STREET

In one school, a Year 4 teacher developed a project to enhance her students' connection with their community. The children began by discussing their ideas of community before considering the question 'How is our street a community and how can I impact upon it?' They then divided into small groups and ventured into the street in small groups (each supervised by an adult) to collect data from different angles and perspectives. One group focused on the changing sounds, a second group noted traffic hazards and talked about how to solve them, while a third group used small items of litter to deduce something about the life of the street. Others photographed houses of different ages. One pupil commented, 'I really enjoyed today because it got me looking at the street in ways I don't normally'. Back at school, each group used a planning sheet to develop a project they felt would create a positive change in their local community. They were supported by a town planner, an architect, a geography lecturer and a scientist (gathered from the teacher's friends and school governors) to develop their project.

■ **Figure 15.3** Some children considered ways of redesigning the street outside their school as part of their project on the local community

Source: photo by Jonathan Barnes

TIME, LIFE AND LANDSCAPE: WAVING TO MR HENSHAW

Peter Vujakovic

If there is one common theme that unites most young children, it is an abiding fascination with lost landscapes and animals of the past. Dinosaurs, trilobites, mammoths and sabre-toothed cats populate their imaginations of 'deep time' and appear to have particular appeal in early and middle childhood. Understanding life and landscapes can be enhanced through this fascination, by encouraging children to see themselves as part of a grand narrative; as occupying a point in both space and time from which they have a grandstand view of environmental processes, and an understanding of the geology beneath their feet.

This theme offers wide scope for use of visual material; on video and in dioramas published in popular books on the subject. Fossils and models of extinct or speculative organisms can be deployed creatively in the class ('show and tell') or even outside. Pupils can be engaged by asking what it would have been like to live in these environments (consider climate, biomes and habitats), and prompted to question the veracity of 'staged' constructions. Is nature always 'red in tooth and claw' as many images of 'deep time' suggest?

During key stage one, you can help pupils to develop their ideas about time using sequencing exercises. Young children in particular find it difficult to distinguish human and geological time scales. Things which happened to their parents and grandparents become confused with much more ancient events such as the Fire of London. They may muddle historical periods like the Roman Empire with the age of the dinosaurs or geological eras. Arranging pictures and drawings of the past along a line of string suspended on a display board or across the corner of the classroom is one way to build children's sense of chronology. Images might range from exploding volcanoes or fossils of sea creatures, to Queen Victoria and the Egyptian pyramids. Consider including creatures which have become extinct like the mammoth or the dodo. Get pupils to display the pictures in a sequence using clothes pegs to fix them to the line at appropriate points. Once they are familiar with the idea of a time line you might want to change or add to the images, perhaps to match the work you are doing in history. Don't worry too much about the order being 'correct'. The main aim is get children thinking and talking.

At key stage two, physical geography is a major theme in the geography curriculum. Rivers, mountains, volcanoes, earthquakes and the water cycle are specifically mentioned along with climate zones, biomes and vegetation belts. Engagement with past landscapes and habitats provides a route to understanding the impact of slow but continual changes which have shaped the world around us. There is an extensive range of BBC programmes on landscapes, dinosaurs and very early life, perhaps the most famous of which are David Attenborough's films of the natural world. The sheer number of these films indicates the extent of public engagement with natural histories and 'deep time' tableaux, and the way that they have fired the public imagination. You can use these films as teaching resources and select extracts for the children to discuss.

Children can extend their geographical enquiries inside and outside the classroom by creatively thinking about past and future environments. The UK's rich and complex geological heritage presents teachers everywhere with a wonderful resource, literally beneath their feet. Draw a line in chalk 90 metres long across the playground to represent 4.5 billion years of the Earth's existence, and stand Mr Henshaw at the far end when the Earth began. At this scale each metre will represent 50 million years. Ask the children to place fossils, toy dinosaurs and other animals where they think they should exist in time. The first five metres should be fairly cluttered. The first ten will include all significant fossilised life. A murky bottle of water, representing early life, can be placed within twenty metres of Mr Henshaw. Everyone wave to Mr Henshaw, a very lonely mammal indeed!

Another creative approach is for children to project their understanding of landscape and life into the future. What might new life forms look like? How are they adapted to the world around them? Children can be engaged creatively by constructing their own spec-ulative organisms ('sporgs'), then placing them in real environments and habitats to create dioramas. Pupils can use a digital cameras and video to record these 'habitats' for display. More fancifully they might focus on sea monsters such as the legendary kraken which was believed to live off the coast of Norway and Greenland. These activities encourage chil-dren to think deeply about the links between place and resources. Any models they make can be collected into a 'cabinet of curiosities' as a permanent record of the learning process, pupil's creativity, and as a talking point in its own right. Making links to literacy and stories provides a natural extension which will further fuel their imagination and develop their understanding of 'deep time' (Figure 15.4).

Figure 15.4 Toy creatures such as dinosaurs enable children to create miniature words that engage their imagination

WILDTHINK: A FRAMEWORK FOR CREATIVE AND CRITICAL LEARNING

Paula Owens

'Wildthink' is a new concept which expresses a framework for creative and critical learning and a philosophy for transformative change. The term, originally coined by Owens, Rawlinson and Witt (2012), implies a way of thinking that is not afraid to walk on the wild side and explore the less travelled path. It is arguably an approach that ought to be part of any agenda purporting to enable learners to be both creative and critical actors in their own futures.

In our risk-averse world it has become easy, even acceptable, to focus on what is safe and familiar and to avoid the risky, dangerous, peripheral areas of learning or at least to limit our contact with those treacherous territories. We are also bombarded with a range of stimuli and have learnt to blank out much that stimulates us in order to survive and make progress. Yet, if we are to support courageous learners with the capacity to intrepidly explore the world around them and its many problems, we ought to seek out and explore those shadowy borderlands of uncertainty. Here, in these less pressured places, we can take our time and linger, learning to move slowly, attentively, dialogically and playfully.

Learning experiences are sometimes like river channels that have been straightened and streamlined enabling us to attain clearly defined goals in an efficient and timely way. Yet often, in moving too fast in a linear direction, much peripheral hinterland and secret scenery is missed (Figure 15.5). New ways of knowing the world are needed as there are still so many problems to be solved and on a grand scale. Creative thinkers have perhaps never been needed more desperately. It's not enough to just go over the same old ground: we need to look beyond those familiar horizons and explore the bigger picture. We need to put the meanders back into learning.

Wildthink offers ideas for creative learning on several levels. In putting the meanders back, we reclaim new ways of seeing and exploring what we might otherwise miss. Thus it is a rationale for a form of enquiry that is not afraid of risks and yet which is contemplative and mindful of them nonetheless. Wildthink is also a pedagogy for practice that seeks to slow down and linger, embracing the unexpected dividends that new directions, flexibility and personalised responses can bring.

The Wildthink map (see Figure 15.6) uses the idea of a physical landscape to metaphorically consider the types of learning journeys that we offer children today. In our sanitised classrooms with an overbearing focus on core subjects such as maths and English and driven by target setting and assessment practices, our learning journeys can easily become the shortest distance between two points. We take the superhighway or learning motorway where we can speed along and reach the end objective as quickly as possible – allowing for monitoring and assessment checks that is. Yet by doing this, we are denying children vital opportunities to take risks, admire the scenery and explore hidden corners along the way.

Just as with channelised rivers, surges of learning can, like water, flood the barriers meant to contain them and seep back into the ground of sleeping thoughts. Yet meanders can restore equilibrium and allow those with faster learning inclinations to take the inside bends: everyone is more equitably accommodated. Embracing the landscape of learning and creating opportunities to talk, to stare, to think to explore and to take risks is something we need to do from time to time. Let's develop children's natural curiosity and feed it and encourage new qualities of resilience and self-direction.

■ **Figure 15.5** Student teachers from Winchester University exploring and responding to place in the Brecon Beacons

Wildthink Map

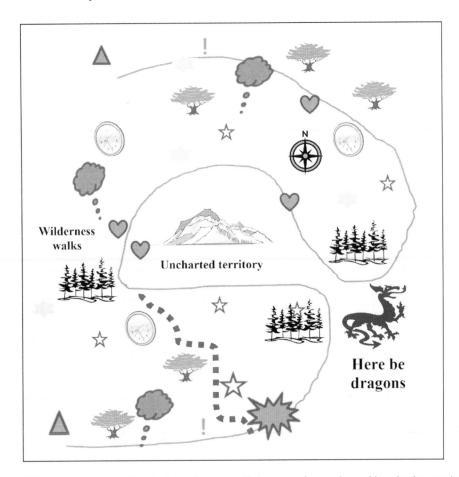

Wildthink puts the meanders back into learning, offering scope for creative and imaginative enquiry.

Linear Learning

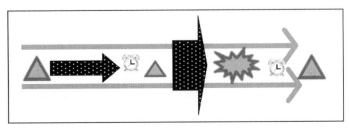

Linear learning can be likened to a channelized river: it cannot cope with additional volume or blockages and overflows its banks. Short narrow channels can also be too tightly packed with assessment, restricting flow.

▨ **Figure 15.6** Creativity is best promoted by slower forms of learning

Map Key		
Icon	Meaning	Implication
△	Assessment checkpoint	Teaching and learning must be an interactive, collaborative process, where teachers can talk with pupils and raise open-ended questions in order to construct and share their understandings. Testing and grading alone do not support great progress. Activating learners as owners of their own learning can be very powerful (Wiliam 2011, Wiliam and Leahy 2015).
✸	Learning barrier or jam	Barriers are opportunities demanding alternative, pioneering routes. Immersive and intuitive – the landscape invites participation (see Gibson's affordance theory in Matthews 1992).
→	Linear learning path	Meanders have been taken out but there's trouble downstream! Any learning too focused on outcomes may miss peripheral scenery along the way. Congestion in the channel causes 'flooding' and loss of learning. *Learning is not found at the end of the road but on its path.*
⏰	Timed Tasks and rote learning	Research data have suggested that overlearning, e.g. of geography facts, is an inefficient strategy for learning material for meaningfully long periods of time. (Rohrer et al. 2004).
∿	Meandering learning path	Putting the meanders back into learning. There is risk, uncertainty and new terrain to be encountered along the way as well as new paths of learning. The unevenness and varied terrain demands different kinds of skills. The risk heightens awareness and perception. Curiosity improves memory by tapping into the brain's reward system (Sample 2014).
◷	Time to stop, think, reflect and be curious	
🌲	Risk	
🌳	Conversations and dialogues	Geographical vocabulary is best learnt in situ and supports knowledge (Ward 1998), while dialogic sharing and evaluation of an environment supports creativity (Lambert and Owens 2012).
💭	Creativity and imagination	
☆	Time for bright ideas	
❄	Awe and wonder	Positive learning experiences in natural settings can trigger pro – environmental behaviours. See summary and extension of research on significant life experiences in Catling et al. (2010).
♥	Emotional encounters	Emotional and cognitive experiences work together to deepen learning through exploratory enquiry (Scoffham 2010).
△	Wild terrain	'The wild of the unknown' can be a powerful catalyst for change (Payne and Wattchow 2009). Outdoor 'back to nature' experiences can trigger transformational learning, challenging existing values and unsettling traditional landscapes (WWF 2009). This is where leaving a traditional and well-trodden path can provide a new enquiry stimulus and offer a different perspective on a familiar problem.
!	Critical thinking opportunity	
⋯	Detours, diversions and shortcuts	

CONCLUSION

Alternative learning settings offer great potential for creative geography teaching. Geographers have always extolled the value of fieldwork but all too often this has been seen in rather utilitarian terms and harnessed to pre-determined learning objectives. A more open-ended and less constrained approach which gives children the freedom to explore the world and brings the magic back into learning deserves a higher profile.

There is a rich literature on children's relationship with the environment that has been explored by Cobb (1977), Chawla (1992) and others. Following in this tradition Catling (2003) has documented the role of play experience in young children's learning. Meanwhile, Wasson-Elham (2010) has combined her classroom experience with a literary perspective to explore how children make use of the space between home and school to negotiate meanings and explore emerging ideas in low stakes situations.

Engagement and interaction with the natural world has been a source of inspiration for people from all walks of life and cultural backgrounds across the ages. It also helps to engender a sense of harmony and appreciation which contributes to our mental health and physical well-being. Learning doesn't happen in a vacuum. It is located in a context which is both temporally and culturally bounded. Some places seem particularly rich at stimulating creative thinking. Kellert, for example, notes that people across the globe typically favour landscapes with clean and flowing water, which enhance sight and mobility and which possess bright and flowering colours because they seem to be instrumental in human survival (Kellert 2009: 29).

The approaches suggested in this chapter seek to shift attention away from measurable targets and outcomes. The aim is to encourage pupils to make unusual connections and to embark on the kind of slow learning which accesses deeper levels of meaning. Research indicates that when we take active control of our learning it literally shapes our brains. By contrast, when we are simply exposed to events and information in a passive manner our brains and bodies are not much affected (Fischer 2009). Neuroscience is thus confirming what cognitive scientists have demonstrated for over a century. Learning and teaching require the active construction of knowledge.

REFERENCES

Capra, F. and Luisi, L. (2014) *The Systems View of Life: A Unifying Vision*. Cambridge: Cambridge University Press.

Catling, S. (2003) Curriculum contested: primary geography and social justice. *Geography* 88(3): 164–210.

Catling, S. Greenwood, R. Martin, F. and Owens, P. (2010) Formative experiences of primary geography educators. *International Research in Geographical and Environmental Education* 19(4): 341–50.

Chawla, L. (1992) Childhood and place attachment. In I. Altman and S. Low (eds), *Place Attachment*, pp. 63–79. New York: Plenum.

Cobb, E. (1977) *The Ecology of Imagination in Childhood*. Dallas TX: Spring.

Csikszentmihalyi, M. (1997) *Creativity: Flow and the Psychology of Discovery and Invention*. London: HarperPerennial.

Fischer, K. (2009) Mind, brain and education: building a scientific groundwork for learning and teaching. *Mind, Brain and Education* 1: 3–16.

Fredrickson, B. (2004) The broaden and build theory of positive emotions. *Philosophical Transactions of the Royal Society* 359(1449): 1367–77.

Kellert, S. (2009) A biocultural basis for an environmental ethic. In S. Kellert and J. Speth (eds), *The Coming Transformation*, pp. 21–38. New Haven, CT: Yale Schools of Forestry and Environmental Studies.

Lambert, D. and Owens, P. (2012) Geography. In R. Jones and Wyse (eds), *Creativity in the Primary Curriculum*, pp. 98–115. Abingdon: David Fulton.

Lucas, B. and Claxton, G. (2011) *New Kinds of Smart*. Maidenhead: Open University Press.

Matthews, M. H. (1992) *Making Sense of Place Children's Understanding of Large Scale Environments*. Hemel Hempstead: Harvester Wheatsheaf.

Moran, S. and John-Steiner, V. (2003) Creativity in the making. In K. Sawyer, V. John-Steiner, S, Moran, R. J. Sternberg, D. H. Feldman, J. Nakamura and Mihaly Csikszentmihalyi, *Creativity and Development*, pp. 61–90. Oxford: Oxford University Press.

Owens, P., Rawlinson, S. and Witt, S. (2012) Environmental immersion, slow pedagogy and serendipitous learning. Paper presented at Charney Manor Primary Geography Research Conference, February.

Payne, P. G. and Wattchow, B. (2009) Phenomenological econstruction, slow pedagogy, and the corporeal turn in wild environmental/outdoor education. *Canadian Journal of Environmental Education* 14: 15–32.

Pickering, S. (ed.) (2016) *Teaching Out of Doors Creatively*. London: Routledge.

Robinson, K. and Aronica, L. (2015) *Creative Schools*. London: Allen Lane.

Rohrer, D., Taylor, K,. Pashler, H., Wixted, J., Cepeda, N. (2004) The effect of overlearning on long-term retention. *Applied Cognitive Psychology* 19: 361–74.

Sample, I. (2014) Curiosity improves memory by tapping into the brain's reward system. Available at www.theguardian.com/science/2014/oct/02/curiosity-memory-brain-reward-system-dopamine (accessed 12 January 2016).

Scoffham, S. (2010) Young Geographers. In S. Scoffham (ed.), *Primary Geography Handbook*, pp. 14–23. Sheffield: Geographical Association.

Scoffham, S. and Barnes, J. (2011) Happiness matters: towards a pedagogy of happiness and well-being. *The Curriculum Journal* 22(4): 535–48.

Waite, S. (ed.) (2011) *Children Learning Outside the Classroom*. London: Sage.

Ward, H. (1998) Geographical Vocabulary in Scoffham (ed.) *Primary Sources: Research Findings in Primary Geography*. Sheffield: Geographical Association.

Wasson-Elham, L. (2010) Children's literatures as springboard to place-based embodied learning. *Environmental Education Research* 16(3–4): 279–94.

Wiliam, D. (2011) *Embedded Formative Assessment*. Bloomington, IN: Solution Tree Press.

Wiliam, D. and Leahy, S. (2015) *Embedding Formative Assessment: Practical Techniques for K-12 Classrooms*. West Palm Beach, FL: Learning Sciences International.

WWF (2009) *Natural Change Psychology and Sustainability*. Available at http://assets.wwf.org.uk/downloads/wwf_naturalchange2.pdf?_ga=1.85461146.202645 7788.1412683861 (accessed 12 January 2016).

CHAPTER 16

GEOGRAPHY, CREATIVITY AND THE FUTURE

Stephen Scoffham and Jonathan Barnes

This chapter explores how geography and creativity can be combined to help build a preferred and hopeful future. It focuses especially on the way that places and environments can be a catalyst for creative thinking. The connections that we make with the world around us, coupled with the uniqueness of every human mind and life, offer far-reaching possibilities for education. Helping children to develop qualities such as hope, co-operation, trust, fairness and love in relation to their surroundings is essential if they are to engage with the world around them and care about its future. There is now ample evidence that issues to do with sustainability in its widest sense will provide the meta-narrative for the twenty first century. It is argued that building children's social, emotional and intellectual capacity alongside these positive qualities can promote the capabilities they will need for sustainable living.

FUTURES THINKING

Futures thinking involves identifying issues, analysing data and research findings, using imagination to envisage different scenarios, and comparing and evaluating solutions. In an increasingly globalised world it also involves making connections, inter-cultural understanding and contextualised awareness. As children deepen their understanding of geography and the future they will begin to engage with complex situations which don't have neat solutions or easy answers. They will also find themselves drawn into a discussion about principles and values. This means that futures thinking has the potential to enrich both curriculum planning and classroom practice with new perspectives.

As a subject, geography is essentially future facing. Predicting the future is notoriously challenging and usually inaccurate. However, some clear trends have emerged which seem set to dominate the years ahead. These include global climate change, the loss of species and biodiversity, planetary environmental stress, global inequalities, human rights and political instability. International studies such as the annual State of the Planet report from the World Wide Fund for Nature (WWF) and the regular updates on global warming from the Intergovernmental Panel on Climate Change (IPCC) confirm the scale of the challenges that lie ahead. There are very good reasons to believe that the twenty-first century will be a time of dramatic and irreversible change. Klein, for example, presents an extensive review of the data on climate change which leads her to conclude that it is nothing less than an 'existential crisis' for the human species (Klein 2014: 15). At the same time, it is increasingly clear that the capitalist economic model which has dominated life in the West since before the Industrial Revolution is coming under ever increasing strain. The Earth has a finite carrying capacity and we are using resources faster than they can be replaced. Current rates of consumption exceed what is available by around fifty per cent and the trend is ever upwards (see Figure 16.1)

There is a danger that learning about daunting economic, environmental and social problems will leave children feeling desperate and powerless. However, rather than allowing negative scenarios to engender a sense of hopelessness, we can use our diversity and imagination to construct alternative narratives and scenarios. Creative and honest interaction with places can serve to empower children and give them a sense of vision. Hicks (2006: 70–71) observes that 'concern for something Other, something better, something not-yet, is an inherent element in the human condition and one of the deep components of human creativity'. More prosaically, the advice on good educational practice from government and other agencies stresses the importance of positive and hopeful engagement with environmental issues. Teaching in a spirit of grounded optimism is one of the ways we can help to equip pupils to thrive in the face of these challenges.

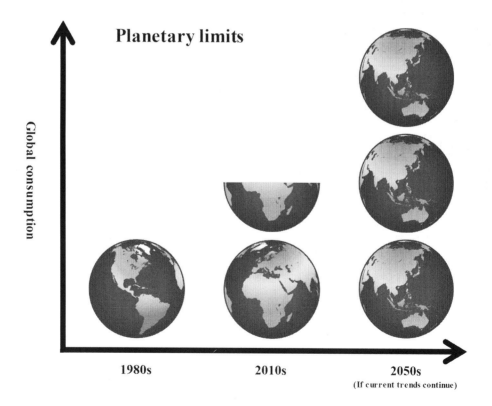

Planetary limits

Global consumption

1980s   2010s   2050s
                              (If current trends continue)

■ **Figure 16.1** We are currently consuming around 50 per cent more resources than the Earth can provide and the trend is ever upwards

GEOGRAPHY AND PLACE

Like any other academic discipline, geography is a constantly evolving. The earliest geographies date back to classical times and were largely descriptions of different, and often unknown, parts of the world. In the sixteenth century, geographical knowledge played a crucial part in the English voyages of exploration and provided support for subsequent colonial adventures. In the nineteenth and early twentieth century geography was largely driven by imperial values and portrayed the British empire in all its glory. Today, geographers continue to investigate and interpret the world using contemporary media and electronic devices to help filter information and process ideas. An historical perspective shows how geographical philosophies and narratives have changed in an increasingly secular and crowded world. However, it also highlights that throughout the centuries geographers have had an enduring interest in place – they are fascinated by what places are like, where they are located, how they are changing and how people interact with them.

Place is a complex notion which has many interpretations. Place can be a physical entity like a town. It can be as small as a street corner or as large as a continent or ocean. Some argue that place is best understood as the intersection and meetings of people. For example, Massey (1999) points out that a village is a node for a network of connections reaching out thousands of miles, brought together at a specific moment in time. With digital technology allowing us to occupy multiple spaces, the notion of place is becoming ever more diffuse. Certainly, we need to recognise that different groups and individuals will be set within the community in contrasting ways and have different understandings of it.

As well as being rooted in space, places are located in time. There will be observable clues that link them to different periods of the past, whether this is measured in terms of hours and days or the great expanses of geological history. Places also anticipate the future in the potential they have for change and development. In addition, places exist at different scales, from the microscopic to the global. The processes of weathering and erosion, for example, impact on small stones and pebbles just as much as entire mountain ranges. One of the features of geographical thinking is that it generates ideas and models that can be applied in widely different contexts which stimulates comparison.

The notion that time, scale and context interact in places in different ways is a theme that runs through this book and serves to structure this chapter. Figure 16.2 shows how the three faces of a cube can be used diagrammatically to illustrate the interactions which combine to create the concept of place. Time (past, present and future) appears on the horizontal axis along with scale (local, national, global). These two dimensions establish the context which is then overlaid by different layers of understanding shown on the vertical axis. Physical geography provides the base and fundamental layer, social and cultural interpretations appear next, imagination is shown at the top. These three layers represent different dimensions or modes of thinking. They interact dynamically in a way that parallels the manner in which a geographical information system (GIS) uses overlays to build up increasing levels of meaning and complexity. Each one acts as a lens which can reveal certain features but which can also hide or obscure others.

An awareness of these dimensions of place has the potential deepen our thinking in significant ways. Physical geographers concentrate on natural features of the Earth's surface and seek to understand the processes which shape them. Social and cultural geographers are more interested in the human dimension and the interactions between people. Arguably neither of these perspectives gives sufficient weight to creativity and imagination. Focusing on the dynamic interaction between people and place generates different forms of meaning.

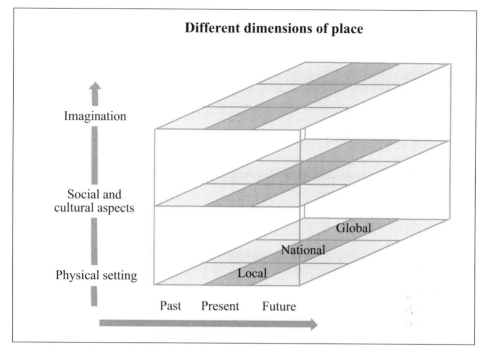

Different dimensions of place

■ **Figure 16.2** Interpreting place through different perspectives or 'lenses', deepens geographical thinking

The growing literature about the geographical imagination (Harvey 1973; Massey 2005), the notion of ethno-geography (Martin 2008) and debate about children's contribution to the curriculum (Catling 2014) all recognise this subjective element.

Harnessing our imagination to create stories about our lives builds our sense of identity and belonging. As we explore the world around us – the external world – there is also a sense in which we are simultaneously learning about our inner selves. This raises some profound and potentially unsettling questions. How do we understand our lives, for example, and where do we position ourselves in the scheme of creation? As we contemplate and interact with the natural world, many people experience a sense of oneness with their surroundings and a feeling of belonging to the universe which transcends every-day cares and concerns. Such transcendent moments are encapsulated in the notion of mindfulness and are, as Capra and Luisi (2014) point out, often accompanied by a sense of awe and wonder and feelings of profound humility. These experiences are extremely hard to capture in words because they represent something which is beyond language. Carl Jung, the Swiss psychologist, alluded to what might be called the 'inexpressible' in the following terms as he reflected on the mystery of existence:

> At times I feel as if I am spread over the landscape and inside things, and am myself living in every tree, in the plashing of the waves, in the clouds and the animals that come and go, in the procession of the seasons … Here everything has its history, and mine; here is space for the spaceless kingdom of the world's and the psyche's hinterland.

> (Jung 1975: 252)

One of the strengths of a layered approach to place is it that it acknowledges the importance of the inner world and personal perspectives. People can never be really objective observers or totally detached from the world around them. Rather, they screen and interpret what they see in the light of their previous experiences, attitudes and beliefs. Furthermore, how we respond to different circumstances is strongly influenced by the significance we attach to them. This is particularly apparent in the realm of sustainability and environmental issues. For example, there are those who see grasslands, forests, rivers, seas and other natural resources simply as wealth to be exploited. Others view them as habitats which need to be carefully guarded, both to protect wildlife and to maintain ecological diversity. Our ideas about what matters and our sense of who are will be two of the key factors influencing the way we think.

AN EDUCATIONAL CHALLENGE

The importance of narratives and personal scripts is an acknowledged part of current academic thinking. In school and classroom settings, recognising that knowledge has a subjective dimension and that it is complex and contested is not always easy. Such an approach runs counter to traditional notions of the curriculum which focus on established wisdoms and truths. It also requires new pedagogical approaches which value questions and dilemmas alongside answers and solutions. Living with uncertainty can be challenging, especially for those who prefer more settled modes of thinking.

In recent years there has been a growing dissatisfaction with many aspects of formal education. Critics point out that the current school system has its roots in the Industrial Revolution and was strongly associated with social control and power structures. At that time, one of the primary aims of education was to provide workers who could take their place on production lines or work on the land performing menial tasks. Standardisation and conformity mattered much more than individuality and creativity. Despite the huge social and technological changes which happened since those days, schools and the curriculum have changed remarkably since Victorian times. The school system is still largely geared towards uniformity, and examinations and assessment still only focus on remarkably narrow objectives, as is confirmed in current political debates. This leads Robinson and Aronica (2015) and many other critics to argue that much of what happens in education today is inappropriate and outdated. It also fails to meet the needs of many pupils and is extremely wasteful of talent.

Modern research into teaching and learning is adding to the momentum for change. One key finding is that intelligence, rather than being fixed, can actually be enhanced and developed. Lucas and Claxton (2011) cite evidence indicating that the qualities we receive at birth provide a broad 'envelop of possibility', which can be heavily modified and influenced by experience. Meanwhile, it is now recognised that nearly everything that we do and think has an emotional as well as an intellectual component. High level cognitive skills, Immordino Yang and Damasio (2007: 3) contend, do not function as disembodied systems and most types of thinking are 'profoundly affected by and subsumed within the processes of emotion'. Furthermore, empirical studies in neuroscience have established that learning is social, multi-sensory and depends on experience (Goswami 2015). International agencies acknowledge these developments. For example, a report by UNESCO (2014) on global citizenship education, refers to a shift in discourse and practice and highlights the way education is moving beyond the development of knowledge and cognitive skills to the building of values and attitudes learners will need in a more just, peaceful and sustainable world. Creative geography teaching can contribute to this trend and help to forge new approaches to teaching and learning. It is a process which is sharpened by futures thinking which is necessarily riddled with uncertainty.

CLASSROOM ACTIVITIES

How then can a multi-layered and principled approach to the study of place be interpreted in terms of teaching and classroom experience? The suggestions below illustrate how the physical, social and imaginative dimensions of place can be explored from a futures perspective at different scales. Nine different aspects derived from Figure 16.2 are examined in turn. These overlap in different ways and combine to build an increasingly mature understanding of place.

Physical focus

ENERGY USE (LOCAL SCALE)

Children could start by investigating how energy is used in their school. Making a survey of how lights are used and whether they are turned off is a popular starting point. Finding out about the amount of electricity used week by week will broaden the study. As pupils become more involved they may start to ask questions about insulation and ways to reduce energy consumption. They may also investigate the opportunities for installing solar panels and other renewables. The costs involved in establishing new systems needs to be set against potential benefits and will lead to some interesting work in maths as well as debate about priorities.

WIND POWER (NATIONAL SCALE)

The UK is particularly well placed geographically to generate wind and tidal power. Pupils could use the internet and other sources to find out about current renewable energy schemes and carbon reduction targets. The debate about the pros and cons of different proposals and how they affect the landscape has the potential to engage children at both an emotional and cognitive level.

CLIMATE CHANGE (GLOBAL SCALE)

As global temperatures rise the polar ice caps are melting and sea levels are rising. Around the world many major cities are on the coast at or close to current levels. Bangladesh, home to over 100 million people, is particularly vulnerable and some island nations such as Tuvalu and the Maldives could disappear completely. As well as finding out about these threats, children could learn about how nations are trying to work together to tackle climate change. Can they think of ways their own school can contribute, or changes they could make in their own lives? Small actions, when repeated by many individuals, make a significant impact and are fundamental to our sense of integrity.

Social/cultural focus

COHESIVE COMMUNITIES (LOCAL SCALE)

Primary schools often form particularly strong communities with a common ethos and shared values. Children can investigate the facilities and attitudes which create situations in which everyone has a chance to flourish. One way to do this is to become involved in an award scheme. The UNICEF Rights Respecting Schools Award, for example, has been found to have a profound effect on participating schools, and has helped pupils to develop positive attitudes towards inclusion and diversity (Sebba and Robinson 2010). Moreover, the sense of belonging which results from cohesive practices such as paired, group and whole class work is an excellent way to counter radicalisation.

DIVERSITY (NATIONAL SCALE)

The UK is one of the most ethnically diverse countries in the world and respecting other faiths cultures and beliefs has been identified as a core British value. Studying the physical and human geography of the UK, especially in groups and during fieldwork, is one way to start thinking about different societies. The way that modern Britain combines ideas and influences from around the world can be illustrated in studies as varied as food, language, music, religion and culture. Geography provides a relatively neutral context for investigating such issues.

MIGRATION (GLOBAL SCALE)

There are more people on the move today than at any time in history – over 200 million people currently live outside their country of origin. What makes people want to move? What parts of the world are most affected? What will be the likely impact now and in the future? These are complex questions with a strong geographical dimension which younger children can begin to explore by tracing the journeys and fortunes of individual migrants through picture books such as the *Silence Seekers* (Morley 2009) and teaching packs from Oxfam and other agencies. The opportunities for developing values such as tolerance and mutual respect are an integral part of such studies and, as Barnes and Ntung (2015) point out, schools are one of the best places in a community to consider positive attitudes and hopeful solutions to integration.

Imagination focus

CHANGE ALL AROUND US (LOCAL SCALE)

How do children think their local area will have changed by 2050? Talk about current trends and how change is continually affecting the built and natural environment. What changes have the children seen in their lifetime? Now get the pupils to consider three different future scenarios – possible, probable and preferred. Challenge them to draw maps, plans, pictures and diagrams to illustrate their ideas.

VISIONS FOR THE FUTURE (NATIONAL SCALE)

It was the vision of social reformers such as Octavia Hill which led to the creation of the National Trust in the nineteenth century. Similarly, the idea of the 'garden city', originally pioneered by Ebenezer Howard, provides the underpinning for the 'new towns' which were created in the UK before and after the Second World War. Get the children to find how different people have tried to make the UK a better place to live. What ideas can they themselves come up with to address the needs of the future?

BIODIVERSITY (GLOBAL SCALE)

Making wise choices is essential part of building a sustainable future. Working in groups, get the children to consider a biodiversity issue such as the threat to tigers or whales around the world. One scenario might involve establishing conservation areas which could halt the decline in numbers. Another scenario would see the continuing hunting and habitat destruction leading to extinction. A third scenario could focus on a new international law to prevent the international trade in tiger products. Representing the possible outcomes and their knock on effects in a diagram such as a 'consequences wheel' will highlight links and connections and raise questions which will draw pupil into research and investigations.

ETHICAL ATTITUDES FOR THE FUTURE

The studies outlined above all focus firmly on places in the future. They are also about developing universal attitudes and values. Environmental and sustainability issues require the next generation to be confident, values-literate citizens. Building a better future thus leads us into an ethical domain in which we are obliged to clarify our values. Craft (2011) points out that these challenges, which are both local and global, will oblige us to draw on our creative potential perhaps more urgently than at any other time in our history. Geography, with its focus on place and the future is centrally placed to explore these issues and is particularly well positioned to provide a suitable context for critical debate. The links to the UK national curricula which are summarised in Figure 16.3 indicate some of the possibilities.

The national curricula for the different countries of the UK provide a range of statements that support sustainability and futures thinking in geography. In England, the interaction of human and physical processes and the changes which occur over time are identified in the overall purpose of the curriculum for KS1 and KS2. In Scotland, 'sustainable development', 'international education' and 'creativity' are all identified as important curriculum themes. The curriculum for Northern Ireland contains a number of statements relating to sustainability in the area of learning entitled 'the world around us'. Meanwhile, in Wales the geography curriculum for KS2 specifically states that pupils need to understand the importance of sustainability, develop an informed concern about the quality of their environment and recognize that they are global citizens

■ **Figure 16.3** Sustainability and futures thinking in the UK national curricula

Questions about justice, human rights and global equity are central to the sustainability debate. Learning about sustainability and environment also raises questions about inclusion. Booth and Ainscow (2011) make a powerful point when they argue that we have a responsibility not only to those around us but to distant people and future generations. This is a commitment that cannot be postponed. Earth's resources are very unequally shared and the damage caused by human activity is already undermining the lives of millions of poor people around the world on a daily basis. Booth and Ainscow conclude that environmental inclusion is central to sustainability and that 'the most fundamental aim of education is to prepare children and young people for sustainable ways of life' (*ibid*.: 24).

There are those who would rather avoid teaching children about controversial issues and argue that they are too complex for them to understand but this is not the case. Without an early exposure to their surroundings and a grounding in aspects of biodiversity and human stewardship, children are less likely to appreciate their environment and engage with it as they grow older. Hicks (2014) argues that the responding to these dilemmas is both affirmative and empowering. Furthermore, if we fail to engage there is a danger that we will turn inwards and pretend that nothing is wrong. Hicks concludes that teachers who enter into denial or who turn a blind eye to current events are abrogating their responsibilities. Such an approach, he declares, amounts to 'an educational crime' (*ibid*.: 23).

CONCLUSION

A positive future requires people with a high degree of respect for each other and their environment. To be respectful, students need to learn self-confidence as well as sensitivity to others. They need to take an interest in both local and global issues. Self-confidence and empathy may both arise from an increased sense of belonging to a locality and by appreciating the unique patterns and relationships evident in every place. Networks and connections are fundamental in understanding the character of a locality. And these links and connections can only be fully appreciated when they are considered on a national and global as well as a local scale.

Many of the studies which geographers undertake contribute directly to planetary awareness. As Bonnett (2008: 55) puts it, 'the twin pillars of modern geography are environmental and international knowledge'. To participate in a relevant and responsible geography curriculum, learners must ask similar questions as those at the frontiers of the subject. Today, even Earth's wildest places are affected by human influences and this impact needs mediation in order to be positive and sustainable. The built environment is full of examples of creative endeavour. The questions that stimulate creative thinking about places are simple and fundamental:

▨ Where exactly is this place?
▨ What characterises it?
▨ What are its links to other places?
▨ How is it changing?
▨ How can we protect it or improve it now and in the future?
▨ How can I contribute?

These and other similar questions have occupied geographers for centuries and are best addressed by creative, collaborative thought and action. The future of every place on this planet is therefore the central concern of geography education.

It is our hope that creative geography teaching will foster creativity and knowledge in pupils helping them to become joyful and imaginative learners. At the same time education can also enhance their capacity to contribute to building a better world – a world in which co-operation, fairness, sensitivity and kindness to each other and the environments that sustain us become our guiding values. Establishing such shared human values is an essential base on which to support, build and sustain a preferred future which will enable us to live within planetary limits. At a time when there is overwhelming evidence of damaging ecological, environmental and social stress, this is an agenda which is becoming ever more urgent and cannot be ignored.

REFERENCES

Barnes, J. and Ntung, A. (2015) *Education in a Diverse UK*. Dover: Migrant Help.

Bonnett, A. (2008) *What is Geography?* London: Sage.

Booth, T. and Ainscow, M. (2011) *Index for Inclusion: Developing Learning and Participation in Schools* (3rd edition). Bristol: Centre for Studies in Inclusive Education.

Capra, F. and Luisi, L. (2014) *The Systems View of Life*. Cambridge: Cambridge University Press.

Catling, S. (2014) Giving younger children voice in primary geography: empowering pedagogy – a personal perspective. *International Research in Geography and Environmental Education* 23(4): 350–72.

Craft, A. (2011) *Creativity and Education Futures*. Stoke on Trent, Trentham.

Goswami, U. (2015) *Children's Cognitive Development and Learning*. York: Cambridge Primary Review Trust.

Harvey, D. (1973) *Social Justice and the City*. Oxford: Blackwell.

Hicks, D. (2006) *Lessons for the Future*. Victoria, BC: Trafford. Available at www.teaching4abetterworld.co.uk/books/download21.pdf.

Hicks, D. (2014) *Educating for Hope in Troubled Times*. London: Institute of Education.

Immordino-Yang, H. and Damasio, A. (2007) We feel, therefore we learn: the relevance of affective and social neuroscience to education. *Mind, Brain and Education* 1(1): 3–10.

Jung, C. (1975) *Memories, Dreams, Reflections*. London: Collins.

Klein, N. (2014) *This Changes Everything*. London: Penguin.

Lucas, B. and Claxton, G. (2011) *New Kinds of Smart*. Maidenhead: Open University Press.

Martin, F. (2008) Ethnogeography: towards liberatory geography education. *Children's Geographies* 6(4): 437–50.

Massey, D. (1999) The social space. *Primary Geographer* 37: 46.

Massey, D. (2005) *For Space*. London: Sage.

Morley, B. (2009) *Silence Seeker*. London: Tamarind.

Robinson, K. and Aronica, L. (2015) *Creative Schools*. London: Allen Lane.

Sebba, J. and Robinson, C. (2010) *Evaluation of UNICEF's UK Rights' Respecting Schools Award*. Final report. London: UNICEF.

UNESCO (2014) *Global Citizenship Education: Preparing Learners for the Challenges of the 21st Century*. Paris: UNESCO.

Welsh Assembly Government (2008) *Geography in the National Curriculum for Wales: Key Stages 2–3*. Cardiff: Welsh Assembly Government. Available at http://learning.gov.wales/docs/learningwales/publications/130424-geography-in-the-national-curriculum-en.pdf

WWF (2014) *Living Planet Report 2014*. Gland: World Wide Fund for Nature. Available at http://wwf.panda.org/about_our_earth/all_publications/living_planet_report

APPENDIX
National Curriculum
links

The following tables identify how each of the chapters in *Teaching Geography Creatively* relates to the National Curriculum. There are separate tables for each of the four jurisdictions of the UK. Every chapter is broadly focused on high-quality geography teaching, and each one explores the curriculum in a different way. The result is that there is considerable overlap. For a more detailed breakdown of themes and topics please refer to the index that follows this appendix.

England Geography programme of study KS1 and KS2.

Main themes	Locational knowledge	Place knowledge	Human and physical geography	Geographical skills and fieldwork
Chapter 1				✓
Chapter 2	✓		✓	✓
Chapter 3		✓	✓	
Chapter 4		✓		✓
Chapter 5	✓			✓
Chapter 6		✓		✓
Chapter 7			✓	
Chapter 8			✓	
Chapter 9		✓	✓	
Chapter 10	✓			✓
Chapter 11		✓		✓
Chapter 12	✓	✓		
Chapter 13		✓	✓	
Chapter 14			✓	✓
Chapter 15		✓		✓
Chapter 16		✓	✓	

Wales Geography programme of study KS1 and KS2.

Main themes	Locating places, environments and patterns	Understanding places, environments and processes	Investigating	Communicating
Chapter 1			✓	✓
Chapter 2	✓	✓	✓	✓
Chapter 3		✓	✓	✓
Chapter 4		✓	✓	✓
Chapter 5	✓	✓		✓
Chapter 6	✓		✓	✓
Chapter 7		✓	✓	✓
Chapter 8		✓	✓	✓
Chapter 9	✓		✓	✓
Chapter 10	✓		✓	✓
Chapter 11			✓	✓
Chapter 12	✓	✓		✓
Chapter 13		✓	✓	✓
Chapter 14		✓	✓	✓
Chapter 15		✓	✓	✓
Chapter 16		✓	✓	✓

Scotland   Social studies (people, place and environment) experiences and outcomes.

Generalised themes	Local area	Weather and climate and habitats	Sustainability and environmental change	Global/local connections
Chapter 1				
Chapter 2	✓	✓	✓	✓
Chapter 3	✓		✓	
Chapter 4	✓			
Chapter 5	✓			✓
Chapter 6	✓		✓	✓
Chapter 7	✓			✓
Chapter 8	✓	✓		
Chapter 9	✓		✓	
Chapter 10	✓			
Chapter 11	✓	✓		✓
Chapter 12	✓			✓
Chapter 13	✓		✓	✓
Chapter 14	✓		✓	✓
Chapter 15	✓		✓	
Chapter 16			✓	✓

Northern Ireland   The world around us Strand 3 place KS1 and KS2.

Generalised themes	Local area	Weather and climate and habitats	Sustainability and environmental change	Global/local connections
Chapter 1				
Chapter 2	✓	✓	✓	✓
Chapter 3	✓		✓	
Chapter 4	✓			
Chapter 5	✓			✓
Chapter 6	✓		✓	✓
Chapter 7	✓			✓
Chapter 8	✓	✓		
Chapter 9	✓		✓	
Chapter 10	✓			
Chapter 11	✓	✓		✓
Chapter 12	✓			✓
Chapter 13	✓		✓	✓
Chapter 14	✓		✓	✓
Chapter 15	✓		✓	
Chapter 16			✓	✓

INDEX

Aboriginal art 81, 83, 102: dreamings 81
acrostics 19
addresses 59–60
aerial photographs 23, 62, 65, 77, 82, 85, 114, 122
Africa 16, 24, 32, 33, 36, 42, 43, 49, 63, 68, 70, 166, 171, 209
Alexander, R. 4, 151, 166, 167, 168
anagrams 16
Andes mountains 33, 80, 92, 93
animals 14, 20. 33, 45, 84 (*see also* zoos)
Antarctic circle 71
Antarctica 22, 34, 43
'apps' 20, 24, 137, 140
Arctic circle 71
art xvi, 76–87, 101–2, 143, 147–62
artefacts 124, 149, 158, 188, 206–9
Arts Council 148, 159
Asia 32, 43. 84, 202, 209
assemblies 20, 171
assessment 10, 18, 27, 51, 55, 127, 136, 142, 216, 219, 226
atlases 24, 25, 61–74, 79, 85, 86, 137, 173, 196, 208
Attenborough, D. 214
autism 169
awe and wonder 22, 53, 133, 135, 143, 155, 182, 219, 225

banana 38, 208–9
Barnaby Bear 20, 27, 59
Barrow Bridge 121, 12, 125–7
bears 19, 22, 39, 60
beauty 1, 35, 52, 84, 122, 143, 148, 150, 182, 186
biodiversity 67, 177, 208, 222, 229, 230
biomes 67, 113–15, 214

bi-sociation 2
brain 8, 13, 14, 167, 192, 193, 200, 206, 220
Brazil 21, 71, 170–2
British empire 224
British Isles 62, 67, 70, 72, 172
British values 169, 228
built environment 121, 133, 182, 186, 212, 230

cabinet of curiosities 215
Cambridge Primary Review xvii, 151
care 10, 38, 51, 101, 178, 181, 188, 201–2, 222
Catling, S. 12, 50, 51, 55, 88, 108, 118, 180, 181, 192, 220, 225
change 37, 127–8, 214, 228
Children's Society 7
cities 16, 62, 71–2, 173
citizenship 129: global citizenship 175, 226
climate change 113, 177, 183–7, 199–200, 208, 223, 227
climate zones 114, 214
cognitive dissonance 6
Coll, Isle of 85
collaborative learning 187
colour 35, 77; colour codes 72, 113, 114; colour matching 212; soil colour 101
community 36–8, 47, 81, 113, 119, 157, 166, 170, 187, 188, 213;
community cohesion 129, 228
compass directions 71, 72, 78, 82, 84, 140, 141, 173, 211
complexity 83, 150, 166, 182, 185, 193, 224
consequences wheel 229
continents 24, 26, 58–74, 84, 105, 198
controversial issues 10, 154, 230
Cotopaxi 80

counting 33, 134, 136, 140
countries 16, 24, 60–72, 170–2
Craft, A. xvi, xvii, 2, 4, 7, 229
Creative arts 147–62
creative curriculum 1163, 179
creativity xv–xviii, 1–11, 12–15; definitions of 2–3
Cremin, T. xv–xviii, 5. 6, 15, 32, 89. 153, 186
critical thinking 30, 179–80, 203, 216
cross-curricular approach 95, 118–30, 131–46, 147–62
crosswords 6, 18
Csikzentmihalyi, M. xvi, 7, 13, 14, 148, 210
culture 2–3, 21, 35, 49, 164, 166, 171–2
curiosity 3, 15, 38, 45, 84, 137, 147
curriculum making 55, 119

Damasio. A. 4, 193, 226
dance 6, 21, 147–53, 159, 160, 166, 185
De Bono, E. 2, 92
debates 154
deep thinking 202
dens 47, 50–1
development goals 178
dialogic ethnography 167–8
differentiation 18, 126, 136–42
digital technologies 9–10, 58, 101, 224
dingbats 17–18
dioramas 214–15
discussion 38–41, 134–5
displays 6, 26, 135
distributed intelligence 210
diversity 7, 36, 169, 172, 228
drama 6, 20, 37, 39, 41, 51, 124, 147–54, 159–60, 185
Dublin 109

early years 12, 19, 136, 151
earth movements 92, 202
Ecuador 80–1
education for sustainability (ESD) 143, 177–91
elves 52–3
emotions 4–5, 13, 53, 128, 152, 166–7, 170–1, 193, 210, 226
empathy 47, 170, 185–6, 208, 230
energy 188–9, 208, 227
engagement 13
England 59, 157
English as an Additional Language (EAL) 169
English Heritage 154
enjoyment 10, 13–14, 45, 170
enquiry process 105, 119–28, 147, 168
entry points 5, 12, 210
entry points 5, 14, 19, 210
environment 32–5, 47–51, 199–202, 206; environmental issues 37–8, 183–5, 223
erosion 17, 21, 92–7, 112, 224

estate agents 51, 154
ethno-geography 225
Europe 9, 16, 24, 62, 64; European artists 76; European Union 24
Exeter Extending Literacy Project 158

fairy tales 19. 186
fieldwork 45, 64–5, 78, 108–13, 118–30, 181–2, 210–13
flags 24, 27, 71, 143
floods 109, 110, 199, 200, 202
flow (state of) 7–8, 14, 210
focus exercises 210–13
food 67, 200, 208; food analogies 88–100; food miles 201
food miles 201
fossils 98–100, 206–7, 214–15; ammonite 98; echinoid 99; trilobite 99
Fredrickson, B. 210
freeze frames 23, 152, 154
fridge magnets 207, 212
fun 12–29, 45, 49, 52, 72, 76, 109, 136, 173
future 9, 10, 46, 51, 119, 127, 177–81. 201, 215, 222–31

Gage, Phineas 192
Gaia hypothesis 198, 199
games 14, 26–7, 196
garden cities chap 14
gardens 37, 101, 143, 229
Gardner, H. 14, 193
generating ideas 4 111, 120
geocaching 140, 141
Geographical Association i, iii, 45, 59, 76, 107, 180, 181
geographical concepts 36, 49, 84, 88, 105, 127, 143, 164, 206–9
geographical imagination 51, 164, 166–7, 181, 188, 225
geography: cultural geography 163–4; ethno-geography 225; history of 224; living geography 181; local and global 131, 227–9; pedagogy 10; personal geographies 48, 55, 166, 168
global citizenship 226
Global Learning Programme 185
global perspective 35–7, 68
global warming 184–5, 208, 222
globalisation 36, 181
globe 24, 32, 61, 62, 67–74, 86, 114, 143, 171, 196
'Google Earth' 23, 24, 67, 72, 76, 77, 79, 82, 193, 196
graphicacy 77, 84, 85, 86
grids 25, 71, 72, 158

habitats 75, 115, 154, 183, 208, 214–15, 226; habitat loss 67, 202, 229

haikus 21, 212 (*see* poems)
Hawk and Owl Trust 183
health and safety 41, 44, 55, 88, 90, 210;
    safeguarding 20
Hicks, D. 177, 180, 183, 187, 223, 230
hidden agendas 188
historical maps 84
history 118–30
Hockney, David 76, 7, 79, 83, colour plate
    section
holidays 20, 26, 143, 183, 196–7
holistic education 53, 151, 178
homework 70, 71, 111, 112
hope 10, 36, 171, 171, 187, 22: hopelessness
    223
houses 47, 52, 182
human rights 177, 22, 230
Hundertwasser, F. 82–3; colour plate section

identity 6, 10, 59, 65, 118, 129, 164; music
    and identity 165, 166, 169; national identity
    172, 181
illustrations 20, 30–41, 186
images 20–3; post-colonial images 153;
    satellite images 59, 79, 82, 8; visual images
    86, 155
imagination 4, 9, 32, 47, 51–4, 228–9
imagined worlds 124
immigrants 36, 166
inclusion 7, 64, 168–70, 228, 230
intuition 5

Jerusalem 84, 172
jigsaws 62, 200
jokes 15
journey sticks 212
journeys 24, 33–5, 68, 79, 153, 172, 212
junk models 126, 127
justice 36, 177, 178, 230

Kenya 20, 36
kinaesthetic learning 38, 149
Koestler, A. 2, 3, 158

land use 65, 77, 124, 141
landmarks 23–7, 61, 65, 78,79, 121, 212
landscapes 44, 76–80, 83, 88–103, 157,
    214–15
learning out of doors 44–57, 205–20
learning styles 28, 30
Learning Through Landscapes 47
learning with peers 141
leaves 102, 139, 156, 182
lesson planning 5, 104–6, 119–20
linear learning 218–19
literacy 15, 25, 30, 95, 215; emotional literacy
    171; visual literacy 35,77, 84, 155
litter 124, 156, 187

living maps
locational knowledge 58–75, 173
London 16, 33, 212; London Underground 79,
    208
Louv, R. 45
Lovelock, J. 199
Lucas and Claxton 2, 5, 13, 210, 226

Maathai, Wangari 36
map games 27–8
map keys 71
'Mappa Mundi' 84
map skills 32, 58–75, 84–5, 143, 193–6,
    210–11
map symbols 9, 25, 71, 77, 82, 210
Martin F. 12, 55, 118, 163, 168, 170, 179,
    225
Massey, D. 163, 166, 224, 225
mathematics 131–46
Maximap 67
mental maps 58–75
metaphors 5, 35, 174, 198, 216
middle childhood 44–53, 214
migration 132, 228
mime 152, 153, 158, 159
mindfulness 225
minerals 88–91, 207
minibeasts 136
misconceptions xvi, 104, 106, 107
mobile phones 58, 209
models 20, 26, 62, 78, 153, 215
modern languages 195
mountains 215, 23, 24, 92, 93, 106, 206–7
multicultural dimension 3, 129, 143
murals 37, 155, 157
music 21–22, 153, 163–76, 211

National Advisory Committee on Creativity
    and Cultural Education xv, 2, 147
national anthems 166, 172
National Curriculum 13, 27, 60, 118–20, 131,
    136, 226, 232–4
National Gallery 147, 157
National Trust 154, 229
natural environment 36, 45, 104, 140, 144,
    208, 228
nature 35, 36, 38, 44–57, 82, 104, 124, 214:
    nature reserve 184
nature deficit disorder 45
neighbourhood 24, 36, 51, 118, 186
nested hierarchy 64
neuroscience 4, 13, 192, 220, 226
New York 20, 22, 164, 173
news reports 36, 40, 58, 60, 70, 114, 154, 183,
    202
north pole 46
northern and southern hemispheres 62
numbers 131–46

oceans 20, 24, 60, 199
Ofsted 45, 49, 61, 178–80, 188
Olympic Games 172, 202
Ordnance Survey 24, 25, 64, 78, 84, 121, 126, 195
Oxfam 70, 196, 228

paintings 76–87, 102, 148, 153, 157
Paris 16
pattern 77, 82, 137; weather patterns 114, 206
perspective 32, 85–6
Philosophy for Children 198
photo packs 22
photographs 21, 23, 51, 78–9, 156, 193, 200
    (see aerial photographs)
photomontage 156
Piaget, J. 13, 107
picture-books 20, 30–43, 64–5, 153, 186, 228
place 224–6; attachment 47, 118, 133, 151,
    165; place-making 49–50; place names 17,
    21, 126, 164; sense of place 119, 133, 155,
    158; special places 47, 155–7
Planning for Real 47
play 3–4, 13–14, 140; playful learning 44–57,
    169, 216, outdoor play 45–9
playground 26, 72, 121, 132, 157, 194, 205,
    214
poems 19–21, 38; fridge magnet poems 212;
    haikus 21, 212   ; limericks 21; riddles 20
population 9, 71, 100, 143, 166
possibility thinking xvii, 2, 7
postage stamps 20
postcards 51, 71, 77, 115, 122
postcodes 59
prevent agenda 129, 130
Prime Meridian 62, 71
problem solving 1, 38, 49, 70, 139, 142, 177,
    192–204
progression 120
pupil participation 186–7
puppets 140, 153, 154, 158
puzzles 15–27 (see games)

Quechen paintings 80
questions 26, 46, 71, 91, 104–17, 155, 168,
    178, 185–8, 200, 230

radicalisation 228
rainforest 22, 47, 114, 115
recycling 38, 143, 201
reflection 47, 120
refugees 36–7, 132
reluctant learners
re-modelling 158
research findings 5, 44–9, 50–2, 61–4, 107–8,
    167, 192, 226
resources (see energy)
respect agenda 130

risk assessment 41
River Tolka 109. 110
rivers 16–21, 35, 67, 106, 109–10
Roberts Report 6
Roberts, M. 49, 119, 120, 123, 128, 168
rocks 88–103, 104, 111–12, 206; conglomerate
    97–8; sandstone 93–4; sedimentary 95
Rocky Mountains 208
role play 6, 14, 15, 20, 38, 51, 124, 140, 147,
    151, 153–4, 159, 160, 185
routes 25, 64, 65, 79, 83, 137, 140, 208
rubbish and waste 38, 200

safe learning environments 15, 49, 148, 168,
    186
scale 32, 49, 195–6, 214, 224, 227–9
school corridor 134
school grounds 25, 46, 48, 13, 115, 156, 157,
    182
school partnerships
Scotland 21, 131, 157, 172, 229
sea level rise chap 14
seaside 20
self-esteem 51. 59, 148, 169
sensory learning 45, 46, 49, 52, 167, 210, 226
settlement 47, 77, 78, 122, 123
simulations 14, 27, 47, 154
small world play 140, 153
smart phones 140
Sobel, D. 44, 45, 49, 50, 52, 53
soils 17, 88, 92, 95, 100–2, 104, 106, 107,
    111–13, 115
solitary learning 5, 131
songs 21–2, 38, 164, 165, 170, 172–3
sounds 22, 38, 125, 172, 181, 182;
    soundscapes 38; sound maps 210–11
South Africa 71, 166, 209
space 224–5
Special Educational Needs and Disabilities
    (SEND) 126, 169
sports events 24, 172
St Lucia 19, 185
stereotypes 5, 153, 171
stories 19–20, 30–43, 66, 81, 140, 153, 157,
    186, 206–9
street furniture 122, 124, 126
stress 8, 13, 200, 231
sustainability 143, 177–91, 200–1, 229–30

tally charts 136
Tanner, J. 181
Tanzania 33
tigers chap 202, 229
time 214–15, 224–5
trails 131–46
transport 32, 33, 41, 133, 141, 183
transportation (geology) 92
travel agent 196–7

trees 36, 37, 45, 122, 132, 136, 139, 148, 157, 176
tropics 62, 71, 209
tsunamis 152, 183

United Kingdom (UK) 2, 6, 18, 21, 31, 59–62, 66, 71, 81, 157, 172, 185, 207–9, 214, 227–9
United Nations 185
USA 59, 71, 111, 151, 158, 173

values 1, 10, 148, 177, 178, 181, 206, 222–31; ethical attitudes 229–30; moral framework 8
videos 22, 27
villages 118, 121, 193, 224
visual artists 158
visual arts 150, 155–7
vocabulary 15–19, 46, 51, 65, 95, 108, 125, 126, 136, 181, 185
volcanoes 24, 58, 80, 104–6, 116, 117, 202, 214; volcanic eruptions 92, 106, 152

Wales 59, 131, 157, 229; Welsh artists 157

Warwick Commission 6
water 100, 106, 126, 143, 199, 206; water cycle 206, 214; water vapour 106
waterfall 17, 22, 123, 152
waves 20, 21, 47, 54, 152, 225
weather 12, 16, 17, 21, 32, 79, 104, 113–15, 142, 152, 156, 157, 172, 197, 206
weathering 107, 112, 224
well-being 7, 14, 44, 45, 51–2, 147, 151, 166, 177, 220
wheelchairs 211
Wiegand, P. 61, 64, 76, 106
Wildthink 216–19
wind turbines 189
word association 16
word games 15–21
world map 24, 60–72, 114, 115, 143
World Wide Fund for Nature (WWF) 179, 222
writing frames 142

zoos 31, 39–41, 153

Taylor & Francis eBooks

Helping you to choose the right eBooks for your Library

Add Routledge titles to your library's digital collection today. Taylor and Francis ebooks contains over 50,000 titles in the Humanities, Social Sciences, Behavioural Sciences, Built Environment and Law.

Choose from a range of subject packages or create your own!

Benefits for you

- » Free MARC records
- » COUNTER-compliant usage statistics
- » Flexible purchase and pricing options
- » All titles DRM-free.

Benefits for your user

- » Off-site, anytime access via Athens or referring URL
- » Print or copy pages or chapters
- » Full content search
- » Bookmark, highlight and annotate text
- » Access to thousands of pages of quality research at the click of a button.

REQUEST YOUR FREE INSTITUTIONAL TRIAL TODAY

Free Trials Available
We offer free trials to qualifying academic, corporate and government customers.

eCollections – Choose from over 30 subject eCollections, including:

Archaeology	Language Learning
Architecture	Law
Asian Studies	Literature
Business & Management	Media & Communication
Classical Studies	Middle East Studies
Construction	Music
Creative & Media Arts	Philosophy
Criminology & Criminal Justice	Planning
Economics	Politics
Education	Psychology & Mental Health
Energy	Religion
Engineering	Security
English Language & Linguistics	Social Work
Environment & Sustainability	Sociology
Geography	Sport
Health Studies	Theatre & Performance
History	Tourism, Hospitality & Events

For more information, pricing enquiries or to order a free trial, please contact your local sales team:
www.tandfebooks.com/page/sales

Routledge
Taylor & Francis Group

The home of
Routledge books

www.tandfebooks.com